Hugh Johnson's Pocket Encyclopedia of Wine

Simon and Schuster/New York

KEY TO SYMBOLS

r.	red	
p.	rosé	} (in brackets) means relatively unimportant
w.	white	
br.	brown	
sw.	sweet	
s/sw.	semi-sweet	
dr.	dry	
sp.	sparkling	

★	plain, everyday quality
★★	above average
★★★	well known, highly reputed
★★★★	grand, prestigious, expensive
☐	usually particularly good value in its class

70 71 etc.
    recommended years which may be currently available.

70' etc. Vintage regarded as particularly successful for the property in question.

70 etc. years in **bold** should be ready for drinking (the others should be kept). Where both reds and whites are indicated the red is intended unless otherwise stated.
N.B. German vintages are codified by a different system. See note on p. 76.

D.Y.A. drink the youngest available

NV vintage not normally shown on label

Cross-references are in SMALL CAPS

See p. 5 for extra explanation

A quick-reference vintage chart for France and Germany appears on p. 176.

Hugh Johnson's Pocket Encyclopedia of Wine
© 1977 by Mitchell Beazley Publishers Limited
Text © 1977, 1978, 1979, 1980, 1981 by Hugh Johnson
Revised edition published 1978, 1979, 1980, 1981
© 1981 Mitchell Beazley Publishers
All rights reserved
including the right of reproduction
in whole or in part in any form
Published by Simon and Schuster
A Division of Gulf & Western Corporation
Simon & Schuster Building
Rockefeller Center
1230 Avenue of the Americas
New York, New York 10020

ISBN 0-671-43995-2
Library of Congress Catalog Card Number 77-79242
Designed by Florianne Henfield
Assistant Editor Kathie Gill
Printed in Hong Kong by Mandarin Offset International (H.K.) Ltd.

Contents

Introduction

This book is an exercise in crowding angels on a pinhead, or students into a telephone box. It is deliberately the shortest book in which I could possibly squeeze a book's-worth of information. Conversely it holds as much information as I could possibly squeeze into a little diary-format book. Hence no prose: the whole work is played staccato.

Its arrangement is intended to be as helpful as possible when you are buying a bottle, whether you are on the nursery slopes or an old hand with a bad memory. You are faced with a list of wines or an array of bottles in a restaurant, wine merchant or bottle store. Your mind goes blank. You fumble for your little book. All you need to establish is what country a wine comes from. Look up the principal words on the label in the appropriate country's section. You will find enough potted information to let you judge whether this is the wine you want.

Specifically, you will find information on the colour and type of wine, its status or prestige, whether it is usually particularly good value, which vintages are good and which are ready to drink — and often considerably more . . . about the quantity made, the grapes used, ownership and the rest. Hundreds of cross-references help you go further into the matter if you want to.

The introduction to each national section will help you to establish which label-terms are the ones that count. In many cases you will find you can look up almost all the words on the label: estate, grape, shipper, quality-rating, bottling-information. . . .

Note on Revised and Enlarged 1981/82 Edition
This fifth edition has been totally revised and enlarged with 20 more pages of information. All the sections have been updated and expanded as necessary and critical comment sharpened wherever possible. Completely new sections deal with the emerging quality wine-producers of New Zealand and the Pacific North-west.

There is a major new dimension to the information on the Châteaux of Bordeaux. I have consulted all their proprietors on the relative success of their last ten vintages (see page 54). Extra notes scattered through the book give more background on vintages, quantities, strengths, aperitifs, decanting and other topics.

Finally, to give readers a toe-hold on what is becoming a mountain of information, I have included a Personal Choice for the year on pages 6 and 7.

How to read an entry

The top line of most entries consists of the following information in an abbreviated form.

1. Which part of the country in question the wine comes from. (References to the maps in this book.)
2. Whether it is red, rosé or white (or brown/amber), dry, sweet or sparkling, or several of these.
3. Its general standing as to quality: a necessarily rough and ready guide based principally on the following ascending scale:

   * plain, everyday quality
   ** above average
   *** well known, highly reputed
   **** grand, prestigious, expensive

So much is more or less objective. Additionally there is a subjective rating: a box round the stars of any wine which in my experience is usually particularly good (which means good value) within its price range. There are good everyday wines as well as good luxury wines. The box system helps you find them.

4. Vintage information: which were the more successful of the recent vintages which *may* still be available. And of these which are ready to drink this year, and which will probably improve with keeping. Your first choice for current drinking should be one of the vintage years printed in **bold** type. Buy light-type years for further maturing.

The German vintage information works on a different principle: see the Introduction to Germany, page 76.

Acknowledgements

This store of detailed recommendations comes partly from my own notes and partly from those of a great number of kind friends. Without the generous help and co-operation of every single member of the wine trade I have approached, I could not have attempted it. I particularly want to thank the following for giving me material help with research or in the areas of their special knowledge.

Martin Bamford
Anthony Barton
Jean Claude Berrouet
Michael Broadbent M.W.
Teresa Carlisle
Sheila Cavanagh-Bradbury
Jan Critchley-Salmonson
Len Evans
Francis Fouquet
Jean-Paul Gardère
Robert Hart M.W.
Peter Hasslacher
Graham Knox
Matt Kramer
Tony Laithwaite
Michael Longhurst
Tim Marshall

Patrick Matthews
Dr. Franz Werner Michel
Christian Moueix
Reginald Nicholson
Anders Ousback
David Peppercorn M.W.
Alain Querre
Jan and Maite Read
Dr. Bruno Roncarati
Steven Spurrier
David Stevens M.W.
Keith Stevens
Serena Sutcliffe M.W.
Hugh Suter M.W.
Bob Thompson
Peter Vinding-Diers
James Walker

A Personal Choice

As this book has grown to the point where its 3,000-odd entries refer to at least twice that number of wines it is not surprising that many readers have asked for a few clues or short-cuts. "Surely there is an inside track" is what they are saying. "Who can possibly find his way around in all that lot?"

I grant the difficulty. More and more good wines are being made every year. The object of this book is to be encyclopedic. But where do you look for inspiration in such a list?

You can of course skim through the pages of, say, Bordeaux châteaux or California wineries looking for the ones with four stars (if you are rich) or one star-with-a-box (if you are not). Or you can start with the food you are going to eat. You can look up the bottles on the wine-merchants' shelves. Or you can just browse.

As a further means of inspiration and access I also list here a selection of entries that have given me particular pleasure over the last year—a personal choice. It is not, I add emphatically, my choice of the world's best buys: just a random list of pleasures which will, if you follow the appropriate alphabetical entries, give you pleasure too.

Some of these entries refer to regions, some to particular wines and some to individual growers and/or merchants. Some are famous; some simply offer something unusual and worthwhile at a fair price.

Next year the list will be different: no repeat entries. I am not trying to establish a new classification—only to pass the word around about where exciting wines are coming from.

These are some ideas for 1982.

France

Aligoté
Beaumes de Venise
Beyer, Leon
Coteaux du Layon
Blanquette de Limoux
Bordeaux-Côtes-de Castillon
Chablis Premier Cru
Côtes du Luberon
Fixin
Gaillac Perlé
Gratien, Alfred
Jadot, Louis
Listel
Maufoux, Prosper
Morey-St-Denis
Minervois
Passe-tout-grains
Pol Roger

St-Joseph
Seyssel

Châteaux of Bordeaux

d'Angludet
Branaire-Ducru
Cissac
Fieuzal
Grand-Puy-Lacoste
La Lagune
Langoa-Barton
Magdelaine
de Pez
Potensac
Prieuré-Lichine
La Tour de By

Germany

Castell'sches
Deidesheim
Durbach
Escherndorf
Heilbronn
Munster
Ockfen
Scharzhofberger
Traisen
Ungstein
Winkel

Italy

Antinori
Attems
Bricco Manzoni
Castel S. Michele
Cellatica
Chiaretto
Dolcetto d'Alba
Gaja
Gavi
Marino
Montecarlo
Montepulciano del Molise
Nebbiolo d' Alba
Pomino
Torgiano
Venegazzú

Spain

Campo Viejo
Codorniu
La Rioja Alta
Lopez de Heredia
Marques de Caceres Blanco
Muga
Señorio de Sarria
Torres

Portugal

Barca Velha
Conde de Santar
Evel
Palacio do Brejoeira
Serradayres

Austria

Burgenland
Heiligenkreuz, Stift
Lenz Moser
Siegendorf, Klosterkeller

Hungary

Eger
Kadarka
Szekszárdi Vörös
Vilány

Yugoslavia

Kosovo
Prokupac
Traminac
Zilavka

Bulgaria

Cabernet
Mavrud

Greece

Carras, John

California

Alexander Valley
Almaden
Carneros Creek
Chateau St Jean
Christian Brothers
Domaine Chandon
Dry Creek
Giumarra
Jordan
Mondavi
Round Hill
Trefethen

Australia

Brand
Brown
Houghton
Petaluma
Leasingham
Tollana
Tyrrell

South Africa

Fleur du Cap Cabernet
Meerlust
Nederburg
Twee Jongegezellen
Zandvliet

Grape varieties

The most basic of all differences between wines stems from the grapes they are made of. Centuries of selection have resulted in each of the long-established wine-areas having its favourite single variety, or a group of varieties whose juice or wine is blended together. Red burgundy is made of one grape, the Pinot Noir; red Bordeaux of three or four: two kinds of Cabernet, Merlot, Malbec and sometimes others. The laws say which grapes must be used, so the labels assume it.

So in newer vineyards the choice of a grape is the planter's single most crucial decision. Where he is proud of it, and intends his wine to have the character of a particular grape, the variety is the first thing he puts on the label—hence the useful, originally Californian, term "varietal wine".

A knowledge of grape varieties, therefore, is the single most helpful piece of knowledge in finding wines you will like wherever they are grown. Learn to recognize the characters of the most important. At least seven—Cabernet, Pinot Noir, Riesling, Sauvignon Blanc, Chardonnay, Gewürztraminer and Muscat—have memorable tastes and smells distinct enough to form international categories of wine.

Further notes on grapes will be found on page 146 (for California) and in the sections on Germany, Italy, central and south-east Europe, South Africa, etc.

The following are the best and commonest wine grapes.

Grapes for white wine

Aligoté

Burgundy's second-rank white grape. Crisp (often sharp) wine, needs drinking young. Perfect for mixing with cassis (blackcurrant liqueur) to make a "Kir". Also grown in the USSR.

Blanc Fumé

Another name for SAUVIGNON BLANC, referring to the "smoky" smell of the wine, particularly on the upper Loire. Makes some of California's best whites.

Bual

Makes sweet Madeira wines.

Chardonnay

The white burgundy grape, one of the grapes of Champagne, and the best white grape of California. Gives dry wine of rich complexity. Trials in Australia and eastern Europe are also successful.

Chasselas

A prolific and widely grown early-ripening grape with little flavour, also grown for eating. Best known as Fendant in Switzerland, Gutedel in Germany. Perhaps the same as Hungary's Leanyka and Romania's Feteasca.

Chenin Blanc

The leading white grape of the middle Loire (Vouvray, Layon, etc.). Wine can be dry or sweet (or very sweet), but always retains plenty of acidity—hence its popularity in California, where it rarely distinguishes itself. See also Steen.

Clairette

A dull neutral grape widely used in the s. of France.

Fendant
>> See Chasselas

Folle Blanche
>> The third most widely grown grape of France, though no-where making fine wine. High acid and little flavour makes it ideal for brandy. Known as Gros Plant in Brittany, Picpoul in the Midi. At its best in California.

Furmint
>> A grape of great character: the trade mark of Hungary both in Tokay and as vivid vigorous table wine with an appley flavour. Called Sipon in Yugoslavia.

Gewürztraminer (or Traminer)
>> The most pungent wine grape, distinctively spicy to smell and taste. Wines are often rich and soft, even when fully dry. Best in Alsace; also good in Germany, eastern Europe, Australia, California.

Grüner Veltliner
>> An Austrian speciality. Round Vienna and in the Wachau and Weinviertel can be delicious: light but lively. For drinking young.

Italian Riesling
>> Grown in n. Italy and all over central eastern Europe. Inferior to German or Rhine Riesling with lower acidity, but a good all-round grape. Alias Wälschriesling, Olaszriesling (or often just "Riesling").

Kerner
>> The most successful of a wide range of recent German var-ieties, largely made by crossing Riesling and Sylvaner (but in this case Riesling and [red] Trollinger). Early-ripening; flowery wine with good acidity. Popular in RHEINPFALZ.

Malvasia
>> Known as Malmsey in Madeira, Malvasia in Italy: also grown in Greece, Spain, eastern Europe. Makes rich brown wines or soft whites of no great character.

Müller-Thurgau
>> Dominant variety in Germany's Rheinhessen and Rhein-pfalz; said to be a cross between Riesling and Sylvaner. Ripens early to make soft flowery wines to drink young. Makes good sweet wines. Grows well in Austria, England.

Muscadet
>> Makes light, very dry wines round Nantes in Brittany. Recently some have been sharper than they should.

Muscat (many varieties)
>> Universally grown easily recognized pungent grape, mostly made into perfumed sweet wines, often fortified (as in France's VIN DOUX NATURELS). Muscat d'Alsace is alone in being dry.

Palomino
>> Alias Listan. Makes all the best sherry.

Pedro Ximénez
>> Said to have come to s. Spain from Germany. Makes very strong wine in Montilla and Malaga. Used in blending sherry. Also grown in Australia, California, South Africa.

Pinot Blanc
>> A close relation of CHARDONNAY without its ultimate nobility. Grown in Champagne, Alsace (increasingly), n. Italy (good sparkling wine), s. Germany, eastern Europe, California. Called Weissburgunder in German.

Pinot Gris
>> Makes rather heavy full-bodied whites with a certain spicy style. Known as Tokay in Alsace, Tocai in n.e. Italy and Yugoslavia, Ruländer in Germany.

Pinot Noir

Superlative black grape (see under Grapes for red wine) used in Champagne and occasionally elsewhere for making white wine, or a very pale pink "vin gris".

Riesling

Germany's finest grape, now planted round the world. Wine of brilliant sweet/acid balance, flowery in youth but maturing to subtle oily scents and flavours. Successful in Alsace (for dry wine), Austria, parts of eastern Europe, Australia, California, South Africa. Often called White, Johannisberg or Rhine Riesling.

Sauvignon Blanc

Very distinctive aromatic, herby and sometimes smoky scented wine, can be austere (on the upper Loire) or buxom (in Bordeaux, where it is combined with SEMILLON, and parts of California). Also called Fumé Blanc.

Scheurebe

Spicy-flavoured German Riesling × Silvaner cross, very successful in Rheinpfalz, esp. for Ausleses.

Semillon

The grape contributing the lusciousness to great Sauternes; subject to "noble rot" in the right conditions. Makes soft dry wine. Often called "Riesling" in Australia.

Sercial

Makes the driest wine of Madeira—where they claim it is really Riesling.

Seyval Blanc

French-made hybrid between French and American vines. Very hardy and attractively fruity. Popular and successful in the eastern States and England.

Steen

South Africa's best white grape: lively fruity wine. Said to be the Chenin Blanc of the Loire.

Sylvaner (Silvaner)

Germany's workhorse grape: wine rarely better than pleasant except in Franconia. Good in the Italian Tyrol and useful in Alsace. Wrongly called Riesling in California.

Tokay

See Pinot Gris. Also a table grape in California and a supposedly Hungarian grape in Australia.

Traminer

See Gewürztraminer

Trebbiano

Important grape of central Italy, used in Orvieto, Chianti, Soave, etc. Also grown in s. France as Ugni Blanc, and Cognac as "St-Emilion".

Ugni Blanc

See Trebbiano

Verdelho

Madeira grape making excellent medium-sweet wine.

Verdicchio

Gives its name to good dry wine in central Italy.

Vernaccia

Grape grown in central and s. Italy and Sardinia for strong wine inclining towards sherry.

Viognier

Rare but remarkable grape of the Rhône valley, grown at Condrieu to make very fine soft and fragrant wine.

Welschriesling (or Wälschriesling)

See Italian Riesling

Weissburgunder

See Pinot Blanc

Grapes for red wine

Barbera
One of several good standard grapes of Piemonte, giving dark, robust, fruity and often rather sharp wine. High acidity makes it a good grape for California.

Cabernet Franc
The lesser of two sorts of Cabernet grown in Bordeaux; the Cabernet of the Loire making Chinon, etc., and rosé.

Cabernet Sauvignon
Grape of great character; spicy, herby and tannic. The first grape of the Médoc, also makes the best Californian, Australian, South American and eastern European reds. Its wine always needs ageing and usually blending.

Carignan
By far the commonest grape of France, covering hundreds of thousands of acres. Prolific with dull but harmless wine. Also common in North Africa, Spain and California.

Cinsaut
Common bulk-producing grape of s. France; in S. Africa crossed with Pinot Noir to make Pinotage.

Gamay
The Beaujolais grape: light fragrant wines at their best quite young. Makes even lighter wine on the Loire and in Switzerland and Savoie. Known as Napa Gamay in California, Blaufräukisch in Germany.

Gamay Beaujolais
Not Gamay but a variety of PINOT NOIR grown in California.

Grenache
Useful grape giving strong and fruity but pale wine: good rosé. Grown in s. France, Spain, California and usually blended.

Grignolino
Makes one of the good cheap table wines of Piemonte. Also used in California.

Merlot
Adaptable grape making the great fragrant and rich wines of Pomerol and St-Emilion, an important element in Médoc reds, and making lighter but good wines in n. Italy, Italian Switzerland, Yugoslavia, Argentina, etc.

Nebbiolo (also called Spanna)
Italy's best red grape, the grape of Barolo, Barbaresco, Gattinara and Valtellina. Intense, nobly fruity and perfumed wine taking years to mature.

Pinot Noir
The glory of Burgundy's Côte d'Or, with scent, flavour, texture and body unmatched anywhere. Less happy elsewhere; makes light wines of no great distinction in Germany, Switzerland, Austria; good ones in Hungary. The great challenge to the wine-makers of California.

Sangiovese
The main red grape of Chianti and much of central Italy.

Spätburgunder
German for Pinot Noir

Syrah (alias Shiraz)
The best Rhône red grape, with heavy purple wine, which can mature superbly. Said by some to come from Shiraz in Persia; others say Syracuse in Sicily. Very important as "Shiraz" in Australia.

Zinfandel
Fruity adaptable grape peculiar to California.

Wine & Food

There are no rules and regulations about what wine goes with what food, but there is a vast body of accumulated experience which it is absurd to ignore.

This list of dishes and appropriate wines records most of the conventional combinations and suggests others that I personally have found good. But it is only a list of ideas intended to help you make quick decisions. Any of the groups of recommended wines could have been extended almost indefinitely, drawing on the whole world's wine list. In general I have stuck to the wines that are widely available, at the same time trying to ring the changes so that the same wines don't come up time and time again—as they tend to do in real life.

The stars refer to the rating system used throughout the book: see opposite Contents.

Before the Meal—Aperitifs

The traditional aperitif wines are either sparkling (epitomized by champagne) or fortified (epitomized by sherry). The current fashion for a glass of white wine before eating calls for something light and stimulating, dry but not acid, with a degree of character, such as:

France:
> Alsace Edelzwicker, Riesling or Sylvaner; Chablis; Muscadet; Sauvignon de Touraine; Graves Blanc; Mâcon Blanc; Crépy.

Germany:
> Any Kabinett wine.

Italy:
> Soave; Orvieto Secco; Frascati; Pinot Bianco; Montecarlo; Vernaccia; Tocai; Lugano; Albana di Romagna.

Spain:
> Rioja Blanco Marqués de Caceres or Faustino V, or Albariño, but fino sherry or Montilla is even better.

Portugal:
> Any vinho verde.

Eastern Europe:
> Riesling.

California:
> "Chablis"; Chenin Blanc; Riesling; French Colombard; Emerald Riesling; Fumé Blanc.

Australia:
> Riesling.

South Africa:
> Steen.

England:
> English white.

References to these wines will be found under their national A–Z sections.

First courses

Aïoli
> A thirst-quencher is needed with so much garlic. ★→★★★ white Rhône, or Verdicchio, and mineral water.

Antipasto (see also Hors d'oeuvre)
> ★★ dry or medium white, preferably Italian (e.g. Soave) or light red, e.g. Valpolicella, Bardolino or young ★ Bordeaux.

Artichoke

    ★ red or rosé.

    vinaigrette ★ young red, e.g. Bordeaux.

    hollandaise ★ or ★★ full-bodied dry or medium white, e.g. Mâcon Blanc, Rheinpfalz or California "Chablis".

Asparagus

    ★★→★★★ white burgundy or Chardonnay, or Tavel rosé.

Assiette anglaise (assorted cold meats)

    ★★ dry white, e.g. Chablis, Graves, Muscadet, Dão.

Avocado

    with prawns, crab, etc. ★★→★★★ dry to medium white, e.g. Rheingau or Rheinpfalz Kabinett, Graves, California Chardonnay or Sauvignon, Cape Stein, or dry rosé.

    vinaigrette ★ light red, or fino sherry.

Bisques

    ★★ dry white with plenty of body: Verdicchio, Pinot Gris, Graves.

Bouillabaisse

    ★→★★ very dry white: Muscadet, Alsace Sylvaner, Entre-Deux-Mers, Pouilly Fumé, Cassis.

Caviare

    ★★★ champagne or iced vodka.

Cheese fondue

    ★★ dry white: Fendant du Valais, Grüner Veltliner.

Chicken Liver Pâté

    Appetizing dry white, e.g. ★★ white Bordeaux, or light fruity red; Beaujolais, Gamay de Touraine or Valpolicella.

Clams and Chowders

    ★★ big-scale white, not necessarily bone dry: e.g. Rhône, Pinot Gris, Dry Sauternes.

Consommé

    ★★→★★★ medium-dry sherry, dry Madeira, Marsala, Montilla.

Crudités

    ★→★★ light red or rosé, e.g. Côtes-du-Rhône, Beaujolais, Chianti, Zinfandel.

Eggs (see also Soufflés)

    These present difficulties: they clash with most wine and spoil good ones. So ★→★★ of whatever is going.

Empanadas

    ★→★★ Chilean Cabernet, Zinfandel.

Escargots

    ★★ red or white of some substance: e.g. Burgundy; Côtes-du-Rhône, Chardonnay, Shiraz, etc.

Foie gras

    ★★★→★★★★ white. In Bordeaux they drink Sauternes. Others prefer vintage champagne or a rich Gewürztraminer Vendange tardive.

Gazpacho

    Sangria (see Spain) is refreshing, but to avoid too much liquid intake dry Manzanilla or Montilla is better.

Grapefruit

    If you must start a meal with grapefruit try port, Madeira or sweet sherry with it.

Ham, raw

    See Prosciutto

Herrings, raw or pickled

    Dutch gin or Scandinavian akvavit, or ★★ full-bodied white Mâcon-Villages, Graves or Dão.

Hors d'oeuvre (see also Antipasto)

    →* clean fruity sharp white: Sancerre or any Sauvignon Alsace Sylvaner, Muscadet, Cape Stein—or young light re Bordeaux, Rhône or equivalent.

Mackerel, smoked

    →* full-bodied tasty white: e.g. Gewürztraminer, Tokay d'Alsace or Chablis Premier Cru.

Melon

    Needs a strong sweet wine: ** Port, Bual Madeira, Muscat Oloroso sherry or Vin doux naturel.

Minestrone

    * red: Grignolino, Chianti, etc.

Omelettes

    See observations under Eggs

Onion/Leek tart

    *→*** fruity dry white, e.g. Alsace Sylvaner or Riesling Mâcon-Villages of a good vintage, California or Australian Riesling.

Pasta

    *→** red or white according to the sauce or accompaniments e.g.

    with fish sauce (vongole, etc.) Verdicchio or Soave.
    meat sauce Chianti, Beaujolais or Côtes-du-Rhône.
    tomato sauce Barbera or Sicilian red.
    cream sauce Orvieto or Frascati.

Pâté

    ** dry white: e.g. Chablis, Mâcon Blanc, Graves.

Peppers or aubergines (egg-plant), stuffed

    ** vigorous red: e.g. Bull's Blood, Chianti, Zinfandel.

Pizza

    Any ** dry Italian red or a ** Rioja, Australian Shiraz or California Zinfandel.

Prawns or Shrimps

    →* dry white: burgundy or Bordeaux, Chardonnay or Riesling. ("Cocktail sauce" kills wine.)

Prosciutto with melon

    →* full-bodied dry or medium white: e.g. Orvieto o Frascati, Fendant, Grüner Veltliner, Alsace Sylvaner California Gewürztraminer, Australian Riesling.

Quiches

    *→** dry white with body (Alsace, Graves, Sauvignon) o young red according to the ingredients.

Ratatouille

    ** vigorous young red, e.g. Chianti, Zinfandel, Bull's Blood young red Bordeaux.

Salade niçoise

    ** very dry not too light or flowery white, e.g. white (or rosé Rhône, white Spanish, Dão, California Sauvignon Blanc.

Salads

    As a first course: any dry and appetizing white wine. After main course: no wine.
    N.B. Vinegar in salad dressings destroys the flavour of wine If you want salad at a meal with fine wine, dress the sala with wine instead of vinegar.

Salami

    *→** powerfully tasty red or rosé: e.g. Barbera, youn Zinfandel, Tavel rosé, young Bordeaux.

Salmon, smoked

    A dry but pungent white, e.g. fino sherry, Alsace Gewürz traminer, Chablis Grand Cru.

Soufflés

As show dishes these deserve ★★→★★★ wines.

Fish soufflés Dry white, e.g. burgundy, Bordeaux, Alsace, Chardonnay, etc.

Cheese soufflé Red burgundy or Bordeaux, Cabernet Sauvignon, etc.

Taramasalata

Calls for a rustic southern white of strong personality; not necessarily the Greek Retsina.

Terrine

As for pâté, or the equivalent red: e.g. Beaune, Mercurey, Beaujolais-Villages, fairly young ★★ St-Emilion, California Cabernet or Zinfandel, Bulgarian or Chilean Cabernet, etc.

Trout, smoked

Sancerre, Pouilly Fumé, or California Fumé Blanc.

Fish

Abalone

★★→★★★ dry or medium white: e.g. Sauvignon Blanc, Chardonnay, Verdicchio.

Bass, striped

Same wine as for sole.

Cod

A good neutral background for fine dry or medium whites, e.g. ★★→★★★ Chablis, cru classé Graves, German Kabinetts and their equivalents.

Coquilles St. Jacques

An inherently slightly sweet dish, best with medium-dry white wine.

in cream sauces ★★★ German wines.

grilled or fried Hermitage Blanc, Gewürztraminer, California Chenin Blanc or Riesling.

Crab, cold, with salad

★★★California or Rheinpfalz Riesling Kabinett or Spätlese.

Eel, smoked

Either strong or sharp wine, e.g. fino sherry or Bourgogne Aligoté.

Haddock

★★→★★★ dry white with a certain richness: e.g. Meursault, California Chardonnay.

Herrings

Need a white with some acidity to cut their richness. Burgundy Aligoté or Gros Plant from Brittany or dry Sauvignon Blanc. **Kippers:** a good cup of tea, preferably Ceylon.

Lamproie à la Bordelaise

★★ young red Bordeaux, especially St-Emilion or Pomerol.

Lobster or Crab

salad ★★→★★★★ white. Non-vintage champagne, Alsace Riesling, Chablis Premier Cru.

richly sauced Vintage champagne, fine white burgundy, cru classé Graves, California Chardonnay, Rheinpfalz Spätlese, Hermitage Blanc.

Mackerel

★★ hard or sharp white: Sauvignon Blanc from Bergerac or Touraine, Gros Plant, vinho verde, white Rioja.

Mullet, red

★★ Mediterranean white, even Retsina, for the atmosphere.

Mussels

★→★★ Gros Plant, Muscadet, California "Chablis".

Oysters

    →* white. Champagne (non-vintage), Chablis or (better) Chablis Premier Cru, Muscadet or Entre-Deux-Mers.

Salmon, fresh

    *** fine white burgundy: Puligny- or Chassagne-Montrachet, Meursault, Corton-Charlemagne, Chablis Grand Cru, California Chardonnay, or Rheingau Kabinett or Spätlese, California Riesling or equivalent.

Sardines, fresh grilled

    *→** very dry white: e.g. vinho verde, Dão, Muscadet.

Scallops

    See Coquilles St. Jacques

Shad

    →* white Graves or Meursault.

Shellfish (general)

    Dry white with plain boiled shellfish, richer wines with richer sauces.

Shrimps, potted

    Fino sherry or Chablis.

Skate with black butter

    ** white with some pungency (e.g. Alsace Pinot Gris) or a clean one like Muscadet.

Sole, Plaice, etc.

    plain, grilled or fried An ideal accompaniment for fine wines: * up to **** white burgundy, or its equivalent.

    with sauce Depending on the ingredients: sharp dry wine for tomato sauce, fairly sweet for Sole véronique, etc.

Trout

    Delicate white wine, e.g. *** Mosel.

    Smoked, a full-flavoured **→*** white: Gewürztraminer, Pinot Gris, Rhine Spätlese or Australian Hunter white.

Turbot

    Fine rich dry white, e.g. *** Meursault or its Californian equivalent.

Meat

Beef, boiled

    ** red: e.g. Cru Bourgeois Bordeaux (Bourg or Fronsac), Côtes-du-Rhône-Villages, Australian Shiraz or Claret.

Beef, roast

    An ideal partner for fine red wine. *→**** red of any kind.

Beef stew

    →* sturdy red, e.g. Pomerol or St-Emilion, Hermitage, Shiraz.

Beef Strogonoff

    →* suitably dramatic red: e.g. Barolo, Valpolicella, Amarone, Hermitage, late-harvest Zinfandel.

Cassoulet

    ** red from s.w. France, e.g. Cahors or Corbières, or Barbera or Zinfandel.

Chicken or Turkey, roast

    Virtually any wine, including your very best bottles of dry or medium white and fine old reds.

Chili con carne

    *→** young red: e.g. Bull's Blood, Chianti, Mountain Red.

Chinese food

    ** dry to medium-dry white: e.g. Jugoslav Riesling, Mâcon Villages, California "Chablis".

Choucroute

    Lager.

Confit d'Oie

 ★★→★★★ rather young and tannic red Bordeaux helps to cut the richness. Alsace Tokay or Gewürztraminer matches it.

Coq au Vin

 ★★→★★★★ red burgundy. In an ideal world one bottle of Chambertin in the dish, one on the table.

Corned beef hash

 ★★ Zinfandel, Chianti, Côtes-du-Rhône red.

Curry

 ★→★★ medium-sweet white, very cold: e.g. Orvieto abboccato, certain California Chenin Blancs, Jugoslav Traminer.

Duck or Goose

 ★★★ rather rich white, e.g. Rheinpfalz Spätlese or Alsace Réserve Exceptionelle, or ★★★ Bordeaux or burgundy.

 Wild Duck ★★★ big-scale red: e.g. Hermitage, Châteauneuf-du-Pape, Calif. or S. African Cabernet, Australian Shiraz.

Frankfurters

 ★→★★ German or Austrian white, or Beaujolais.

Game birds

 Young birds plain roasted deserve the best red wine you can afford. With older birds in casseroles ★★→★★★ red, e.g. Gevrey-Chambertin, St-Emilion, Napa Cabernet.

Game Pie

 ★★★ red wine.

Goulash

 ★★ strong young red: e.g. Zinfandel, Bulgarian Cabernet.

Grouse

 See under Game birds

Ham

 ★★→★★★ fairly young red burgundy, e.g. Volnay, Savigny, Beaune, Corton, or a slightly sweet German white, e.g. a Rhine Spätlese, or Chianti or Valpolicella.

Hamburger

 ★→★★ young red: e.g. Beaujolais, Corbières or Minervois, Chianti, Zinfandel.

Hare

 Jugged hare calls for ★★→★★★ red with plenty of flavour: not-too-old burgundy or Bordeaux. The same for saddle.

Kebabs

 ★★ vigorous red: e.g. Greek Demestica, Turkish Doluca, Hungarian Pinot Noir, Chilean Cabernet, Zinfandel.

Kidneys

 ★★→★★★ red: Pomerol or St-Emilion, Rhône, Barbaresco, Rioja, California or Australian Cabernet.

Lamb cutlets or chops

 As for roast lamb, but less grand.

Lamb, roast

 One of the traditional and best partners for very good red Bordeaux—or its equivalents.

Liver

 ★★ young red: Beaujolais-Villages, Rhône, Médoc, Italian Merlot, Zinfandel.

Meatballs

 ★★→★★★ red: e.g. Mercurey, Madiran, Rubesco, Dão, Zinfandel.

Mixed Grill

 A fairly light easily swallowable red; ★★ red Bordeaux from Bourg, Fronsac or Premières Côtes; Chianti; Bourgogne Passetoutgrains.

Moussaka

 ★→★★ red or rosé: e.g. Chianti, Corbières, Côtes de Provence, California Burgundy.

Oxtail

    →* rather rich red: e.g. St-Emilion or Pomerol, Burgundy, Barolo or Chianti Classico, Rioja Reserva, California Cabernet.

Paella

    ** Spanish red, dry white or rosé, e.g. Panades or Rioja or vinho verde.

Partridge, pheasant

    See under Game birds

Pigeons or squabs

    →** red Bordeaux, Chianti Classico, Cabernet Sauvignon, etc.

Pork, roast

    The sauce or stuffing has more flavour than the meat. Sharp apple sauce or pungent sage and onion need only a plain young wine. Pork without them, on the other hand, is a good neutral background to very good white or red wine.

Rabbit

    *→*** young red: Italian for preference.

Ris de veau

    See Sweetbreads

Sauerkraut

    Beer.

Shepherd's Pie

    *→** rough and ready red seems most appropriate, but no harm would come to a good one.

Steak and Kidney Pie or Pudding

    Red Rioja Reserva or mature **→*** Bordeaux.

Steaks

    Au poivre a fairly young *** Rhône red or Cabernet.

    Tartare ** light young red: Bergerac, Valpolicella.

    Filet or Tournedos *** red of any kind (but not old wines with Béarnaise sauce).

    T-bone **→*** reds of similar bone-structure: e.g. Barolo, Hermitage, Australian Cabernet.

    Fiorentina (bistecca) Chianti Classico.

    Ostrich South African Pinotage.

Stews and Casseroles

    A lusty full-flavoured red, e.g. young Côtes-du-Rhône, Corbières, Barbera, Shiraz, Zinfandel, etc.

Sweetbreads

    These tend to be a grand dish, suggesting a grand wine, e.g. *** Rhine Kabinett or Spätlese, or well-matured Bordeaux or Burgundy, depending on the sauce.

Tongue

    Ideal for favourite bottles of any red or white.

Tripe

    *→** red: Corbières, Mâcon Rouge, etc., or rather sweet white, e.g. Liebfraumilch.

Veal, roast

    A good neutral background dish for any old red which may have faded, or a *** German white.

Venison

    *** big-scale red (Rhône, Bordeaux of a grand vintage) or rather rich white (Rheinpfalz Spätlese or Tokay d'Alsace).

Wiener Schnitzel

    →* light red from the Italian Tyrol (Alto Adige) or the Médoc: or Austrian Riesling, Grüner Veltliner or Gumpoldskirchener.

Cheese

Very ripe cheese completely masks the flavour of wine. Only serve fine wine with mild cheeses.

Bleu de Bresse, Dolcelatte, Gorgonzola

Need fairly emphatic accompaniment: young ✹✹ red wine (Barbera, Dolcetto, Moulin-à-Vent, etc.) or sweet white.

Cream cheeses: Brie, Camembert, Bel Paese, Edam, etc.

In their mild state go perfectly with any good wine, red or white.

English cheeses

On the whole are strong and acidic. Sweet or strong wine is needed.

Cheddar, Cheshire, Wensleydale, Stilton, Gloucester, etc. Ruby, tawny or vintage-character (not vintage) port, or a very big red: Hermitage, Châteauneuf-du-Pape, Barolo, etc.

Goat cheeses

✹✹→✹✹✹ white wine of marked character, either dry (e.g. Sancerre) or sweet (e.g. Monbazillac, Sauternes).

Hard Cheese, Parmesan, Gruyère, Emmenthal

Full-bodied dry whites, e.g. Tokay d'Alsace or Vernaccia.

Roquefort, Danish Blue

Are so strong-flavoured that only the youngest, biggest or sweetest wines stand a chance.

Desserts

Apple pie, apple strudel

✹✹→✹✹✹ sweet German, Austrian or Hungarian white.

Apples, Cox's Orange Pippins

Vintage port (55, 60, 63 or 66).

Baked Alaska

Sweet champagne or Asti Spumante.

Cakes

Bual or Malmsey Madeira, Oloroso or cream sherry.

Cheesecake

✹✹→✹✹✹ sweet white from Vouvray or Coteaux du Layon.

Chocolate cake, mousse, soufflés

No wine.

Christmas pudding

Sweet champagne or Asti Spumante.

Creams and Custards

✹✹→✹✹✹ Sauternes, Monbazillac or similar golden white.

Crème brûlée

The most luxurious dish, demanding ✹✹✹→✹✹✹✹ Sauternes or Rhine Beerenauslese, or the best Madeira or Tokay.

Crêpes Suzette

Sweet champagne or Asti Spumante.

Fruit flans (i.e. peach, raspberry)

✹✹✹ Sauternes, Monbazillac or sweet Vouvray.

Fruit, fresh

Sweet Coteaux du Layon white, light sweet muscat (e.g. California).

Fruit salads, orange salad

No wine.

Nuts

Oloroso sherry, Bual, Madeira, vintage or tawny port.

Sorbets, ice-creams

No wine.

Stewed fruits, i.e. apricots, pears, etc.
> Sweet Muscatel: e.g. Muscat de Beaumes de Venise, Moscato di Pantelleria.

Strawberries and cream
> ✶✶✶ Sauternes or Vouvray.

Wild strawberries Serve with ✶✶✶ red Bordeaux poured over them and in your glass (no cream).

Summer Pudding
> Fairly young Sauternes of a good vintage (e.g. 70, 71, 75).

Treacle Tart
> Too sweet for any wine but a treacly Malmsey Madeira.

Trifle
> No wine: should be sufficiently vibrant with sherry.

Sweet Soufflés
> Sweet Vouvray or Coteaux du Layon.

Zabaglione
> Light gold Marsala.

Savoury

Cheese straws
> Admirable meal-ending with a final glass (or bottle) of a particularly good red wine.

Temperature

Temperature
No single aspect of serving wine makes or mars it so easily as getting the temperature right. White wines almost invariably taste dull and insipid served warm and red wines have disappointingly little scent or flavour served cold. The chart below gives an indication of what is generally found to be the best and most satisfactory temperature for serving each class of wine.

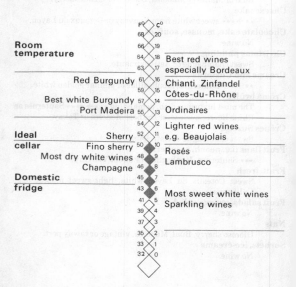

	F°	C°	
	68	20	
Room	66	19	
temperature	64	18	Best red wines
	63	17	especially Bordeaux
Red Burgundy	61	16	Chianti, Zinfandel
	59	15	Côtes-du-Rhône
Best white Burgundy	57	14	
Port Madeira	56	13	Ordinaires
	54	12	Lighter red wines
Ideal Sherry	52	11	e.g. Beaujolais
cellar Fino sherry	50	10	
Most dry white wines	48	9	Rosés
Champagne	46	8	Lambrusco
Domestic	45	7	
fridge	43	6	
	41	5	Most sweet white wines
	39	4	Sparkling wines
	37	3	
	35	2	
	33	1	
	32	0	

Wine Newspeak

The last ten years have seen a revolution in wine technology. They have also heard a matching revolution in wine-talk. Attempts to express the characters of wines used to get little further than terms as vague as "fruity" and "full-bodied". Your modern wine-lover is made of sterner stuff. He is satisfied with nothing less than the jargon of laboratory analysis. Rather than expound the old imagery (which should after all be self-explanatory) I therefore give below a summary of the new hard-edge wine-talk.

The most frequent references are to the ripeness of grapes at picking; the resultant alcohol and sugar content of the wine; various measures of its acidity; the amount of sulphur dioxide used as a preservative, and the amount of "dry extract"—the sum of all the things that give wine its characteristic flavours.

The **sugar** in wine is mainly glucose and fructose, with traces of arabinose, xylose and other sugars that are not fermentable by yeast, but can be attacked by bacteria. Each country has its own system for measuring the sugar content or ripeness of grapes, known as the "**must-weight**". The chart below relates the three principal ones (German, French and American) to each other, to specific gravity, and to the potential alcohol of the resulting wine if all the sugar is fermented out.

Specific Gravity	°O °Oechsle	Baumé	Brix	% Potential Alcohol v/v
1.065	65	8.8	15.8	8.1
1.070	70	9.4	17.0	8.8
1.075	75	10.1	18.1	9.4
1.080	80	10.7	19.3	10.0
1.085	85	11.3	20.4	10.6
1.090	90	11.9	21.5	11.3
1.095	95	12.5	22.5	11.9
1.100	100	13.1	23.7	12.5
1.105	105	13.7	24.8	13.1
1.110	110	14.3	25.8	13.8
1.115	115	14.9	26.9	14.4
1.120	120	15.5	28.0	15.0

Residual sugar is the sugar left after fermentation has finished or been artificially stopped, measured in grammes per litre.

Alcohol content (mainly ethyl alcohol) is expressed as a percentage by volume of the total liquid.

Acidity is both fixed and volatile. **Fixed acidity** consists principally of tartaric, malic and citric acids which are all found in the grape, and lactic and succinic acids, which are produced during fermentation. **Volatile acidity** consists mainly of acetic acid, which is rapidly formed by bacteria in the presence of oxygen. A small amount of volatile acidity is inevitable and attractive. With a larger amount the wine becomes "pricked"—i.e. starts to turn to vinegar.

Total acidity is fixed and volatile acidity combined. As a rule of thumb for a well-balanced wine it should be in the region of 1 gramme/thousand for each 10°Oechsle (see above).

pH is a measure of the strength of the acidity, rather than its volume. A pH above 7 is alkaline; below is acid; the lower the figure the more acid. Wine normally ranges in pH from 2.8 to 3.8. Cold northerly climates with less ripe grapes tend to lower pHs; winemakers in hot climates can have problems getting the pH low enough. Lower pH gives better colour, helps prevent bacterial spoilage, allows more of the SO_2 to be free and active as a preservative.

Sulphur dioxide (SO_2) is added to prevent oxidation and other accidents in wine-making. Some of it combines with sugars, etc., and is known as "bound". Only the "**free SO_2**" that remains in the wine is effective as a preservative. **Total SO_2** is controlled by law according to the level of residual sugar: the more sugar the more SO_2 needed.

France

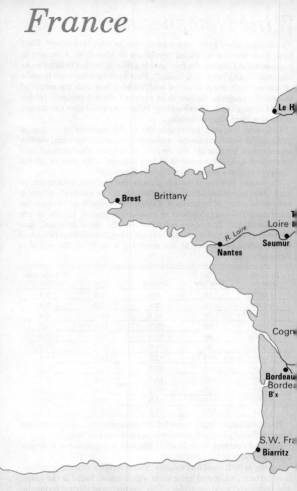

France makes every kind of wine, and invented most of them. Her wine trade, both exporting and importing, dwarfs that of any other country. Tens of thousands of properties make wine over a large part of France's surface. This is a guide to the best known of them and to the system by which the rest can be identified and to some extent evaluated.

All France's best wine regions have Appellations Controlées, which may apply to a single small vineyard or a whole large district: the system varies from region to region, with Burgundy on the whole having the smallest and most precise appellations, grouped into larger units by complicated formulae, and Bordeaux having the widest and most general appellations, in which it is the particular property (or "château") that matters. In between lie an infinity of variations.

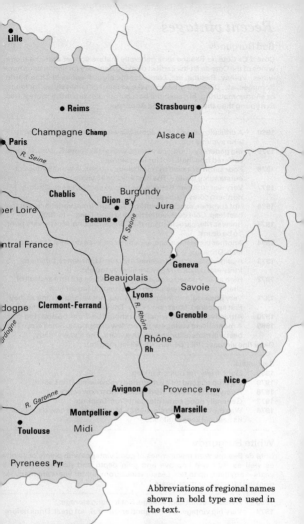

Abbreviations of regional names shown in bold type are used in the text.

An Appellation Controlée is a guarantee of origin and of production method, of grape varieties and quantities produced: not of quality. France does not have a comprehensive quality-testing system as Germany does. The scale of the problem is too vast and the French are too French.

Appellations therefore help to identify a wine and indicate that it comes from a major area. They are the first thing to look for on a label.

Wine regions without the overall quality and traditions required for an appellation can be ranked as Vins Délimités de Qualité Supérieure (VDQS), or (a new third rank created largely to encourage the improvement of mediocre wines in the south of France) Vins de Pays. VDQS wines are often good value, on the Avis principle. Vins de Pays are worth trying for curiosity's sake.

Recent vintages

Red Burgundy

Côte d'Or Côte de Beaune reds generally mature sooner than the bigger wines of the Côte de Nuits. Earliest drinking dates are for lighter commune wines: Volnay, Beaune, etc. Latest for the biggest wines of Chambertin, Romanée, etc. Different growers make wines of different styles, for longer or shorter maturing, but even the best burgundies are much more attractive young than the equivalent red Bordeaux.

1980	A difficult, wet year, but some fair wines from the best growers who avoided rot.
1979	Big generally good ripe vintage with weak spots. S. Côte de Nuits suffered from hail. Not for long storage.
1978	Poor summer saved by miraculous autumn. A small vintage of outstanding quality. The best will live 15 years.
1977	Very wet summer. Better wine than expected, especially in northern côtes. Drink soon.
1976	Hot summer, excellent vintage. As usual great variations, but the best (esp. Côte de Beaune) rich and long-lived—to 1990.
1975	Rot was rife, particularly in the Côte de Beaune. Mostly very poor. To be drunk.
1974	Another big wet vintage; mostly poor, even the best light and lean. Drink up.
1973	Again, vintage rain stretched the crop. Light wines, but many fruity and delicate. Many are already too old.
1972	High acidity posed problems, but the wines are firm and full of character, ageing well. Few need keeping longer now.
1971	Very powerful and impressive wines, not as long-lasting as they first appeared. Most now ready. The best have 10 years ahead.
1970	Attractive soft fruity wines, but should be drunk up now. Big crop.
1969	A magnificent vintage with very few exceptions. Small crop. The best will mature for another five years. The rest are ready.

Older fine vintages: '66, '64, '62, '61, '59 (all mature).

Beaujolais

1980	Light, fruity, for quick drinking.
1979	Big crop of good quick-maturing typical wine. Drink soon.
1978	A very good vintage in profusion. Most now ready.
1977	Generally poor, some pleasant Crus. Drink up.
1976	Was the best vintage since 1971. Most wines are now delicious. Its best will keep until 1983.

White Burgundy

Côte de Beaune Well-made wines of good vintages with plenty of acidity as well as fruit will improve and gain depth and richness for some years—anything up to ten. Lesser wines from lighter years are ready for drinking after two or three years.

1980	A weak, but not bad, vintage. Not for long storage.
1979	Very big vintage. Overall good and useful, not great. Drink before '78s.
1978	Very good wines, firm and well-balanced, to keep till 1990.
1977	Rather light; some well-balanced and good. Drink soon.
1976	Hot summer, rather heavy wines; good but not for laying-down.
1975	Hot summer, then vintage rain. Whites did much better than reds. Chablis best, but all now ready.
1974	Spring frosts reduced the crop. The hot summer made some good wines, but they have aged disappointingly.
1973	Very attractive, fruity, typical and plentiful. Drink up.
1972	Awkward wines to make with high acidity, even greenness, but plenty of character. All are now ready to drink.
1971	Great power and style, some almost too rich, but the best have good balance. Small crop. Generally ready.

The white wines of the Mâconnais (Pouilly-Fuissé, St Véran, Mâcon-Villages) follow a similar pattern, but do not last as long. They are more appreciated for their freshness than their richness.

Chablis Grand Cru Chablis of vintages with both strength and acidity can age superbly for up to ten years. Premier Crus proportionately less. Only buy Petit Chablis of ripe years, and drink it young.

1980	More successful than the rest of Burgundy.
1979	Very big crop. Good easy wines, not for storing.
1978	Excellent wines for fairly early drinking.
1977	Reduced quantity, but typical and fresh like 1974. Drink soon.
1976	A great vintage. Start to drink.
1975	Very good wines maturing rather quickly. Drink.

Red Bordeaux

Médoc/red Graves For some wines bottle-age is optional: for these it is indispensable. Minor châteaux from light vintages need only two or three years, but even modest wines of great years can improve for fifteen years or so, and the great châteaux of these years need double that time.

1980	Small, late harvest, ripe but rained-on. Many respectable wines but no exciting ones. Drink '83–'90.
1979	Abundant harvest of good average quality. '82–'95.
1978	A miracle vintage: magnificent long warm autumn saved the day. Some very good wines. '84–2000.
1977	Pleasant light wine, many better than 1974. Now–'87.
1976	Excessively hot, dry summer; rain just before vintage. Difficult year, but its best wine will be very good, maturing rather quickly. Now–'95.
1975	A splendid summer and very fine vintage, with deep colour, high sugar content and some tannin. For long keeping.
1974	Oceans of disappointing light wines, though the best have good colour and have developed some character. Now–'85.
1973	A huge vintage, attractive to drink young but lacking acidity and tannin. Now–'86.
1972	High acidity from unripe grapes. Do not pay much for '72s. Now.
1971	Small crop. Less fruity than '70 and less consistent. A few châteaux made outstanding wine. Most are ready to drink.
1970	Abundance *and* uniform quality. Big fruity wines with elegance and attractive suppleness. Wines of great distinction for long keeping. Now–2000.
1969	Mean wines lacking fruit and colour. Should all be drunk soon.
1968	This time a wet August was the culprit. Very few drinkable wines.
1967	Never seductive, but characterful in its maturity. Drink soon.
1966	A very fine vintage with depth, fruit and tannin. Still needs time to open out. Classic claret. Now–'90.

Older fine vintages: '62, '61, '59, '55, '53, '52, '50, '49, '48, '47, '45, '29, '28.

St-Emilion/Pomerol

1980	A poor Merlot year; very variable quality. No hurry to buy.
1979	Big rather patchy vintage. A rival to '78; start comparing in '84.
1978	Lovely wine, to everyone's surprise. Will mature fairly early.
1977	Very wet summer. Mediocre with few exceptions.
1976	Very hot, dry summer and early vintage, but vintage rain made complications. Some excellent; the best great. Now–'95.
1975	Most St-Emilions good, the best superb. Frost in Pomerol cut crops and made splendid concentrated wine. '85–2000.
1974	Vintage rain again. Mainly disappointing light wines. Soon.
1973	Good summer, big wet vintage. Pleasant: wines to drink young.
1972	Poor summer but fine for the late vintage. Many unripe wines, but some are pleasant enough. Drink soon, if at all.
1971	Small crop: fine wines with length and depth, on the whole better than Médocs but generally now ready.
1970	Glorious weather and beautiful wines with great fruit and strength throughout the district. Very big crop. Now–'90s.
1969	Fine summer, small wet vintage. At best agreeable.
1968	A disaster. Endless rain.
1967	Large and generally very good; better than Médoc. Now.
1966	Ripe, powerful, round. Maturing well. Now–'90.

Older fine vintages: '64, '61, '59, '53, '52, '49, '47, '45.
For other areas see under A–Z entries.

Ajaccio Corsica r. p. or w. dr. ⋆ NV

The capital of Corsica and its strong plain wines.

Aligoté

Second-rank burgundy white grape and its often sharp wine, often agreeable and with considerable local character when young.

Aloxe-Corton B'y. r. or w. ⋆⋆⋆ 69 71 72 76 77 78 79

Northernmost village of CÔTE DE BEAUNE: best v'yds.: CORTON (red) and CORTON-CHARLEMAGNE (white). Village wines lighter but often good value.

Alsace Al. w. or (r.) ⟦⋆⋆⟧ 71 75 76 77 78 79

Aromatic, fruity dry white of Germanic character from French Rhineland. Normally sold by grape variety (RIESLING GEWÜRZTRAMINER, etc.). Matures well up to 5, even 10, years.

Alsace Grand Cru ⟦⋆⋆⋆⟧

Appellation restricted to the best named v'yds.

Alsace Grand Vin or Réserve

Wine with minimum 11° natural alcohol.

Ampeau, Robert

Leading grower and specialist in MEURSAULT.

Anjou Lo. (r.) p. or w. (sw. dr. or sp.) ⋆→⋆⋆⋆ 69 70 71 73 75 76 78 79

Very various Loire wines, incl. good CABERNET rosé, luscious COTEAUX DU LAYON. Maturity depends on style.

Appellation Contrôlée

Government control of origin and production of all the best French wines (see France Introduction).

Apremont Savoie w. dr. ⋆⋆ D.Y.A.

One of the best villages of SAVOIE for pale delicate whites.

Arbin Savoie r. ⟦⋆⋆⟧ Drink at 1–2 years

Deep-coloured tannic red of Mondeuse grapes, like a good LOIRE Cabernet.

Arbois Jura r. p. or w. (dr. sp.) ⋆⋆ D.Y.A.

Various pleasant light wines; speciality VIN JAUNE.

l'Ardèche, Coteaux de Central France r. (w.dr.) ⟦⋆⟧ D.Y.A.

Light country reds, the best made of SYRAH. A change from BEAUJOLAIS.

Armagnac

Region of s.w. France famous for its excellent brandy, a fiery spirit of rustic character. The chief town is Condom.

Auxey-Duresses B'y. r. or w. ⟦⋆⋆⟧ 71 72 75w. 76 77 78 79

Second-rank CÔTE DE BEAUNE village: has affinities with VOLNAY and MEURSAULT. Best estates: Duc de Magenta, Prunier, Roy, HOSPICES DE BEAUNE Cuvée Boillot.

Avize Champ. ⋆⋆⋆⋆

One of the best white-grape villages of CHAMPAGNE.

Ay Champ. ⋆⋆⋆⋆

One of the best black-grape villages of CHAMPAGNE.

Ayala NV "Château d'Ay" and 71 73 75

Ay-based old-style champagne concern, formerly much better known.

Bandol Prov. r. p. or (w.) ⋆⋆ 73 74 76 78

Little coastal region near Toulon with strong tasty reds.

Banyuls Pyr. br. sw. ⋆⋆ NV

One of the best VIN DOUX NATURELS (fortified sweet red wines) of the s. of France. Not unlike port.

Barsac B'x. w. sw. ⋆⋆→ ⟦⋆⋆⋆⟧ 70 71 75 76 78

Neighbour of SAUTERNES with similar superb golden wines, often more racy and less rich. Top ch'x.: CLIMENS and COUTET.

Barton & Guestier

Important Bordeaux shipper dating from the 18th century, now owned by Seagram's.

Bâtard-Montrachet B'y. w. dr. [★★★★] 69 71 72 73 74 76 77 78 79
Neighbour and almost equal of MONTRACHET, the top white burgundy. As rich in flavour as dry white wine can be.

Béarn S.W. France r. p. or w. dr. ★
VDQS of local interest.

Beaujolais B'y. r. (p. w.) ★ 79 80 D.Y.A.
The simple appellation of the big Beaujolais region: light short-lived fruity red.

Beaujolais de l'année
The Beaujolais of the latest vintage, until the next.

Beaujolais Primeur (or Nouveau)
The same made in a hurry (often only 4–5 days fermenting) for drinking 15 Nov. to the end of Feb. The best come from light sandy soil and are as strong as 12.5% alcohol.

Beaujolais Supérieur B'y. r. (w.) ★ D.Y.A.
Beaujolais 1° of natural alcohol stronger than the 9° minimum. Since sugar is almost always added this makes little difference to the final product.

Beaujolais-Villages B'y. r. ★★ 76 78 79 80
Wine from the better (northern) half of Beaujolais, stronger and tastier than plain Beaujolais. The 9 (easily) best "villages" are the "crus": FLEURIE, BROUILLY, etc. Of the 30 others the best lie around Beaujeu. The crus cannot be released "en primeur" before December 15th.

Beaumes de Venise Rh. (r. p.) br. sw. [★★★] NV
France's best dessert MUSCAT, from the s. Côtes-du-Rhône; high-flavoured, subtle, lingering. The red and rosé from the co-operative are also good.

Beaune B'y. r. or (w. dr.) ★★★ 71 72 76 78 79
Middle-rank classic burgundy. Négociants' "CLOS" wines (usually "Premier Cru") are often best. "Beaune de Château" is a (good) brand of BOUCHARD PÈRE.

Bellet Prov. p. (r. w. dr.) ★★
Highly fashionable, much above average, local wine from near Nice. Tiny production. Very expensive.

Bergerac Dordogne r. or w. sw. or dr. [★★] 78 79 80w.
Light-weight, often tasty, Bordeaux-style. Drink young, the white very young.

Beyer, Leon
Ancient ALSACE family wine business at Eguisheim making forceful dry wines that age well.

Bichot, Maison Albert
BEAUNE-based grower and merchant. V'yds in CHAMBERTIN, CLOS DE VOUGEOT, RICHEBOURG, etc., and Domaine Long-Depaquit in CHABLIS (see MOUTONNE). Said to be the biggest B'y. exporter.

Blagny B'y. r. or w. dr. [★★] 71 72 73 76 78 79
Hamlet between MEURSAULT and PULIGNY-MONTRACHET; affinities with both and VOLNAY for reds. Ages well.

Blanc de Blancs
Any white wine made from (only) white grapes, esp. champagne, which is usually made of black and white.

Blanc de Noirs
White wine made from black grapes.

Blanquette de Limoux Midi w. dr. sp. [★★] NV
Good cheap sparkler from near Carcassonne made by a version of the MÉTHODE CHAMPENOISE. Very dry and clean.

Blaye B'x. r. or w. dr. ★→★★ 70 75 76 78 79
Your average Bordeaux from e. of the Gironde. PREMIÈRES CÔTES DE BLAYE are better.

Bollinger NV "Special Cuvée" and **66 69 70 73** 75
Top champagne house, at AY. Dry full-flavoured style. Luxury wines "Tradition R. D."; and "Vieilles Vignes Françaises" (**69 70 73** 75) from ungrafted vines.

Bommes
Village of SAUTERNES. Best ch'x.: LA TOUR-BLANCHE, LAFAURIE PEYRAGUEY, etc.

Bonnes Mares B'y. r. ★★★★ 66 69 71 72 73 76 77 78 79
37-acre Grand Cru between CHAMBOLLE-MUSIGNY and MOREY-SAINT-DENIS. Often better than CHAMBERTIN.

Bonnezeaux Lo. w. sw. ★★★ **69 70 71 73 75** 76 78 79
Unusual fruity/acidic wine from CHENIN BLANC grapes, the best of COTEAUX DU LAYON.

Bordeaux B'x. r. or (p.) or w. ★ 75 76 78 79 (for ch'x. see p. 54)
Basic catch-all appellation for low-strength Bordeaux wine.

Bordeaux Supérieur
Ditto, with slightly more alcohol.

Bordeaux Côtes-de-Castillon B'x. r. ★ 70 71 75 76 78 79
Fringe Bordeaux from east of ST-EMILION, and not far from some St-Emilions in quality.

Bordeaux Côtes-de-Francs B'x. r. or wh. dr. ★ 75 76 78 79
Fringe Bordeaux from east of ST-EMILION. Light wines.

Borie-Manoux
Bordeaux shippers and château-owners, incl. Ch'x BATAILLEY, HAUT BAGES-MONPELOU, DOMAINE DE L'EGLISE TROTTEVIEILLE, BEAU-SITE.

Bouchard Ainé
Famous and long-established burgundy shipper and grower with 60 acres in Beaune, Mercurey, etc.

Bouchard Père et Fils
Important burgundy shipper (est. 1731) with 200 acres of excellent v'yds., mainly in the CÔTE DE BEAUNE, and cellars at the Château de Beaune.

Bourg B'x. r. or (w. dr.) ★★ 70 75 78 79
Meaty, un-fancy claret from e. of the Gironde. CÔTES DE BOURG are better.

Bourgogne B'y. r. (p.) or w. dr. ★★ 78 79
Catch-all appellation for burgundy, but with theoretically higher standards than basic BORDEAUX. Light but often good flavour. BEAUJOLAIS crus can be sold as Bourgogne.

Bourgogne Grand Ordinaire B'y. r. or (w.) ★ D.Y.A.
The lowest burgundy appellation for Gamay wines. Seldom seen.

Bourgogne Passe-tout-grains B'y. r. or (p.) ★ Age 1–2 years
Often enjoyable junior burgundy. ⅓ PINOT NOIR and ⅔ GAMAY grapes mixed. Not as "heady" as BEAUJOLAIS.

Bourgueil Lo. r. ★★★ 71 75 76 78 79
Delicate fruity CABERNET red from Touraine, the best from St Nicolas de Bourgueil.

Bouvet-Ladubay
Major producer of sparkling SAUMUR, controlled by TAITTINGER.

Bouzy Rouge Champ. r. ★★★ 70 71 73 75 76 79
Still red wine from famous black-grape CHAMPAGNE village.

Brédif, Marc
One of the most important growers and traders of VOUVRAY.

Brouilly B'y. r. ★★★ 79 80
One of the 9 best CRUS of BEAUJOLAIS: fruity, round, refreshing. One year in bottle is enough.

Brut
Term for the driest wines of CHAMPAGNE until recently, when some completely unsugared wines have become available as "Brut Intégrale", "Brut non-dosé", "Brut zéro" etc.

ugey Savoie w. dr. or sp. ★ D.Y.A.
District with a variety of light sparkling, still or half-sparkling wines. The grape is the Rousette (or Roussanne).

abernet
See Grapes for red wine

abernet d'Anjou Lo. p. ★★ D.Y.A.
Delicate, often slightly sweet, grapy rosé.

ahors S.W. France r. ★→ ⟦ ★★ ⟧ 70 75 76 78 79
Very dark, traditionally hard "black" wine, now made more like Bordeaux but can be full-bodied and distinct.

airanne Rh. r. p. or w. dr. ⟦ ★★ ⟧ 76 78 79 80
Village of CÔTE-DU-RHÔNE-VILLAGES. Good solid wines.

alvet
Great family wine business, originally on the Rhône, now important in Bordeaux and Burgundy.

anon-Fronsac
See Côtes-Canon-Fronsac

antenac B'x. r. ★★★
Village of the HAUT-MÉDOC entitled to the Appellation MARGAUX. Top ch'x. include PALMER, BRANE-CANTENAC, etc.

aramany Pyr. r. (w. dr.) ⟦ ★ ⟧ 78 79
New appellation for part of CÔTES DE ROUSSILLON.

assis Prov. (r. p.) w. dr. ★★ D.Y.A.
Seaside village e. of Marseille known for its very dry white, above the usual standard of Provence. Not to be confused with cassis, a blackcurrant liqueur made in Dijon.

ave Cellar, or any wine establishment.

ave co-opérative
Wine-growers' co-operative winery. Formerly viticultural dustbins, most are now well run, well equipped and making some of the best wine of their areas.

épage
Variety of vine, e.g. CHARDONNAY, MERLOT.

érons B'x. w. dr. or sw. ★★ 70 71 75 76 78 79
Neighbour of SAUTERNES with some good sweet-wine ch'x.

hablis B'y. w. dr. ★★ 76 77 78 79
Distinctive full-flavoured greeny gold wine. APPELLATION CONTRÔLÉE essential. Petit Chablis is less fine, but often good.

hablis Grand Cru B'y. w. dr. ⟦ ★★★★ ⟧ 71 75 76 77 78 79
Strong, subtle and altogether splendid. One of the great white burgundies. There are seven v'yds: Blanchots, Bougros, Clos, Grenouilles, Preuses, Valmur, Vaudésir. See also MOUTONNE.

hablis Premier Cru B'y. w. dr. ⟦ ★★★ ⟧ 71 75 76 77 78 79
Second-rank but often excellent and more typical of Chablis than Grands Crus. Best v'yds incl.: Côte de Lechet, Fourchaume, Mont de Milieu, Montmains.

hai Building for storing and maturing wine, esp. in Bordeaux.

hambertin B'y. r. ★★★★ 66 69 70 71 72 73 76 77 78 79
32-acre Grand Cru giving the meatiest, most enduring and often the best red burgundy. 15 growers, incl. LATOUR, JABOULET-VERCHERRE, Rebourseau, ROUSSEAU, Trapet.

hambertin-Clos-de-Bèze B'y. r. ★★★★ 69 70 71 72 73 76 77 78 79
37-acre neighbour of CHAMBERTIN. Similarly splendid wine. Ten growers, incl. CLAIR-DAÜ, DROUHIN, Drouhin-Laroze.

hambolle-Musigny B'y. r. (w.) ⟦ ★★★ ⟧ 69 71 72 76 77 78 79
420-acre CÔTE DE NUITS village with fabulously fragrant, complex wine. Best v'yds.: MUSIGNY, part of BONNES-MARES, Les Amoureuses, Les Charmes. Best growers incl.: de Vogüé, DROUHIN, FAIVELEY, Roumier.

hambré
At (old-fashioned) room temperature; normal for drinking red wines. Modern room temperature is often too high.

Champagne

Sparkling wine from 55,000 acres 90 miles e. of Paris, made by the MÉTHODE CHAMPENOISE: wines from elsewhere, however good, cannot be Champagne. (See also name of brand.)

Champagne, Grande

The appellation of the best area of COGNAC.

Champigny

See Saumur

Chanson Père et Fils

Growers and traders in fine wine at BEAUNE. Reds can be pale but last well.

Chante-Alouette

A famous brand of white HERMITAGE.

Chantovent

Major brand of VIN DE TABLE, largely from MINERVOIS.

Chanturgues Central France r. ★ D.Y.A.

Well-known Gamay local wine of Clermont-Ferrand.

Chapelle-Chambertin B'y. r. ★★★ **69 70 71 72** 76 **77** 78 79

13-acre neighbour of CHAMBERTIN. Similar wine, not quite so full and meaty.

Chapoutier

Long-established family firm of growers and traders of Rhône wines, particularly HERMITAGE.

Chardonnay

See Grapes for white wine

Charmes-Chambertin B'y. r. ★★★ **71 72 76 77** 78 79

76-acre neighbour of CHAMBERTIN.

Chassagne-Montrachet B'y. r. or w. dr. ★★★ **69 71 72** r. **73 74** w. **76** 78 79.

750-acre CÔTE DE BEAUNE village with superlative rich dry whites and sterling hefty reds. Best v'yds.: MONTRACHET, BÂTARD-MONTRACHET, CRIOTS-BÂTARD-MONTRACHET, Ruchottes, Caillerets, Boudriottes (r, w.), Morgeot (r, w.), CLOS-ST-JEAN (r.). Growers incl. RAMONET-PRUDHON, Morey, Magenta, DELAGRANGE-BACHELET.

Château

An estate, big or small, good or indifferent, particularly in Bordeaux. In Burgundy the term "domaine" is used. For all Bordeaux ch'x see pp. 54–70.

Château-Chalon Jura w. dr. ★★★

Unique strong dry yellow wine, almost like sherry. Ready to drink when bottled.

Château Corton-Grancey B'y. r. ★★★ 71 72 **73** 76 **77** 78 79

Famous estate at ALOXE-CORTON, the property of Louis LATOUR. Impressive wine with a long life.

Château d'Eau Entre Deux Mers w. dr. ★ D.Y.A.

Light, refreshing, reliable.

Château de la Chaize B'y. r. ★★★ **78 79 80**

The best-known estate of BROUILLY, with 200 acres.

Château de la Maltroye B'y. r. w. dr. ★★★

First-class burgundy estate at CHASSAGNE-MONTRACHET.

Château de Panisseau Dordogne w. dr. ★★ D.Y.A.

Leading estate of BERGERAC: good dry SAUVIGNON BLANC.

Château de Selle Prov. r. p. or w. dr. ★★ D.Y.A.

Estate near Cotignac, Var. Well-known and typical wines.

Château des Fines Roches Rh. r. ★★★ **67 70 71 72 74 76** 78 79 80

Large (114 acres) and distinguished estate in CHÂTEAUNEUF-DU-PAPE. Strong old-style wine.

Château du Nozet Lo. w. dr. ★★★ **78 79** 80

Biggest and best-known estate of Pouilly (FUMÉ) sur Loire.

Château Fortia Rh. r. ✶✶✶ 67 70 71 72 74 76 78 79 80
First-class property in CHÂTEAUNEUF-DU-PAPE. Traditional methods. The owner's father, Baron Le Roy, also fathered the APPELLATION CONTROLÉE system.

Château-Grillet Rh. w. dr. ✶✶✶✶ 76 78 79 80
3½-acre v'yd. with one of France's smallest appellations. Intense, fragrant, expensive. Drink fairly young.

Burgundy boasts one of the world's most famous and certainly its most beautiful hospital, the Hospices de Beaune, founded in 1443 by Nicolas Rolin, Chancellor to the Duke of Burgundy, and his wife Guigone de Salins. The hospital he built and endowed with vineyards for its income still operates in the same building and still thrives, tending the sick of Beaune without charge, on the sale of its wine. Many growers since have bequeathed their land to the Hospices. Today it owns 125 acres of prime land in Beaune, Pommard, Volnay, Meursault, Corton and Mazis-Chambertin. The wine is sold by auction every year on the third Sunday in November.

Château-Gris B'y. r. ✶✶✶ 71 72 76 78 79
Famous estate at NUITS-ST-GEORGES.

Châteaumeillant Lo. r. p. or w. dr. ✶ D.Y.A.
Small VDQS area near SANCERRE.

Châteauneuf-du-Pape Rh. r. (w. dr.) ✶✶✶ 67 70 71 72 76 77 78 79 80
7,500 acres near Avignon. Best estate ("domaine") wines are dark, strong, long-lived. Others may be light and/or disappointing. The white is heavy: at best rich, almost sweet.

Château Rayas Rh. r. (w. dr.) ⌷✶✶✶⌷ 69 70 71 72 76 77 78 79 80
Excellent old-style property in Ch'neuf-du-Pape.

Château Simone Prov. r. p. or w. dr. ✶✶ D.Y.A.
Well-known property in Palette; the only one in this appellation near Aix-en-Provence.

Château Vignelaure Prov. r. ⌷✶✶⌷ 70 71 73 74 75 76 77 78
Very good Provençal estate near Aix making Bordeaux-style wine with CABERNET grapes.

Chatillon-en-Diois Rh. r. p. or w. dr. ✶ D.Y.A.
Small VDQS e. of the Rhône near Die. Good GAMAY reds; white mostly made into CLAIRETTE DE DIE.

Chavignol
Village of SANCERRE with famous v'yd., Les Monts Damnés.

Chauvenet, F.
Merchant at NUITS-ST-GEORGES controlled by MARGNAT.

Chénas B'y. r. ✶✶✶ 76 78 79 80
Good Beaujolais cru, neighbour to MOULIN-À-VENT and JULIÉNAS. One of the weightier Beaujolais.

Chenin Blanc
See Grapes for white wine

Chevalier-Montrachet B'y. w. dr. ✶✶✶✶ 69 71 73 76 77 78 79
17-acre neighbour of MONTRACHET with similar luxurious wine, perhaps a little less powerful. Includes Les Demoiselles. Growers incl. BOUCHARD PÈRE, LEFLAIVE.

Cheverny Lo. w. dr. ✶ D.Y.A.
Light sharp Loire country wine from near Chambord.

Chignin Savoie w.dr. ⌷✶⌷ D.Y.A.
Light soft white of Jacquère grapes.

Chinon Lo. r. ✶✶✶ 71 75 76 78 79
Delicate fruity CABERNET from TOURAINE. Drink cool when young. Good vintages age like Bordeaux.

Chiroubles B'y. r. ✶✶✶ 78 79 80
Good but tiny Beaujolais cru next to FLEURIE; freshly fruity silky wine for early drinking.

Chusclan Rh. r. p. or w. dr. ⭐ 78 79 80

Village of CÔTE-DU-RHÔNE-VILLAGES. Good middle-weight wines from the co-operative.

Cissac

HAUT-MÉDOC village just w. of PAUILLAC.

Clair-Daü

First-class 100-acre burgundy estate of the northern CÔTE DE NUITS, with cellars at MARSANNAY-la-Côte.

Clairet

Very light red wine, almost rosé.

Clairette

Mediocre white grape of the s. of France.

Clairette de Bellegarde Midi w. dr. ⭐ D.Y.A.

Plain neutral white from near Nîmes.

Clairette de Die Rh. w. dr. or s./sw. sp. ⭐⭐ NV

Popular dry or semi-sweet rather MUSCAT-flavoured sparkling wine from the e. Rhône, or straight dry CLAIRETTE white, surprisingly ageing well 3–4 years.

Clairette du Languedoc Midi w. dr. ⭐ D.Y.A.

Plain neutral white from near Montpellier.

La Clape Midi r. p. or w. dr. ⭐

Full-bodied VDQS wines from near Narbonne. The red gains character after 2–3 years.

Claret

Traditional English term for red BORDEAUX.

Climat

Burgundian word for individual named v'yd., e.g. Beaune Grèves, Chambolle-Musigny les Amoureuses.

Clos

A term carrying some prestige, reserved for distinct, usually walled, v'yds., often in one ownership. Frequent in Burgundy and Alsace.

Clos-de-Bèze

See Chambertin-Clos-de-Bèze

Clos de la Roche B'y. r. ⭐⭐⭐ 69 70 71 72 76 77 78 79

38-acre Grand Cru at MOREY-ST-DENIS. Powerful complex wine like CHAMBERTIN. Producers incl. BOUCHARD PÈRE.

Clos des Lambrays B'y. r. ⭐⭐⭐ 71 72 73 76 78

15-acre Premier Cru v'yd. at MOREY-ST-DENIS. Changed hands in 1979 after a shaky period. Being replanted.

Clos des Mouches B'y. r. or w. dr. ⭐⭐⭐

Well-known Premier Cru v'yd. of BEAUNE.

Clos de Tart B'y. r. ⭐⭐⭐ 71 72 76 77 78 79

18-acre Grand Cru at MOREY-ST-DENIS owned by MOMMESSIN. Relatively delicate wines, recently much improved.

Clos de Vougeot B'y. r. ⭐⭐⭐ 66 69 70 71 72 73 76 78 79

124-acre CÔTE-DE-NUITS Grand Cru with many owners. Variable, sometimes sublime. Maturity depends on the grower's technique and his position on the hillside.

Clos du Chêne Marchand

Well-known v'yd. at Bué, SANCERRE.

Clos du Roi B'y. r. ⭐⭐⭐

Part of the Grand Cru CORTON; also a Premier Cru of BEAUNE.

Clos St Denis B'y. r. ⭐⭐⭐ 69 71 72 73 76 77 78 79

16-acre Grand Cru at MOREY-ST-DENIS. Splendid sturdy wine.

Clos St Jacques B'y. r. ⭐⭐⭐ 69 71 72 73 76 77 78 79

17-acre Premier Cru of GEVREY-CHAMBERTIN. Excellent powerful wine, often better (and dearer) than some of the CHAMBERTIN Grands Crus.

Clos St Jean B'y. r. ⭐⭐⭐ 69 71 72 73 76 78 79

36-acre Premier Cru of CHASSAGNE-MONTRACHET. Very good red, more solid than subtle.

Cognac
> Town and region of w. France and its brandy.

Collioure Pyr. r. ⭐ 76 78 79
> Strong dry RANCIO red from BANYULS area. Small production.

Condrieu Rh. w. dr. ⭐⭐⭐ D.Y.A.
> Outstanding soft fragrant white of great character (and price) from the Viognier grape. CH.-GRILLET is similar.

Corbières Midi r. or (p.) or (w.) ⭐ 78 79 80
> Good vigorous cheap VDQS reds, steadily improving.

Corbières de Roussillon Midi r. (p.) or (w.) ⭐ 76 78 79 80
> The same from slightly farther s.

Cordier, Ets D.
> Important Bordeaux shipper and château-owner, including Ch'x. GRUAUD-LAROSE, TALBOT.

Cornas Rh. r. ⭐⭐ 71 72 73 76 78 79 80
> Small area near HERMITAGE. Typical sturdy Rhône wine of good quality from the SYRAH grape.

The Confrèrie des Chevaliers du Tastevin is Burgundy's wine fraternity and the most famous of its kind in the world. It was founded in 1933 by a group of Burgundian patriots, headed by Camille Rodier and Georges Faiveley, to rescue their beloved Burgundy from a period of slump and despair by promoting its inimitable products. Today it regularly holds banquets with elaborate and sprightly ceremonial for 500 guests at its headquarters, the old château in the Clos de Vougeot. The Confrèrie has branches in many countries and members among lovers of wine all over the world.

Corse
> The island of Corsica. Strong ordinary wines of all colours. Better appellations include PATRIMONIO, SARTÈNE, AJACCIO.

Corton B'y. r. ⭐⭐⭐⭐ 69 70 71 72 73 76 77 78 79
> The only Grand Cru red of the CÔTE DE BEAUNE. 200 acres in ALOXE-CORTON incl. les Bressandes and le CLOS DU ROI. Rich powerful wines.

Corton-Charlemagne B'y. w. dr. ⭐⭐⭐⭐ 69 71 72 73 74 75 76 77 78 79
> The white section (one-third) of CORTON. Rich spicy lingering wine. Behaves like a red wine and ages magnificently.

Coste, Pierre
> Influential wine-broker and maker of LANGON, B'x.

Costières du Gard Midi r. p. or w. dr. ⭐ D.Y.A.
> VDQS of moderate quality from the Rhône delta.

Coteaux Champenois Champ. r. (p.) or w. dr. ⭐⭐⭐ D.Y.A.
> The appellation for non-sparkling champagne.

Coteaux d'Aix-en-Provence Prov r. p. or w. dr. ⭐ NV
> Agreeable country wines tending to improve. CH. VIGNELAURE is far above average.

Coteaux d'Ancenis r. p. w. dr. ⭐ D.Y.A.
> Light Cabernet and Gamay reds and pinks; sharpish whites from MUSCADET country.

Coteaux de la Loire Lo. w. dr. sw. ⭐⭐⭐ 71 75 76 78 79
> Forceful and fragrant CHENIN BLANC whites from Anjou. The best are in SAVENNIÈRES. Excellent as aperitif.

Coteaux de l'Aubance Lo. p. or w. dr./sw. ⭐⭐ D.Y.A.
> Light and typical minor Anjou wines.

Coteaux de Pierrevert Rh. r. p. or w. dr. or sp. ⭐ D.Y.A.
> Minor southern VDQS from nr. Manosque. Well-made co-op wine.

Coteaux de Saumur Lo. w. dr./sw. ⭐⭐ D.Y.A.
> Pleasant dry or sweetish fruity CHENIN BLANC.

Coteaux des Baux-en-Provence　Prov. r. p. or w. dr. ★ NV
　　A twin to COTEAUX D'AIX, sharing the same VDQS.

Coteaux du Giennois　r. w. dr. ★
　　Minor Loire area n. of SANCERRE.

Coteaux du Languedoc　Midi r. p. or w. dr.　[★]　D.Y.A.
　　Scattered better-than-ordinary Midi areas with VDQS status.
　　The best (e.g. Faugères, St Saturnin) age for a year or two.

Coteaux du Layon　Lo. w. s./sw. or sw.　[★★]　71 75 76 78 79
　　District centred on Rochefort, s. of Angers, making sweet
　　CHENIN BLANC wines above the general Anjou standard.

Coteaux du Loir　Lo. r. p. or w. dr./sw. ★★ 64 69 71 73 76 78 79
　　Small region n. of Tours. Occasionally excellent wines. Best
　　v'yd.: JASNIÈRES. The Loir is a tributary of the Loire.

Coteaux du Tricastin　Rh. r. p. or w. dr. ★★ D.Y.A.
　　Fringe CÔTES-DU-RHÔNE of increasing quality from s. of
　　Valence.

Coteaux du Vendomois　Lo. r. p. or w. dr. ★ D.Y.A.
　　Fringe Loire from n. of Blois.

> **Côte(s)**
> 　　Means hillside; generally a superior vineyard to those on
> 　　the plain. Many appellations start with either Côtes or
> 　　Coteaux, which means the same thing. In ST-EMILION it
> 　　distinguishes the valley slopes from the higher plateau.

Côte Chalonnaise　B'y. r. w. dr. sp.　[★★→★★★]
　　Lesser-known v'yd. area between BEAUNE and MÂCON. See
　　Mercurey, Givry, Rully, Montagny.

Côte de Beaune　B'y. r. or w. dr. ★★→★★★★
　　Used geographically: the s. half of the CÔTE D'OR. Applies as
　　an appellation only to parts of BEAUNE.

Côte de Beaune-Villages　B'y. r. or w. dr. ★★
　　Regional appellation for secondary wines of the classic area.
　　They cannot be labelled "Côte de Beaune" without either
　　"Villages" or the village name.

Côte de Brouilly　B'y. r. ★★★ 76 78 79
　　Fruity, rich, vigorous Beaujolais cru. One of the best. Leading
　　estate: Ch. Thivin.

Côte de Nuits　B'y. r. or (w. dr.) ★★→★★★★
　　The northern half of the CÔTE D'OR.

Côte de Nuits-Villages　B'y. r. (w.) ★★ 71 76 78 79
　　A junior appellation, rarely seen but worth investigating.

Côte d'Or
　　Département name applied to the central and principal
　　Burgundy v'yd. slopes, consisting of the CÔTE DE BEAUNE
　　and CÔTE DE NUITS. The name is not used on labels.

Côte Rôtie　Rh. r. ★★★ 69 70 71 73 76 78 79 80
　　The finest Rhône red, from just s. of Vienne; achieves complex
　　delicacy with age. Very small production. Top growers in-
　　clude JABOULET, CHAPOUTIER, VIDAL-FLEURY, Jasmin.

(Côtes) Canon-Fronsac　B'x. r.　[★★]　70 71 73 75 76 78 79
　　Attractive solid reds from small area w. of ST-EMILION. Ch'x
　　include Bodet, Canon, Junayme, Moulin-Pey-Labrie,
　　Pichelèvre, Toumalin. The appellation can be simply "Canon
　　Fronsac". See also FRONSAC.

Côtes d'Auvergne　Central France r. p. or (w. dr.) ★ D.Y.A.
　　Flourishing small VDQS area near Clermont-Ferrand. Red (at
　　best) like light Beaujolais.

Côtes de Blaye　B'x. w. dr. ★ D.Y.A.
　　Run-of-the-mill Bordeaux white from BLAYE.

Côtes de Bordeaux Saint-Macaire　B'x. w. dr./sw. ★ D.Y.A.
　　Run-of-the-mill Bordeaux white from e. of Sauternes.

Côtes de Bourg B'x. r. `*→**` 70 75 76 78 79
> Appellation used for many of the better reds of BOURG. Ch'x incl. de Barbe, La Barde, du Bousquet, de la Croix-Millorit, Eyquem, Font-Guilhem, Lamothe, Mendoce, Mille-Secousses, Domaine de Christoly, Domaine de Taste.

Côtes de Buzet S.W. France r. or w. r. ** 76 78 79
> Good light wines from just s.e. of Bordeaux. Promising area with well-run co-operative. Best wine: Cuvée Napoléon.

Côtes de Duras Dordogne r. or w. dr. `*` 78 79
> Neighbour to BERGERAC. Similar light wines.

Côtes de Francs See Bordeaux—Côtes de Francs.

Côtes de Fronsac B'x. r. `*→**` 70 71 75 76 78 79
> Some of the best slopes of FRONSAC, making considerable slow-maturing reds. Ch'x incl. la Dauphine, Mayne-Vieil, la Rivière, Rouet, Tasta.

Côtes de Jura Jura r. p. or w. dr. (sp.) * NV
> Various light tints and tastes. ARBOIS is better.

Côtes de Montravel Dordogne w. dr./sw. `*` NV
> Part of BERGERAC; trad. medium-sw. wine, now often dry.

Côtes de Provence Prov. r. p. or w. dr. *→** NV
> The wine of Provence; often more alcohol than character. Standards have recently been improving. A dozen properties have the right to say "Cru Classé".

Côtes de Roussillon Pyr. r. p. or w. dr. `*→**` 75 76 78 79
> Country wine of e. Pyrenees. The hefty dark reds are best. Some whites are sharp VINS VERTS.

Côtes de Toul E. France r. p. or w. dr. * D.Y.A.
> Very light wines from Lorraine; mainly VIN GRIS (rosé).

Côtes du Forez Central France r. or p. `*` D.Y.A.
> Light Beaujolais-style red, can be good in warm years.

Côtes du Fronton S.W. France r. or p. `*` D.Y.A.
> The local wine of Toulouse, locally admired.

Côtes du Haut-Roussillon S.W. France br. sw. *→** NV
> Sweet-wine area n. of Perpignan.

Côtes du Luberon Rh. r. p. or w. dr. sp. `*` D.Y.A.
> Improving country wines from northern Provence; especially the sparkling, and Château de Sannes.

Côtes du Marmandais Dordogne r. or w. dr. * D.Y.A.
> Undistinguished light wines from s.e. of Bordeaux.

Côtes-du-Rhône Rh. r. p. or w. dr. * 78 79 80
> The basic appellation of the Rhône valley. Best drunk young. Wide variations of quality due to grape ripeness, therefore rising with degree of alcohol. See CÔTES-DU-RHÔNE-VILLAGES.

Côtes-du-Rhône-Villages Rh. r. p. or w. dr. **→ `**` 76 78 79 80
> The wine of the 14 best villages of the southern Rhône. Substantial and on the whole reliable.

Côtes du Vivarais Prov. r. p. or w. dr. * NV
> Pleasant country wines from s. Massif Centrale.

Côtes Frontonnais See Côtes du Fronton

Coulée de Serrant Lo. w. dr./sw. *** 64 69 71 73 75 76 78 79
> 10-acre v'yd. on n. bank of Loire at Savennières, Anjou. Intense strong fruity/sharp wine, ages well.

La Cour Pavillon
> Reliable brand of red and white Bordeaux from Gilbey's.

Cour-Cheverny Lo. w. dr. * D.Y.A.
> Fragile, often sharp Touraine white.

Crémant
> In Champagne means "Creaming"—i.e. half-sparkling. Also high-quality sparkling wines from other parts of France.

Crémant de Loire w. dr./sp. ** NV
> High-quality semi-sparkling wine from ANJOU and TOURAINE. The leading brand is Sablant.

Crépy Savoie w. dr. ✹✹ D.Y.A.

Light, Swiss-style white from s. shore of La. Geneva. "Crépit ant" has been coined for its faint fizz.

Criots-Bâtard-Montrachet B'y. w. ✹✹✹ 69 71 73 74 76 77 78 79

7-acre neighbour to BÂTARD-MONTRACHET. Similar wine.

Crozes-Hermitage Rh. r. or (w. dr.) ✹✹ 72 73 76 78 79 80

Larger and less distinguished neighbour to HERMITAGE Robust and often excellent reds but choose carefully.

Cru "Growth", as in "first-growth"—meaning vineyard.

Cru Bourgeois

Rank of Bordeaux château below CRU CLASSÉ.

Cru Bourgeois Supérieur

Official rank one better than the last.

Cru Classé

Classed growth. One of the first five official quality classes of the Médoc, classified in 1855. Also any classed growth of another district.

Cru Exceptionnel

Official rank above CRU BOURGEOIS SUPÉRIEUR, immediately below CRU CLASSÉ.

Cruse et Fils Frères

Long-established Bordeaux shipper famous for fine wine Owner of CH. D'ISSAN.

Cubzac, St.-André-de B'x. r. or w. dr. ✹ 75 76 78 79

Town 15 miles n.e. of Bordeaux, centre of the minor Cubzaguais region. Sound reds have the appellation Bordeaux Estates include: Ch. du Bouilh, Ch. de Terrefort-Quancard Ch. Timberley, Domaine de Beychevelle.

The curiously inefficient shape of the traditional shallow champagne-glass known as a "coupe" is accounted for (at least in legend) by the fact that it was modelled on Queen Marie Antoinette's breast. Admirable though that organ undoubtedly was, it was not designed for dispensing sparkling wine. Champagne goes flat and gets warm almost as fast in a coupe as it would in your cupped hand. The ideal champagne glass is a tall, thin "tulip".

Cussac

Village just s. of ST. JULIEN. Appellation Haut-Médoc.

Cuve Close

Short-cut way of making sparkling wine in a tank. The sparkle dies away in the glass much quicker than with MÉTHODE CHAMPENOISE wine.

Cuvée

The quantity of wine produced in a "cuve" or vat. Also a word of many uses, incl. "blend". In Burgundy interchangeable with "Cru". Often just refers to a "lot" of wine.

d'Angerville, Marquis

Famous burgundy grower with immaculate estate in VOLNAY

Danglade, L. et Fils

Shipper of St-Emilion and Pomerol, now owned by J-P MOUEIX of Libourne.

Degré alcoolique

Degrees of alcohol, i.e. per cent by volume.

Delagrange-Bachelet

One of the leading proprietors in CHASSAGNE-MONTRACHET.

Delas Frères

Long-established firm of Rhône-wine specialists at Tournor v'yds. at CÔTE RÔTIE, HERMITAGE, CORNAS etc.

Delor, A. et Cie
Bordeaux shippers owned by the English Allied Breweries.

Delorme, André
Leading merchants and growers of the CÔTE CHALONNAISE. Specialists in sparkling wine.

De Luze, A. et Fils
Bordeaux shipper and owners of Ch'x. CANTENAC-BROWN and PAVEIL-DE LUZE; owned by Bowater.

Demi-Sec
"Half-dry": in practice more than half-sweet.

Depagneux, Jacques et Cie
Well-regarded merchants of BEAUJOLAIS.

Deutz & Geldermann NV, rosé **71 73 75**, Blanc de Blancs **73** and **66 69 70 71 73 75**
One of the best of the smaller champagne houses. Luxury brand: Cuvée William Deutz.

Domaine
Property, particularly in Burgundy.

Domaine de Belair
A light-weight branded red Bordeaux of reliable quality made by SICHEL.

Domaine de l'Eglantière
CHABLIS estate with 120 acres and the highest standards.

Dom Pérignon **66 69 70 71** 73 75
Luxury brand of MOËT ET CHANDON named after the legendary blind inventor of champagne. Also occasionally a rosé (**69**).

Dopff "au Moulin"
Ancient family wine-house at Riquewihr, Alsace. Best wines: Riesling Schoenenbourg, Gewürztraminer Eichberg.

Dopff & Irion
Another excellent Riquewihr (ALSACE) business. Best wines include Muscat les Amandiers, Riesling de Riquewihr.

Doudet-Naudin
Burgundy merchant and grower at Savigny-lès-Beaune. V'yds. incl. BEAUNE CLOS DE ROI. Rather heavy wines.

Dourthe Frères
Well-reputed Bordeaux merchant representing a wide range of ch'x., mainly good Crus Bourgeois, incl. Ch'x. MAUCAILLOU, TRONQUOY-LALANDE, BELGRAVE.

Doux Sweet.

Drouhin, J. et Cie
Prestigious Burgundy grower and merchant. Offices in BEAUNE, v'yds. in MUSIGNY, CLOS DE VOUGEOT, etc.

Duboeuf, Georges
Top-class BEAUJOLAIS merchant at Romanèche-Thorin.

Duclot, Ets
Bordeaux merchant specializing in the top growths. Controlled by MOUEIX.

Dujac, Domaine
Perfectionist burgundian grower at MOREY-ST-DENIS with v'yds in that village, ECHÉZEAUX, BONNES-MARES, GEVREY-CHAMBERTIN, etc.

Echézeaux B'y. r. ★★★ **69 71 72 73 76 77 78 79**
74-acre Grand Cru between VOSNE-ROMANÉE and CLOS DE VOUGEOT. Superlative fragrant burgundy without great weight.

Edelzwicker Alsace w. ★ D.Y.A.
Light white from mixture of grapes, often fruity and good.

Entre-Deux-Mers B'x. w. dr. ★ D.Y.A.
Standard dry white Bordeaux from between the Garonne and Dordogne rivers. Often a good buy.

Les Epenots B'y. r. ★★★

Famous Premier Cru v'yd. of POMMARD. Also spelt Epeneaux for the 12-acre Clos des Epeneaux owned by Comte Armand.

Eschenauer, Louis

Famous Bordeaux merchants, owners of Ch'x. RAUSAN-SÉGLA and SMITH-HAUT-LAFITTE, De Lamouroux and LA GARDE in GRAVES. Controlled by John Holt, part of the Lonrho group.

l'Etoile Jura (r.) (p.) or w. dr./sw./sp. ★★

Sub-region of the Jura with typically various wines, incl. VIN JAUNE like CHÂTEAU-CHALON.

Faiveley, J.

Family-owned growers (with 250 acres) and merchants at NUITS-ST-GEORGES, with v'yds. in CHAMBERTIN-CLOS-DE-BÈZE, CHAMBOLLE-MUSIGNY, CORTON, NUITS and MERCUREY (150 acres).

Faugères Midi r. (p. or w. dr.) ⌑ 76 77 78 79 80

Isolated village of the COTEAUX DU LANGUEDOC making above-average wine.

Fitou Midi r. ★★ 75 76 78 79

Superior CORBIÈRES red; powerful and ages well.

Fixin B'y. r. ⌑★★ 71 72 73 76 78 79

A worthy and under-valued neighbour to GEVREY-CHAMBERTIN. Often splendid reds. Best v'yd.: Clos du Chapitre.

Fleurie B'y. r. ⌑★★★ 76 78 79 80

The epitome of a Beaujolais cru: fruity, scented, silky, racy.

Frais Fresh or cool.

Frappé Ice-cold.

Froid Cold.

Fronsac B'x. r. ⌑★→★★ 70 75 76 78 79

Pretty hilly area of good reds just w. of St-Emilion. CÔTES-CANON-FRONSAC and CÔTES DE FRONSAC are the appellations of the best wines. For ch'x see these entries.

Frontignan Midi br. sw. ⌑ NV

Strong sweet and liquorous muscat wine.

Gaillac S.W. France r. p. or w. dr./sw. or sp. ★ NV

Generally dull but usually adequate everyday wine. Slightly fizzy "Perlé" is good value.

Gamay

See Grapes for red wine

Geisweiler et Fils

One of the biggest merchant-houses of Burgundy. Cellars and 50 acres of v'yds. at NUITS-ST-GEORGES. Also 150 acres at Bevy in the HAUTES CÔTES DE NUITS and 30 in the CÔTE CHALONNAISE.

Gevrey-Chambertin B'y. r. ★★★ 71 72 73 76 78 79

The village containing the great CHAMBERTIN and many other noble v'yds. as well as some more commonplace.

Gewürztraminer

The speciality grape of ALSACE: perfumed and spicy, whether dry or sweet.

Gigondas Rh. r. or p. ⌑★★ 70 71 72 76 77 78 79 80

Worthy neighbour to CHÂTEAUNEUF-DU-PAPE. Strong full-bodied wine.

Gilbey, S.A.

British firm long-established as Bordeaux merchants at Ch. LOUDENNE in the MÉDOC. Now owned by International Distillers and Vintners.

Ginestet

Third-generation Bordeaux merchants and former owners of CH. MARGAUX.

Gisselbrecht, Louis

High-quality Alsace shippers at Dambach-la-ville.

Givry B'y. r. or w. dr. `**` 76 78 79

Underrated village of the CÔTE CHALONNAISE: light but tasty and typical burgundy.

Gouges, Henri

Leading burgundy grower of NUITS-ST-GEORGES. Outstanding reds and very rare white "La Perrière".

Goulet, Georges NV, rosé 73 75 76, Crémant Blanc de Blancs 74 75, and 71 73 75 76

High-quality Reims champagne house. Abel Lepitre is label for cheaper range. Luxury brand: Cuvée du Centenaire 73 74

Goût

Taste, e.g. "goût anglais"—as the English like it (i.e. dry).

Grand Cru

One of the top Burgundy v'yds. with its own Appellation Controlée. Similar in Alsace but more vague elsewhere.

Grand Roussillon Midi br. sw. `**` NV

Broad appellation for muscat and other sweet fortified wines of eastern Pyrenees.

Grands-Echézeaux B'y. r. `****` 69 71 72 73 76 78 79

22-acre Grand Cru next to CLOS DE VOUGEOT. Superlative rich burgundy.

Gratien, Alfred and Gratien & Meyer

Good smaller champagne house (fine, very dry, long-lasting wine) and its counterpart at SAUMUR on the Loire.

Graves B'x. r. or w. `* → ****`

Large region s. of Bordeaux city. Its best wines are red, but the name is used chiefly for its dry or medium golden-whites.

Graves de Vayres B'x r. or w. `*`

Part of ENTRE-DEUX-MERS; of no special character.

Les Gravières B'y. r. `***`

Famous Premier Cru v'yd. of SANTENAY.

Griotte-Chambertin B'y. r. `***` 69 71 72 73 76 77 78 79

14-acre Grand Cru adjoining CHAMBERTIN. Similar wine, but less masculine and more "tender". Growers incl. DROUHIN.

Gros Plant du Pays Nantais Lo. w. `*` D.Y.A.

Junior cousin of MUSCADET, sharper and lighter; made of the COGNAC grape also known as Folle Blanche, Ugni Blanc etc.

Haut Comtat Rh. r. or p. `**` 76 78 79 80

Small appellation n. of Avignon. Sound strong wines.

Hautes-Côtes de Beaune B'y. r. or w. dr. `**` 76 78 79

Appellation for a dozen villages in the hills behind the CÔTE DE BEAUNE. Light wines, worth investigating.

Hautes-Côtes de Nuits B'y. r. or w. dr. `**` 71 76 78 79

The same for the CÔTE DE NUITS. An area on the way up.

Haut-Médoc B'x. r. `** → ***` 66 70 71 73 75 76 77 78 79

Big appellation including all the best areas of the Médoc. Most wines have château names: those without should still be above average.

Haut-Montravel Dordogne w. sw. `*` 76 78 79

Medium-sweet BERGERAC.

Haut Poitou

Up-and-coming VDQS area s. of ANJOU. Co-operative makes good whites, incl. CHARDONNAY and SAUVIGNON BLANC.

Heidsieck, Charles NV and 66 69 70 71 73 75 76

Leading champagne house of Reims, family-owned, now merged with Champagne Henriot. Luxury brand: Cuvée Royal Champagne.

Heidsieck, Dry Monopole   NV, rosé 71 73 and 71 73 75 76 79
Important champagne merchant and grower of Reims. Luxury brand: Diamant Bleu (71 73)

Henriot   NV, Blanc de Blancs
Old family champagne house now linked with CHARLES HEIDSIECK. Very dry style. Luxury brand: Réserve Baron Philippe de Rothschild.

Hérault   Midi
The biggest v'yd. *département* in France with 400,000 hectares of vines. Chiefly vin ordinaire.

Hermitage   Rh. r. or w. dr.   [★★★]   66 69 70 71 72 73 76 78 79 80
The "manliest" wine of France. Dark, powerful and profound. Needs long ageing. The white is heady and golden.

Hospices de Beaune
Hospital in BEAUNE, with excellent v'yds. in MEURSAULT, POMMARD, VOLNAY, BEAUNE, CORTON, etc. See panel on page 31.

Hugel Père et Fils
The best-known ALSACE growers and merchants. Founded at Riquewihr in 1639 and still in the family. Best wines: Cuvées Exceptionnelles.

Imperiale
Bordeaux bottle holding 8½ normal bottles.

Irancy   B'y. r. or (p.)   [★★]   76 78 79
Good light red made near CHABLIS. The best vintages are long-lived and mature well.

Irouléguy   S.W. France (r.) or w. dr. ★★ D.Y.A.
Agreeable local wine of the Basque country.

Irroy
Formerly important champagne house.

l'Isle de Beauté
Name given to VINS DU PAYS from CORSICA.

Jaboulet, Paul
Old family firm at Tain, leading growers of HERMITAGE etc.

Jaboulet-Vercherre et Cie
Well-known Burgundy merchant-house with v'yds. (34 acres) in POMMARD, etc., and cellars in Beaune.

Jadot, Louis
Much-respected top-quality Burgundy merchant-house with v'yds. (50 acres) in BEAUNE, CORTON, etc.

Jardin de la France
Name given to VINS DU PAYS of the LOIRE.

Jasnières   Lo. (r.) (p.) or w. dr. ★★★ 70 71 73 75 76 78 79
Rare VOUVRAY-like wine of n. Touraine.

Jeroboam
In Bordeaux a 6-bottle bottle, or triple magnum; in Champagne a double magnum.

Juliénas   B'y. r. ★★★ 76 78 79 80
Leading cru of Beaujolais: vigorous fruity wine.

Jura   See Côtes de Jura

Jurançon   S.W. France w. sw. or dr. ★★ 73 75 76 78 79
Unusual high-flavoured and long-lived speciality of Pau in the Pyrenean foothills. Ages well for several years.

Kressman, E. S. & Cie
Family-owned Bordeaux merchants and owners of CH. LATOUR-MARTILLAC in GRAVES. "Monopole Rouge" is very good.

Kriter
Popular low-price sparkling wine processed in Burgundy by PATRIARCHE.

Krug   "Grande Cuvée" and 66 69 71 73
Small but very prestigious champagne house known for full-bodied very dry wine of the highest quality.

Kuentz-Bas

High-quality ALSACE grower and merchant at Husseren-les-Châteaux.

Labarde

Village just s. of MARGAUX and included in that appellation. Best ch.: GISCOURS.

Lalande de Pomerol B'x. r. ★★ 70 71 73 75 **76** 78 79

Neighbour to POMEROL. Wines similar but considerably less fine. Ch. BEL-AIR is well known.

Langlois-Château

Producer of sparkling SAUMUR, controlled by BOLLINGER.

Langon

The principal town of the s. GRAVES/SAUTERNES district.

Lanson Père et Fils NV rosé NV, and 69 71 75

Important growers and merchants of Champagne, cellars at Reims. Luxury brand: Red Label.

Laroche, Domaine

Important growers of CHABLIS marketed by the house of Bacheroy-Josselin.

Latour, Louis

Top Burgundy merchant and grower with v'yds. (120 acres) in CORTON, BEAUNE, etc. Among the best, esp. for whites.

Latour de France r. (w. dr.) ★→★★ 78 79

New appellation in CÔTES DE ROUSSILLON.

Latricières-Chambertin B'y. r. ★★★ 69 70 71 72 73 76 78 79

17-acre Grand Cru neighbour of CHAMBERTIN. Similar wine, but lighter and "prettier".

Laudun rh. r. p. or w. dr. ★

Village of CÔTES-DU-RHÔNE-VILLAGES. Attractive wines from the co-operative.

Laurent-Perrier NV, rosé brut and 66 70 71 73 75

Well-known champagne house of Tours-sur-Marne. Luxury brand: Cuvée Grand Siécle. New in 1981: Ultra Brut.

Leflaive, Domaine

Top-quality burgundy grower at PULIGNY-MONTRACHET.

Léognan B'x.

Leading village of the GRAVES. Best ch'x.: DOMAINE DE CHEVALIER, MALARTIC-LAGRAVIÈRE and HAUT-BAILLY.

Leroy

Important burgundy merchants at AUXEY-DURESSES, part-owners and distributors of the DOMAINE DE LA ROMANÉE-CONTI.

Lichine, Alexis et Cie

Successful post-war Bordeaux merchants, proprietors of CH. LASCOMBES, now controlled by Bass Charrington Ltd.

Lie, sur

"On the lees." Muscadet is often so bottled, for maximum freshness.

Limoux Pyr. r. or w. dr. ★ D.Y.A.

The non-sparkling version of BLANQUETTE DE LIMOUX and a claret-like red: Anne des Joyeuses.

Lirac Rh. r. p. or (w. dr.) ★★ **76** 78 79 80

Neighbouring village to TAVEL. Similar wine; the red becoming more important than the rosé.

Listel Midi r. p. w. dr. ★ D.Y.A.

Estate in the Camargue owned by the giant Salins du Midi, making pleasant light "vins des sables". Domaine du Bosquet is a fruity red.

Listrac B'x. r. ★★

Village of HAUT-MÉDOC next to MOULIS. Best ch'x.: FOURCAS-HOSTEN and FOURCAS-DUPRÉ.

Loire

The major river of n.w. France. See under wine names.

Loron et Fils

Big-scale burgundy grower and merchant, specialist in BEAUJOLAIS.

Loupiac B'x. w. sw. [**] 67 70 71 75 76 79 80

Neighbour to SAUTERNES with similar but less good wine.

Ludon

HAUT-MÉDOC village s. of MARGAUX. Best ch.: LA LAGUNE.

Lugny ("Macon-Lugny") B'y. r. w. dr. [**] 78 79

Village next to VIRÉ with active and good co-operative. Wine of Les Genevrières v'yd. is sold by LOUIS LATOUR.

Lupé-Cholet et Cie

Merchants and growers at NUITS-ST-GEORGES controlled by Bichot of BEAUNE. Best estate wine: Château Gris.

Lussac-Saint-Emilion B'x. r. [**] 70 75 76 78 79

North-eastern neighbour to ST-EMILION. Often good value. Co-operative makes "Roc de Lussac".

Macau

HAUT-MÉDOC village s. of MARGAUX. Best ch.: CANTEMERLE.

macération carbonique

Traditional Beaujolais technique of fermentation with whole bunches of unbroken grapes in an atmosphere saturated with carbon dioxide. Fermentation inside each grape eventually bursts it, giving vivid and very fruity mild wine for quick consumption. Now much used in the Midi.

Burgundy: a grower's own label

MISE EN BOUTEILLES AU DOMAINE	Domaine is the burgundy equivalent of château.
NUITS ST GEORGES	The Appellation Contrôlée is Nuits St Georges.
LES PRULIERS	The individual v'yd. in Nuits is called Les Pruliers.
APPELLATION CONTRÔLÉE DOMAINE HENRI GOUGES A NUITS ST GEORGES, CÔTE D'OR	The name and address of the grower/producer. (The word propriétaire is often also used.)

A merchant's label

SANTENAY	The village.
LES GRAVIERES	The vineyard.
	The wine qualifies for the Appellation Santenay.
APPELLATION CONTRÔLÉE PROSPER MAUFOUX NEGOCIANT À SANTENAY	Prosper Maufoux is a Négociant, or merchant, who bought the wine from the grower to mature, bottle and sell.

Machard de Gramont

Family estate in Burgundy with cellars in NUITS. Recently enlarged with v'yds. in NUITS, SAVIGNY, BEAUNE, POMMARD, CLOS DE VOUGEOT. Traditional wines for laying down.

Mâcon B'y. r. (p.) or w. dr. ** 76 77w. 78 79 80

Southern district of sound, usually unremarkable, reds and tasty dry (CHARDONNAY) whites. Wine with a village name (e.g. Mâcon-Prissé) is better. POUILLY-FUISSÉ is best appellation of the region. See also Mâcon-Villages.

Mâcon-Lugny see Lugny

Mâcon Supérieur

The same but slightly stronger from riper grapes.

Mâcon-Villages B'y. w. dr. [**] 75 76 77 78 79

Increasingly well-made and typical white burgundies. Mâcon-Prissé, MÂCON-VIRÉ are examples.

Mâcon-Viré

See Mâcon-Villages and Viré

Madiran S.W. France r. ☐******☐ 70 71 73 75 76 78
> Dark vigorous red from ARMAGNAC. Needs ageing.

Magnum
> A double bottle.

Mähler-Besse
> First-class Dutch wine-merchants in Bordeaux, with a
> majority shareholding in Ch. PALMER.

Maire, Henri
> The biggest grower and merchant of JURA wines.

Marc Grape skins after pressing; also the strong-smelling brandy
> made from them.

Margaux B'x. r. **→**** 66 67 70 71 73 75 76 78 79
> Village of the HAUT-MÉDOC making the most "elegant" red
> Bordeaux. The name includes CANTENAC and several other
> villages as well. Top ch'x. include MARGAUX, LASCOMBES, etc.

Margnat
> Major producer of everyday VIN DE TABLE.

Marque déposée
> Trade mark.

Marsannay B'y. (r.) or p. *** 76 78 79
> Village near Dijon with excellent light red and delicate rosé,
> perhaps the best rosé in France.

Martillac
> Village in the GRAVES appellation, Bordeaux.

Maufoux, Prosper
> Family firm of burgundy merchants at SANTENAY. Solid,
> reliable wines with good keeping qualities.

Maury Pyr. r. sw. *→** NV
> Red VIN DOUX NATUREL from ROUSSILLON.

Mazis-Chambertin B'y. r. *** 70 71 72 73 76 78 79
> 30-acre Grand Cru neighbour of CHAMBERTIN. Lighter wine.

Médoc B'x. r. ** 70 75 76 78 79
> Appellation for reds of the less good (n.) part of Bordeaux's
> biggest and best district. Typical but light wines. HAUT-MÉDOC
> is better.

Ménétou-Salon Lo. r. p. or w. dr. ** D.Y.A.
> Attractive light wines from w. of SANCERRE. SAUVIGNON
> white; CABERNET red.

Mercier et Cie NV and 70 71 73 75
> One of the biggest champagne houses, at Epernay. Controlled
> by MOËT & CHANDON.

Mercurey B'y. r. or w. dr. ** 71 76 78 79
> Leading red-wine village of the CÔTE CHALONNAISE. Good
> middle-rank burgundy.

méthode champenoise
> The traditional laborious method of putting the bubbles in
> champagne by refermenting the wine in its bottle.

Meursault B'y. (r.) w. dr. ☐*******☐ 69 71 73 75 76 77 78 79
> CÔTE DE BEAUNE village with some of the world's greatest
> whites: rich, smooth, savoury, dry but mellow. Best v'yds.
> incl. Perrières, Genevrières, Charmes.

Meursault-Blagny See Blagny

Midi General term for the south of France. When used of wine is
> often derogatory, though standards have risen consistently in
> recent years.

Minervois Midi r. or (p.) (w.) or br. sw. ☐***→****☐ 76 78 79 80
> Hilly VDQS area with some of the best wines of the Midi: lively
> and full of flavour. Also sweet MUSCAT de St. Jean de M.

mise en bouteilles au château, au domaine
> Bottled at the château, at the property or estate. N.B. dans nos
> caves (in our cellars) or dans la région de production (in the
> area of production) mean little.

Moelleux

Mellow. Used of the sweet wines of VOUVRAY, etc.

Moët & Chandon NV, rosé 75 and **70 71 73** 75

The biggest champagne merchant and grower, with cellars in Epernay and sparkling wine branches in Argentina, Brazil and California. Luxury brand: DOM PÉRIGNON.

Moillard

Big firm of growers and merchants in NUITS-ST-GEORGES.

Mommessin, J.

Major Beaujolais merchant and owner of CLOS DE TART.

Monbazillac Dordogne w. sw. ⭐⭐ **71 73 75 76 78** 79 80

Golden SAUTERNES-style wine from BERGERAC. Ages well. Ch. Monbazillac is best known.

Mondeuse

Red grape of SAVOIE. Good, deep-coloured wine.

Monopole

Vineyard in single ownership.

Montagne-Saint-Emilion B'x. r. ⭐⭐ **70 71 75 76** 78 79

North-east neighbour of ST-EMILION with similar wines.

Montagny B'y. w. dr. ⭐⭐ →⭐⭐⭐ **76 77 78 79**

CÔTE CHALONNAISE village between MÂCON and MEURSAULT, both geographically and gastronomically.

Montée de Tonnerre B'y.

Famous and excellent PREMIER CRU of CHABLIS.

Monthélie B'y. r. ⭐⭐⭐ **71 76** 78 79

Little-known neighbour and almost equal of VOLNAY. Excellent fragrant reds. Best estate: Château de Monthélie.

Montlouis Lo. w. sw./dr. ⭐⭐ **64 69 71 73 74 75 76** 78 79

Neighbour of VOUVRAY. Similar sweet or dry long-lived wine.

Montrachet B'y. w. dr. ⭐⭐⭐⭐ **69 70 71 73 74 75 76 77** 78 79 80

19-acre Grand Cru v'yd. in both PULIGNY and CHASSAGNE-MONTRACHET. The greatest white burgundy: strong, perfumed, intense, dry yet luscious. (The "ts" are silent.)

Montravel

See Côtes de Montravel

Mont-Redon, Domaine de Rh. r. (w. dr.) ⭐⭐⭐ **70 71 76 77** 78 79 80

Outstanding 215-acre estate in CHÂTEAUNEUF-DU-PAPE.

Moreau et Fils

CHABLIS merchant and grower with 170 acres. Also major table-wine producer.

Morey-Saint-Denis B'y. r. ⭐⭐⭐ **66 69 70 71 72 73** 76 77 78 79

Small village with four Grands Crus between GEVREY-CHAMBERTIN and CHAMBOLLE-MUSIGNY. Glorious wine, often overlooked.

Morgon B'y. r. ⭐⭐⭐ **76 78** 79 80

The "firmest" cru of Beaujolais, needing time to develop its rich flavour.

Moueix, J-P et Cie

The leading proprietor and merchant of St-Emilion and Pomerol. Ch'x. incl. MAGDELAINE, LAFLEUR-PETRUS, and part of PETRUS.

Moulin-à-Vent B'y. r. ⭐⭐⭐ **71 76 78** 79 80

The "biggest" and best wine of Beaujolais; powerful and long-lived when not unbalanced by too much added sugar.

Moulis B'x. r. ⭐⭐→⭐⭐⭐

Village of the HAUT-MÉDOC with its own appellation and several good, not top-rank ch'x.: CHASSE-SPLEEN, POUJEAUX-THEIL, etc.

Mousseux

Sparkling.

Mouton Cadet

Best-selling brand of red Bordeaux.

Moutonne

CHABLIS GRAND CRU *honoris causa* owned by BICHOT.

Mumm, G. H. & Cie NV "Cordon Rouge", rosé **73**, Crémant and **69 71** 73 75 76

Major champagne grower and merchant owned by Seagram's. Luxury brand: Président René Lalou.

Muscadet Lo. w. dr. ⟦★★⟧ D.Y.A.

Popular, good-value, often delicious dry wine from round Nantes in s. Brittany. Perfect with fish.

Muscadet de Sèvre-et-Maine

Wine from the central and usually best part of the area.

Muscat

Distinctively perfumed grape and its (usually sweet) wine.

Muscat de Beaumes de Venise

The best French muscat (see Beaumes de Venise).

Muscat de Frontignan Midi br. sw. ★★ D.Y.A.

Sweet Midi muscat.

Muscat de Lunel Midi br. sw. ★★ NV

Ditto. A small area but good.

Muscat de Mireval Midi br. sw. ★★ NV

Ditto, from near Montpellier.

Muscat de Rivesaltes Midi br. sw. ★ NV

Sweet muscat from a big zone near Perpignan.

Musigny B'y. r. (w. dr.) ★★★★ 66 69 70 71 72 73 76 77 78 79

25-acre Grand Cru in CHAMBOLLE-MUSIGNY. Often the best, if not the most powerful, of all red burgundies (and a little white). Best growers: DE VOGÜÉ, DROUHIN.

Nature Natural or unprocessed, esp. of still champagne.

Néac B'x. r. ★★

Village n. of POMEROL. Wines sold as LALANDE-DE-POMEROL.

Négociant-éleveur

Merchant who "brings up" (i.e. matures) the wine.

Nicolas, Ets.

Paris-based wholesale and retail wine merchants; one of the biggest in France and one of the best.

Nuits-St-Georges r. ★★→★★★ 66 69 70 71 72 73 76 77 78 79

Important wine-town: wines of all qualities, typically sturdy and full-flavoured. Name can be shortened to "Nuits". Best v'yds. incl. Les St-Georges, Vaucrains, Les Pruliers, Clos des Corvées, Les Cailles, etc.

Ordinaire

Commonplace, everyday: not necessarily pejorative.

Ott, Domaine

Important producer of high-quality PROVENCE wines.

Pacherenc-du-Vic-Bilh S.W. France w. sw. ★ NV

Rare minor speciality of the ARMAGNAC region.

Palette Prov. r. p. or w. dr. ★★

Near Aix-en-Provence. Aromatic reds and good rosés.

Pasquier-Desvignes

Very old firm of Beaujolais merchants at St Lager, BROUILLY.

Passe-tout-grains

See Bourgogne Passe-tout-grains.

Patriarche

One of the bigger firms of burgundy merchants. Cellars in Beaune; also owns Ch. de Meursault (100 acres), KRITER, etc.

Pauillac B'x. r. ★★→★★★★ 66 67 70 71 73 75 76 78 79

The only village in Bordeaux (HAUT-MÉDOC) with three first-growths (Ch'x. LAFITE, LATOUR, MOUTON-ROTHSCHILD) and many other fine ones, famous for high flavour and a scent of cedarwood.

Pécharmant Dordogne r. ∗∗ **78 79**

Slightly better-than-typical light BERGERAC red.

Pelure d'oignon

"Onion skin"—tawny tint of certain rosés.

Perlant or Perlé

Very slightly sparkling.

Pernand-Vergelesses B'y. r. or (w. dr.) ⌜∗∗∗⌝ **69 71 72 73** 76 78 79

Village next to ALOXE-CORTON containing part of the great CORTON and CORTON-CHARLEMAGNE v'yds. and one other top v'yd.: Ile des Vergelesses.

Perrier, Joseph NV and 66 69 71 73 75

Family-run champagne house with considerable v'yds. at Chalon-s-Marne. Consistent light and fruity style.

Pèrrier-Jouet NV, **69 71 73** 75 76 and rosé brut **73** 75

Excellent champagne-growers and makers at Epernay. Luxury brand: Belle Epoque.

Pétillant

Slightly sparkling.

Petit Chablis B'y. w. dr. ⌜∗∗⌝ **78 79 80**

Wine from fourth-rank CHABLIS v'yds. Lacks great character but can be good value.

Piat Père et Fils

Important growers and merchants of Beaujolais and Mâcon wines at MÂCON, now controlled by Grand Metropolitan Ltd. V'yds. in MOULIN-À-VENT, also CLOS DE VOUGEOT. BEAUJOLAIS and MÂCON-VIRÉ in special Piat bottles are good value.

Pic, Albert

Well-reputed CHABLIS grower.

Picpoul-de-Pinet Midi w. dr. ∗ NV

Rather dull very dry southern white.

Pineau de Charente

Strong sweet apéritif made of white grape juice and Cognac.

Pinot

See Grapes for white wine

Piper-Heidsieck NV, rosé 75 and **71 73** 75

Champagne-makers of old repute at Reims. Luxury brand: Florens Louis. Also (NV) "Brut Sauvage".

Pol Roger NV, rosé **71 73, Blanc de Blancs 71** 73 and **69 71 73** 75

Excellent champagne house at Epernay. Particularly good non-vintage White Foil.

Pomerol B'x. r. ∗∗→∗∗∗∗ 66 70 71 73 75 76 78 79

The next village to ST-EMILION: similar but more "fleshy" wines, maturing sooner, on the whole reliable and delicious. Top ch.: PETRUS.

Pommard B'y. r. ∗∗∗ **66 69 70 71 72 73** 76 78 79

The biggest and best-known village in Burgundy. No superlative wines, but many warmly appealing ones. Best v'yds.: Rugiens, EPENOTS and HOSPICES DE BEAUNE cuvées.

Pommery & Greno NV, NV rosé and **69 71 73** 75

Very big growers and merchants of champagne at Reims.

Ponnelle, Pierre

Well-established family wine-merchants of BEAUNE.

Pouilly-Fuissé B'y. w. dr. ∗∗→∗∗∗ **76 77 78** 79 80

The best white of the MÂCON area. At its best (e.g. Ch. Fuissé) excellent, but often over-priced. Buy it domaine-bottled.

Pouilly-Fumé Lo. w. dr. ∗∗→∗∗∗ **78 79**

Smoky-fragrant, fruity, often sharp pale white from the upper Loire, next to SANCERRE. Grapes must be SAUVIGNON BLANC. Good vintages improve for 2–3 yrs.

Pouilly-Loché B'y. w. dr. ⌜∗∗⌝

Neighbour of POUILLY-FUISSÉ. Similar wine.

Pouilly-Sur-Loire Lo. w. dr. ★ D.Y.A.

  Inferior wine from the same v'yds. as POUILLY-FUMÉ, but different grapes (CHASSELAS).

Pouilly-Vinzelles B'y. w. dr. ★★

  Neighbour of POUILLY-FUISSÉ. Similar wine.

Pradel

  Well-known brand of Provençal wines, esp. a dry rosé.

Preiss Zimmer, Jean

  Old-established Alsace wine-merchants at Riquewihr.

Premières Côtes de Blaye

  Restricted appellation for better reds of BLAYE. Ch'x. include Barbé, l'Escadre, Menaudat, des Petits-Arnauds.

Premier Cru

  First-growth in Bordeaux (see page 54), but the second rank of v'yds. (after Grand Cru) in Burgundy.

Premières Côtes de Bordeaux B'x. r. (p.) or w. dr. or sw. ★→★★★

  Large area east of GRAVES: a good bet for quality and value, though never brilliant. Ch'x incl. Laffitte (sic).

"Noble rot" (in French pourriture noble, in German Edelfäule, in Latin Botrytis cinerea) is a form of mould that attacks the skins of ripe grapes in certain vineyards in warm and misty autumn weather.

Its effect, instead of rotting the grapes, is to wither them. The skin grows soft and flaccid, the juice evaporates through it, and what is left is a super-sweet concentration of everything in the grape except its water content.

The world's best sweet table wines are all made of nobly rotten grapes. They occur in good vintages in Sauternes, the Rhine, the Mosel (where wine made from them is called Trockenbeerenauslese), in Tokaji in Hungary, in Burgenland in Austria, and occasionally elsewhere—California included. The danger is rain on the pulpy grapes when they are already far gone in noble rot. All too often, particularly in Sauternes, the grower's hopes are dashed by a break in the weather.

Primeur

  Early wine, like early vegetables; esp. of BEAUJOLAIS.

Prissé See Mâcon-Villages

Propriétaire-récoltant

  Owner–manager.

Provence

  See Côtes de Provence

Puisseguin-Saint-Emilion B'x. r. ★★ 75 78 79

  Eastern neighbour of ST-EMILION; wines similar—not so fine but often good value. No famous ch'x. but a good co-operative.

Puligny-Montrachet B'y. w. dr. ★★★ 69 71 73 75 76 77 78 79

  Bigger neighbour of CHASSAGNE-MONTRACHET with equally glorious rich dry whites. Best v'yds.: MONTRACHET, CHEVALIER-MONTRACHET, BÂTARD-MONTRACHET, Bienvenue-Bâtard-Montrachet, Les Combettes, Clavoillon, Pucelles, Champ-Canet, etc.

Quarts de Chaume Lo. w. sw. ★★★ 70 71 73 75 76 78 79

  Famous 120-acre plot in COTEAUX DU LAYON, Anjou. CHENIN BLANC grapes. Long-lasting, intense, rich golden wine.

Quatourze Midi r. (p.) or w. dr. ★ 78 79

  Minor VDQS area near Narbonne.

Quincy Lo. w. dr. ★★ 78 79

  Small area making very dry SANCERRE-style wine of SAUVIGNON BLANC.

Ramonet-Prudhon

> One of the leading proprietors in CHASSAGNE-MONTRACHET with 34 acres. Excellent whites, and red Clos St-Jean.

Rancio

> Term for the tang of wood-aged fortified wine, esp. BANYULS and other VINS DOUX NATURELS.

Rasteau Rh. (r. p. w. dr.) or br. sw. ★★ NV

> Village of s. Rhône valley. Good strong sweet dessert wine is the local speciality.

Ratafia de Champagne

> Sweet apéritif made in Champagne of ⅔ grape juice and ⅓ brandy.

Récolte

> Crop or vintage.

Reine Pedanque, La

> Burgundy growers and merchants at ALOXE-CORTON.

Remoissenet Père et Fils

> Fine growers and merchants of burgundy at BEAUNE.

Rémy Pannier

> Important Loire-wine merchants at Saumur.

Reuilly Lo. (r.p.) w. dr. ★★ 76 78

> Neighbour of QUINCY with similar wine; also good PINOT GRIS.

Richebourg B'y. r. ★★★★ 66 69 70 71 73 76 77 78 79

> 19-acre Grand Cru in VOSNE-ROMANÉE. Powerful, perfumed, fabulously expensive wine, among Burgundy's best.

Riesling

> See Grapes for white wine

Rivesaltes Midi r.w. dr. br. sw. ★★ NV

> Fortified sweet wine, some muscat-flavoured, from e. Pyrenees. An ancient tradition still very much alive.

La Roche-aux-Moines Lo. w. dr./sw. ★★★ 69 71 73 75 76 78 79

> 60-acre v'yd. in Savennières, Anjou. Intense strong fruity/sharp wine ages well.

Roederer, Louis NV, rosé 75 and 69 70 71 73 74 75 76

> One of the best champagne-growers and merchants at Reims. Excellent non-vintage wine. Luxury brand: Cristal Brut (in white glass bottles)

La Romanée B'y. r. ★★★★ 66 69 70 71 72 73 76 77 78 79

> 2-acre Grand Cru in VOSNE-ROMANÉE just uphill from ROMANÉE-CONTI owned by Bichot of BEAUNE.

Romanée-Conti B'y. r. ★★★★ 66 71 72 73 76 77 78 79

> 4½-acre Grand Cru in VOSNE-ROMANÉE. The most celebrated and expensive red wine in the world, though seldom the best.

Romanée-Conti, Domaine de la

> The grandest estate of Burgundy, owning the whole of ROMANÉE-CONTI and LA TÂCHE, major parts of RICHE-BOURG, GRANDS ECHÉZEAUX, ECHÉZEAUX and ROMANÉE-ST-VIVANT (under Marey-Monge label). Also a small part of Le MONTRACHET.

Romanée-St-Vivant B'y. r. ★★★★ 71 72 73 76 77 78 79

> 23-acre Grand Cru in VOSNE-ROMANÉE. Similar to ROMANÉE-CONTI but usually lighter.

Ropiteau

> Burgundy wine-growers and merchants at MEURSAULT controlled by CHANTOVENT. Specialists in Meursault and CÔTE DE BEAUNE wines.

Rosé d'Anjou Lo. p. ★ D.Y.A.

> Pale, slightly sweet, rosé. Cabernet d'Anjou is better.

Rosé de Loire Lo. p. dr. ★→★★ D.Y.A.

> Appellation for dry Loire rosé (Anjou is sweet).

Rosette Dordogne w. s./sw./dr. ★★ D.Y.A.

> Mild BERGERAC white.

Roty, Joseph
> Small grower of classic GEVREY-CHAMBERTIN.

Rousseau, Domaine A.
> Major burgundy grower famous for CHAMBERTIN, etc.

Roussette de Savoie   Savoie w. dr.   [**] D.Y.A.
> Pleasant light fresh white from s. of Geneva.

Roussillon
> See Côtes du Roussillon. "Grands Roussillon" are VINS DOUX
> NATURELS.

Ruchottes-Chambertin   B'y. r. *** 69 70 71 72 73 76 77 78 79
> 7½-acre Grand Cru neighbour of CHAMBERTIN owned by
> Domaine A. ROUSSEAU. Similar splendid long-lasting wine.

Ruinart Père et Fils   NV, rosé 71 and 71 73 75
> The oldest champagne house, now belonging to Moët-
> Hennessy. Luxury brand: Dom Ruinart.

Rully   B'y. r. or w. dr. or (sp.)   [**] 76 78 79
> Village of the CÔTE CHALONNAISE famous for sparkling bur-
> gundy. Still reds and white light but tasty and good value.

Sablant   Lo. w. dr. sp. ** NV
> Brand name for high-quality CRÉMANT DE LOIRE.

Saint-Amour   B'y. r. [**] 78 79 80
> Northernmost cru of BEAUJOLAIS: light, fruity, irresistible.

Saint-Aubin   B'y. (r.) or w. dr.   [**] 71 76 78 79
> Little-known neighbour of CHASSAGNE-MONTRACHET, up a
> side-valley. Not top-rank, but typical and good value. Also
> sold as CÔTE-DE-BEAUNE-VILLAGES.

Saint Bris   B'y. w. dr. [*] D.Y.A.
> Village w. of CHABLIS known for its fruity ALIGOTÉ, making
> good sparkling burgundy, and hillside cherry orchards. See
> also Sauvignon-de-St-Bris.

Saint Chinian   Midi r. [*→**] 76 78 79 80
> Hilly VDQS area of growing reputation. Tasty reds.

Sainte Croix-du-Mont   B'x. w. sw. [**] 67 70 71 75 76 79
> Neighbour to SAUTERNES with similar golden wine. No super-
> latives but well worth trying. Very reasonably priced.

Sainte-Foy-Bordeaux   B'x.
> Part of ENTRE-DEUX-MERS.

Saint-Emilion   B'x. r. **→**** 66 67 70 71 73 75 76 78 79
> The biggest top-quality Bordeaux district; solid, rich, tasty
> wines from scores of ch'x., incl. CHEVAL-BLANC, AUSONE,
> CANON, MAGDELAINE, FIGEAC, etc.

Saint-Estèphe   B'x. r. [**] →**** 66 70 71 73 75 76 77 78 79
> Northern village of HAUT-MÉDOC. Solid, satisfying, occasion-
> ally superlative wines. Top ch'x.: CALON-SÉGUR, COS D'ESTOUR-
> NEL, MONTROSE, etc., and many good CRUS BOURGEOIS.

St-Gall
> Brand-name used by the very good Champagne-growers' Co-
> op at AVIZE.

Saint-Georges-Saint-Emilion
> Part of MONTAGNE-ST-EMILION. Best ch.: ST-GEORGES.

Saint-Joseph   Rh. r. (p. or w. dr.)   [**] 71 72 73 76 78 79 80
> Northern Rhône appellation of second rank but reason-
> able price. Substantial wine often better than CROZES-
> HERMITAGE.

Saint-Julien   B'x. r. ***→**** 66 70 71 73 75 76 77 78 79
> Mid-Médoc village with a dozen of Bordeaux's best ch'x., incl.
> three LÉOVILLES, BEYCHEVELLE, DUCRU-BEAUCAILLOU, GRUAUD-
> LAROSE, etc. The epitome of well-balanced red wine.

Saint-Laurent
> Village next to SAINT-JULIEN. Appellation Haut-Médoc.

Saint-Nicolas-de-Bourgueil   Lo. r. ★★ 71 76 78 79
> The next village to BOURGUEIL: the same light but lively an
> fruity CABERNET red.

Saint-Péray   Rh. w. dr. or sp. ★★ NV
> Rather heavy white from the n. Rhône, much of it mad
> sparkling. A curiosity.

Saint Pourçain   Central France r. p. or w. dr ⋆ D.Y.A.
> The agreeable local wine of Vichy, becoming fashionable i
> Paris. Made from GAMAY and/or PINOT NOIR, the white from
> CHARDONNAY or SAUVIGNON BLANC.

Saint-Sauveur
> HAUT-MÉDOC village just w. of PAUILLAC.

Saint-Seurin-de-Cadourne
> HAUT-MÉDOC village just n. of SAINT-ESTÈPHE.

Saint-Véran   B'y. w. dr. ★★ 76 78 79 80
> Next-door appellation to POUILLY-FUISSÉ. Similar but bette
> value: dry white of real character from the best slopes o
> MÂCON-VILLAGES.

Salon   61 64 66 69 71 73
> The original Blanc de Blancs champagne, from Le Mesni
> Fine very dry wine with great keeping qualities.

Sancerre   Lo. (r. p.) or w. dr. ★★★ 76 78 79 80
> Very fragrant and fresh SAUVIGNON white almost indisting
> uishable from POUILLY-FUMÉ, its neighbour over the Loire
> Drink young. Also light PINOT NOIR red and a little rosé, bes
> drunk very young.

Santenay   B'y. r. or (w. dr.) ★★★ 66 69 70 71 72 73 76 78 79
> Very worthy, rarely rapturous, sturdy reds from the s. of th
> CÔTE DE BEAUNE. Best v'yds.: Les Gravières, Clos de Tavar
> nes, La Comme.

Saumur   Lo. r. p. or w. dr. and sp. ★★→ ★★
> Big versatile district in ANJOU, with fresh fruity whites
> good-value sparklers, pale rosés and increasingly goo
> CABERNET reds, the best from Saumur-Champigny, esp. Cl
> de Chaintres.

Sauternes   B'x. w. sw. ★★ →★★★★ 67 70 71 75 76 78 79 80
> District of 5 villages (incl. BARSAC) making France's bes
> sweet wine: strong (14%+ alcohol) luscious and golden, im
> proving with age. Top ch'x.: D'YQUEM, LA TOUR-BLANCHE
> SUDUIRAUT, COUTET, CLIMENS, GUIRAUD, etc. Also a few heav
> dry wines which cannot be sold as Sauternes.

Sauvignon Blanc
> See Grapes for white wine

Sauvignon-de-St-Bris   B'y. w. dr. ★★ D.Y.A.
> A baby VDQS cousin of SANCERRE from near CHABLIS.

Sauzet, Etienne
> Excellent white burgundy estate at PULIGNY-MONTRACHET.

Savennières   Lo. w. dr./sw. ★★★ 69 70 71 73 75 76 78 79
> Small ANJOU district of pungent, traditionally long-live
> whites, incl. COULÉE DE SERRANT, LA ROCHE AUX MOINES, Clo
> du Papillon. Recent wines show less character.

Savigny-lès-Beaune   B'y. r. or (w. dr.) ★★★ 71 76 77 78 79
> Important village next to BEAUNE, with similar well-balance
> middle-weight wines, often deliciously delicate and fruity
> Best v'yds.: Marconnets, Dominode, Serpentière
> Vergelesses, les Guettes.

Savoie   E. France r. or w. dr. or sp. ★★ D.Y.A.
> Alpine area with light dry wines like some Swiss wine o
> minor Loires. CRÉPY and SEYSSEL are best known whites. Als
> MONDEUSE red.

Schlumberger et Cie
> Excellent Alsace growers and merchants at Guebwiller.

Schröder & Schyler

Old family firm of Bordeaux merchants, owners of CH. KIRWAN.

Sec

Literally means dry, though champagne so-called is medium-sweet.

Selection de Grains Nobles

Description coined by HUGEL for Alsace equivalent to German BEERENAUSLESE. "Grains nobles" are individual grapes with "noble rot" (see page 47).

Sèvre-et-Maine

The *département* containing the central and best v'yds. of MUSCADET.

Seyssel   Savoie w. dr. or sp.   ★★   NV

Delicate pale dry white making admirable sparkling wine.

Sichel & Co.

Famous Bordeaux (and Burgundy and Germany) merchants, owners of CH. D'ANGLUDET and part-owners of CH. PALMER.

Soussans

Village just n. of MARGAUX, sharing its appellation.

Sylvaner

See Grapes for white wine

Syrah

See Grapes for red wine

La Tâche   B'y. r. ★★★★ **62 69 70** 71 72 **73 74** 76 77 78 79

15-acre Grand Cru of VOSNE-ROMANÉE and one of the best v'yds. on earth: dark, perfumed and luxurious wine. Owned by the DOMAINE DE LA ROMANÉE-CONTI.

Paris has one wine school that offers individual amateur as well as professional courses. L'Académie du Vin, 25 rue Royale/24 rue Boissy-D'Anglas, was founded by an English wine merchant, Steven Spurrier, in a little mews near La Madeleine in 1973. It has become a centre for the fashionable pursuit of comparing the best wines of California with those of France.

Taittinger   NV and **69 70 71 73**

Fashionable champagne growers and merchants of Reims. Luxury brand: Comtes de Champagne (also rosé).

Tastevin, Confrèrie du

Burgundy's colourful and successful promotion society. Wine carrying their Tastevinage label has been approved by them and will usually be good. A tastevin is the traditional shallow silver wine-tasting cup of Burgundy. See panel, page 33.

Tavel   Rh. p. ★★★ D.Y.A.

France's most famous rosé, strong and dry, starting vivid pink and fading to orange. Avoid orange bottles.

Tête de Cuvée

Term vaguely used of the best wines of an appellation.

Thomas-Bassot

See Ziltener

Thorin, J.

Fine grower and major merchant of BEAUJOLAIS, at Pontanevaux.

Tokay d'Alsace

See Pinot Gris under Grapes for white wine

Tollot-Beaut

Excellent burgundy grower with some 50 acres in the CÔTE DE BEAUNE, incl. CORTON, BEAUNE, Grèves, SAVIGNY (Les Champs Chevrey) and at Chorey-lès-Beaune.

Touraine Lo. r. p. w. dr./sw./sp. $\boxed{* \rightarrow ***}$

Big mid-Loire province with immense range of wines, incl dry white SAUVIGNON, dry and sweet CHENIN BLANC (e.g Vouvray), red CHINON and BOURGUEIL, light red CABERNETS GAMAYS and rosés. Cabernets, Sauvignons and Gamays o good years are bargains.

Trimbach, F. E.

Distinguished ALSACE grower and merchant at Ribeauvillé Best wines incl. Riesling Clos Ste. Hune; mature magnifi cently.

Vacqueyras Rh. r. $\boxed{**}$ 71 76 77 78 79 80

Up-and-coming village of s. CÔTES-DU-RHÔNE, neighbour t GIGONDAS; comparable with CHÂTEAUNEUF-DU-PAPE but less heavy and more "elegant".

Valençay Lo. w. dr. ∗ D.Y.A.

Neighbour of CHEVERNY: similar pleasant sharpish wine.

Varichon & Clerc

Principal makers and shippers of SAVOIE sparkling wines.

Varoilles, Domaine des

Excellent burgundy estate of 25 acres, principally in GEVREY CHAMBERTIN.

Vaudésir B'y. w. dr. $\boxed{****}$ 69 71 75 76 77 78 79 80

Arguably the best of the 7 Grands Crus of CHABLIS (but ther so are the others).

VDQS Vin Délimité de Qualité Supérieure (see p. 23).

Vendange

Vintage.

Vendange tardive

Late vintage. In ALSACE equivalent to German AUSLESE.

Veuve Clicquot NV and **69 70 73** 75 76

Historic champagne house of the highest standing. Cellars a Reims. Luxury brand: La Grande Dame.

Vidal-Fleury, J.

Long-established shippers and growers of top Rhône wines.

Vieilles Vignes

"Old vines" – therefore the best wine. Used for such wine by BOLLINGER and DE VOGÜÉ.

Viénot, Charles

Grower and merchant of good burgundy, at NUITS-ST-GEORGES 70 acres in Nuits, CORTON, RICHEBOURG, etc.

Vignoble

Area of vineyards.

Vin de garde

Wine that will improve with keeping.

Vin de l'année

This year's wine. See Beaujolais.

Vin de paille

Wine from grapes dried on straw mats, consequently very sweet, like Italian passito. Especially in the JURA.

Vin de Pays

The junior rank of country wines (see Introduction).

Vin de Table

Standard everyday table wine, not subject to particular regu lations about grapes and origin.

Vin Doux Naturel ("VDN")

Sweet wine fortified with alcohol, so scarcely "natural". Com mon in ROUSSILLON. A vin doux liquoreux is several degrees stronger.

Vin Gris

"Grey" wine is very pale pink, made of red grapes pressed before fermentation begins, unlike rosé, which ferments briefly before pressing.

Vin Jaune Jura w. dr. ***
>Speciality of ARBOIS: odd yellow wine like fino sherry. Ready when bottled.

Vin nouveau
>See Beaujolais Nouveau

Vin vert
>A very light, acidic, refreshing white wine, a speciality of ROUSSILLON.

Vinsobres Rh. r. (p. or w. dr.) ⟨**★★**⟩ **76** 78 79 80
>Contradictory name of good s. Rhône village. Strong substantial reds which mature well.

Viré B'y. w. dr. ⟨**★★**⟩ **76 78 79**
>One of the best white-wine villages of Mâcon. Good co-op and excellent Ch. de Viré.

Visan Rh. r. p. or w. dr. ★★ **76** 78 79
>One of the better s. Rhône villages. Reds better than white.

Viticulteur
>Wine-grower.

Vogüé, Comte Georges de
>First-class 30-acre burgundy domaine at CHAMBOLLE-MUSIGNY.

As a simple rule of thumb one vine gives one bottle of top-class table wine. A Bordeaux vineyard is normally planted with 5,269 vines per hectare (2,133 per acre) and produces 4,000 litres (5,333 bottles). 10 per cent of the wine is lost in ageing, so the final figure is 4,800 or 400 dozen. The equivalent in tons of grapes per acre is about 2¼ tons, yielding about 1,942 (162 dozen) finished bottles.

In bulk-wine areas and in Germany, where productivity is often very high, the yield may reach over 10,000 litres (100 hectolitres) per hectare, or six tons per acre. On the other hand, Château Yquem, which uses only grapes dehydrated by noble rot (p.47), produces only about 900 litres per hectare, or 486 bottles per acre.

Volnay B'y. r. *** **66 69 71 72** 76 78 79
>Village between POMMARD and MEURSAULT: the best reds of the CÔTE DE BEAUNE, not strong or heavy but fragrant and silky. Best v'yds.: Caillerets, Clos des Ducs, Champans, Clos des Chênes, etc.

Volnay-Santenots B'y. r. ***
>Excellent red wine from MEURSAULT is sold under this name. Indistinguishable from VOLNAY.

Vosne-Romanée B'y. r. ***→**** **66 69 70 71 72 73** 76 77 78 79
>The village containing Burgundy's grandest Crus (ROMANÉE-CONTI, LA TÂCHE, etc.). There are (or rather should be) no common wines in Vosne.

Vougeot
>See Clos de Vougeot

Vouvray Lo. w. dr./sw./sp. ★★→**★★★★** **64 67 69 70 71 73 75** 76 78 79
>Small district of TOURAINE with very variable wines, at their best intensely sweet and almost immortal. Good dry sparkling.

"Y" (Pronounced ygrec)
>Brand name of powerful dry wine of great character, occasionally made at CH. D'YQUEM.

Ziltener, André
>Important Swiss-owned merchants at GEVREY-CHAMBERTIN.

Châteaux of Bordeaux

Some 300 of the best-known châteaux of Bordeaux are listed below in alphabetical order.

The vintage information for each château has been entirely revised for this edition in consultation with the château-proprietors as well as the many friends who have contributed their notes, as in previous editions, to supplement my own.

A new level of recommendation is added to this section for the first time: the vintages picked out by the man responsible as being his greatest successes of the decade of the '70s (which was, on average, the most successful Bordeaux decade of the century). The vintages marked with an accent "'" are those by which the owner would wish his château to be judged. Whether they are mature yet or will improve with keeping is indicated, as elsewhere in the book, by the style of type.

As in previous editions, but to a much lesser extent, the information is necessarily incomplete, and, since no one person has ever tasted all these wines, it cannot be taken as guaranteed. It does, however, go very much further in guiding you through the complexities of Bordeaux than any previous publication.

General information on the style of each vintage will be found on the vintage charts on page 24 and on page 25. Further information about each village or appellation will be found among the general French entries.

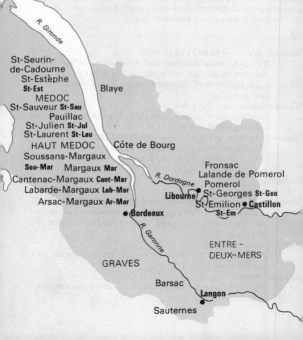

l'Agassac Ludon, Haut-Médoc r. [★★] 75' 76 78 79
14th-century moated fort with 85 acres. Same owners as Ch'x CALON-SÉGUR and DU TERTRE and a growing reputation.

l'Angélus St-Em. r. ★★ 66 70' 75' 76 78 79'
Well-situated classed-growth of 65 acres on the St-Emilion Côtes w. of the town. Recent vintages have not been exciting.

d'Angludet Cant-Mar. r. [★★] 66 70' 73 74 75 76' 78' 79
72-acre British-owned Cru Exceptionnel of classed-growth quality.

d'Arche Sauternes w. sw. ★★ 69 70 71 73 78 79
Substantial second-rank classed-growth of 120 acres. Ch. d'Arche-Lafaurie is its lesser wine.

Ausone St-Em. r. ★★★★ 67 70 71' 75' 76' 78 79
Celebrated first-growth with 18 acres in a commanding position on the Côtes and famous rock-hewn cellars under the v'yd. Off form in the sixties but first class since 1970.

Bahans-Haut-Brion Gr. r. ★★★ N.V.
The second-quality wine of Ch. HAUT-BRION.

Balestard-la-Tonnelle St-Em. r. ★★ 66 67 70' 71 75' 76' 78 79
Historic 25-acre classed-growth on the plateau near the town. Mentioned by the 15c poet Villon and still in the same family (which also owns Ch. Cap-de-Mourlin).

de Barbe Côtes de Bourg r. (w.) [★★] 70' 71 73 75' 76 78 79'
The biggest (122 acres) and best-known ch. of the right bank of the Gironde. Good full-bodied red.

Baret Graves r. and w. dr. ★★ 75 76 77w. 78
Little estate of good quality, better known for its white wine.

Batailley Pauillac r. ★★★ 61 62 64 66 70 71 72 73 75' 76 77 78' 79'
The bigger of the famous pair of fifth-growths (with HAUT-BATAILLEY) on the borders of Pauillac and St-Julien. 125 acres. Firm strong-flavoured wine.

Beaumont Cussac, Haut-Médoc r. ★★ 75 76 78' 79
Considerable Cru Bourgeois, well-known in France for full-bodied, consistent wines. In new hands since '79. Second label: Ch. Moulin d'Arolgny.

Beauregard Pomerol r. [★★★] 70 71 75' 76 77 78' 79
30+ acre v'yd. with pretty 17th-century ch. near LA CONSEILLANTE. Well-made typical "round" wines.

Beauséjour-Bécot St-Em. r. ★★★ 70 71 73 75' 76' 78 79
Half of the famous old Beauséjour estate on the w. slope of the Côtes. 44 acres. Dynamic management; welcomes visitors.

Beauséjour-Duffau-Lagarosse St-Em. r. ★★★ 66 70 71 75 76 78 79
The other half of the above, in old family hands and making traditional wine for long maturing.

Beau Site St-Est. r. [★★] 70' 71 75' 76 78' 79
72-acre Cru Bourgeois in same hands as Ch'x BATAILLEY, TROTTEVILLE, etc. Regular quality.

Belair St-Em. r. [★★★] 70 71 75' 76' 78 79'
Sister-ch. and neighbour of AUSONE with 30+ acres on the Côtes. Steady improvement in recent vintages.

de Bel-Air Lalande de Pomerol r. [★★] 70 71' 73 75' 76' 78
The best-known estate of this village just n. of Pomerol, with very similar wine. 24 acres.

Bel-Air-Marquis d'Aligre Sou-Mar. r. [★★] 70' 71 75' 76 78' 79
Reliable Cru Exceptionnel with 41 acres of old vines.

Belgrave St-Lau. r. ★★
Obscure fifth-growth in St-Julien's back-country. 100+ acres. Recently acquired by DOURTHE.

Bellevue St-Em. r. ★★ 75 76 78 79
Well-known little classed-growth on the w. Côtes.

Bel-Orme-Tronquoy-de-Lalande St-Seurin-de-Cadourne (Haut Médoc) r. **`**`** 70′ 71 75′ 76 78′ 79′
Reputable 62-acre Cru Bourgeois n. of St-Estèphe. Old v'yd producing tannic wines. Same owner as Ch. RAUZAN-GASSIES.

Beychevelle St-Jul. r. **`***`** 61 66 70′ 71 74 75′ 76 78 79
115-acre fourth-growth with the Médoc's finest mansion. Wine of great distinction and more elegance than power.

Le Bourdieu Vertheuil (Haut-Médoc) r. ** 70 71 75′ 76 78′ 79
Cru Bourgeois with sister ch. Victoria (132 acres in all) known for steady typical middle-Médocs.

Bourgneuf-Vayron Pomerol r. ** 75′ 76 78 79
20-acre v'yd. on clay soil making good rather heavy wines.

Bouscaut Graves r. w. dr. **`***`** 70′ 73 74 75′ 76 78′ 79
Neglected classed-growth at Cadaujac brought back to life by American enthusiasts since 1969. Bought in 1980 by Lucien Lurton, owner of Ch. BRANE-CANTENAC, etc. 77 acres red (largely Merlot); 15 acres white.

du Bousquet Côte de Bourg r. **`**`** 75′ 76 78 79
Reliable estate with 100 acres making attractive solid wine.

Boyd-Cantenac Margaux r. **`***`** 66 70′ 71 74 75′ 76′ 78 79
43-acre third-growth regularly producing attractive wine tending to improve. See also Ch. POUGET.

Branaire-Ducru St-Jul. r. **`***`** 61 66 70′ 71 74 75′ 76 78 79′
Fourth-growth of 115 acres producing notably spicy and flavoury wine: attractive and reliable.

Brane-Cantenac Cant-Mar. r. **`***`** 61 66 70 71 75′ 76′ 77 78′ 79
Big (204 acres) well-run and reliable second-growth. Round smooth and delightful wines. Same owners as Chx DURFORT-VIVENS, VILLEGEORGE, CLIMENS, BOUSCAUT, etc.

du Breuil Cissac, Haut-Médoc r. ** 70′ 71′ 73 75′ 76 77 78′ 79
58-acre v'yd. with a 10th-century castle producing full-bodied stylish wine, generally ageing well. Also nuts and melons.

Brillette Moulis, Haut-Médoc r. ** 75 76 78
75-acre v'yd. whose pebbly soil is said to "shine" – hence the name. Reliable rather country-style wine, improving.

A Bordeaux label

> CHATEAU GISCOURS
> GRAND CRU CLASSE
>
> APPELLATION MARGAUX
> CONTROLEE
>
> MIS EN BOUTEILLES AU
> CHATEAU

A château is an estate, not necessarily with a mansion or a big expanse of v'yd. Over 300 are listed in the France A-Z. Reference to the local classification. It varies from one part of Bordeaux to another. The Appellation Controlée: look up Margaux in the France A–Z. "Bottled at the château" — becoming the normal practice with classed-growth wines.

La Cabanne Pomerol r. **`***`** 70′ 71 73 75′ 76 78 79
Highly-regarded 20-acre property near the great Ch. TROTANOY.

Cadet Piola St-Em. r. **`**`** 70′ 71 73 74 75′ 76 78 79
Reliable little property (17 acres) on the plateau just n. of the town of St-Emilion. Ch. Faurie de Souchard has the same owner.

Calon-Ségur St-Est. r. **`***`** 61 62 66 67 70 71 73 75 76 77 78 79
Big (145-acre) third-growth of great reputation. Often the best St-Estèphe but has had off-moments. '78 and '79 suggest a return to excellence.

Camensac St-Lau. r. ⟦******⟧ 66 70′ **71** 73 74 75′ **76** 78′ 79
>Re-emerging 144-acre fifth-growth, replanted in the '60s with new equipment and the same expert direction as LAROSE-TRINTAUDON. Fine vigorous full-bodied wines.

Canon St-Em. r. ******* 66 70 71 75′ 76 78′ 79′
>Famous first-classed-growth with 44+ acres on the plateau w. of the town. Conservative methods; impressive wine.

Canon-la-Gaffelière St-Em. r. ⟦******⟧ 66 70 71 75 76 77 78 79
>50-acre classed-growth on the lower slopes of the Côtes.

Cantemerle Macau r. ⟦*******⟧ 61 62 64 66 70′ **71** 73 74 75′ **76** 78′ 79
>Superb estate at the extreme s. of the Médoc, with a romantic ch. in a wood and 50 acres of vines. Officially fifth-growth: in practice nearer second-growth. Traditional methods make deep, longlasting, richly subtle wine. Changed hands in 1981.

Cantenac-Brown Cant-Mar. r. ******* 61 62 66 70 **71** 73 75 76 78 79
>Formerly old-fashioned 72-acre third-growth, now well run and making classical wine for long development.

Capbern St-Est. r. ******
>80-acre Cru Bourgeois; same owner as Ch. CALON-SÉGUR.

Cap de Mourlin St-Em. r. ******* 70′ **71** 75′ 78 79
>Well-known 40-acre château n. of St-Emilion making reliable, if sometimes rather light, wine.

Carbonnieux Graves r. and w. dr. ******* 70 71 74 75′ **76** 78′ 79
>Historic estate at Léognan making good fairly light wines with modern methods. The white is the much better.

La Cardonne Blaignan (Médoc) r. ******
>Large Cru Bourgeois in the n. Médoc recently bought by the Rothschilds of Ch. LAFITE.

Les Carmes-Haut-Brion Graves r. ****** 75 76 78 79
>Small neighbour of HAUT-BRION. Nothing special.

Caronne-Ste-Gemme St-Lau. (Haut-Médoc) r. ****** 70 73 75′ **76** 77 78 79
>Substantial Cru Bourgeois of 100 acres. Steady quality.

du Castéra Médoc r. ⟦******⟧ 70 73 75 76 78 79
>Beautiful property at St-Germain in the n. Médoc managed by LICHINE. Fine, longlasting wine.

Certan de May Pomerol r. ⟦******⟧ 70 **71** 73 75′ 76 78 79
>Neighbour of VIEUX-CHÂTEAU-CERTAN. Tiny property with fine rather hard wine, needing time to mature.

Certan-Giraud Pomerol r. ******* 71 73 75 76 78 79
>Minute (8½-acre) property next to the great Ch. PETRUS.

Chasse-Spleen Moulis r. ⟦******⟧ 66 70′ **71** 73 74 75′ **76** 77 78′ 79
>12-acre Cru Exceptionnel of classed-growth quality. Consistently good, sometimes outstanding, long-maturing wine.

Cheret-Pitre Graves r. (w. dr.) ****** 70′ 75′ 76 78 79
>29-acre property at Portets making full and meaty wines.

Cheval Blanc St-Em. r. ******** 61 64 66 70′ 71′ 74 75′ 76 78 79
>By reputation the best wine of St-Em. rich, full-blooded, from an old family estate of 80 acres on the border of Pomerol.

Cissac Cissac r. ⟦******⟧ 66 70′ **71** 75′ 76 77 78′ 79
>82-acre Cru Bourgeois with dynamic owners. Traditional methods and style.

Citran Avensan, Haut-Médoc r. ****** 70′ 75 76 78′ 79
>One of the better Crus Bourgeois at present. Full-bodied tough wine. Sadly, rain reduced the '75 crop.

Clarke Listrac, Haut-Médoc r. ******
>Big (330-acre) Cru Bourgeois replanted by a (LAFITE) Rothschild. First vintage 1977. To watch.

Clerc-Milon Pauillac r. ******* 70′ **71** 73 74 75′ **76** 78 79
>Forgotten little fifth-growth until 1970, when it was bought by Baron Philippe de Rothschild. Now 65 acres and new equipment are making first-rate wine.

Climens   Sauternes w. sw.   ★★★   **62 67 70 71'** 73 75' **76'** 78' 79
Famous 75-acre classed-growth at Barsac making some of the best and richest sweet wine in the world. Same owner as Ch. BRANE-CANTENAC, etc.

Clinet   Pomerol r.   ★★   **70 71** 75' 76 78 79
17-acre property in central Pomerol making elegant wine with more finesse than force.

Clos l'Eglise   Pomerol r.   ★★★   **71 73** 75 76 78 79
13-acre v'yd in one of the best sites in Pomerol. Excellent wine.

Clos Fourtet   St-Em. r.   ★★★ 67 70 **73** 75 76 78
Well-known 33-acre first-growth on the plateau with cellars almost in the town. Back on form after a middling patch. Same owner as CLIMENS, etc.

Clos des Jacobins   St-Em. r.   ★★   75' **76** 78 79
Well-known and well-run little (20-acre) classed-growth owned by the shipper CORDIER. Matures rather quickly.

Clos René   Pomerol r.   ★★★   **61 66 67 70** 71 **73** 75 78 79
Leading ch. on the w. of Pomerol. 30 acres making powerful wine which matures to great delicacy. CLOS L'EGLISE is in same hands.

La Clotte   St-Em. r.   ★★   **66 70 71'** 75' 76' 78 79
Côtes classed-growth with attractive "supple" wine.

La Conseillante   Pomerol r. ★★★ **66 67 70'** 71' 75' 76 78 79
30-acre classed-growth on the plateau between PETRUS and CHEVAL BLANC. At its best gloriously rich but less good in the sixties than its position would suggest.

Corbin   St-Em. r. ★★
50-acre classed-growth in n. St-Emilion where a cluster of Corbins occupy the edge of the plateau.

Corbin-Michotte   St-Em. r.   ★★   **66 70 71 73** 75 76 78 79
Well-run small property making attractive and reliable wine.

Cos-d'Estournel   St-Est. r.   ★★★   **61 64 66** 70 **71 73 74** 75' **76'** 78' 79
146-acre second-growth with eccentric chinoiserie building overlooking Ch. LAFITE. Usually full-flavoured, often magnificent, wine. Ch. PETIT-VILLAGE has the same owner.

Cos Labory   St-Est. r. ★★ **66 70'** 71 **73** 75' 76 78' 79'
Little-known fifth-growth neighbour of COS D'ESTOURNEL with 35 acres. Typical robust St-Estèphe, said to be improving in quality.

Coufran   St-Seurin-de-Cadourne (Haut-Médoc) r.   ★★   **70'** 73 74 76' 78' 79
Coufran and Ch. Verdignan, on the northern-most hillock of the Haut-Médoc, are under the same ownership. Mainly Merlot vines; rich soft wine. 144 acres.

Couhins   Graves (r.) w. dr.   ★★   76 77 78 79
25-acre v'yd. at Villenave-d'Ornon producing one of the best dry white Graves.

La Couronne   Pauillac r.   ★★   67 70 **73** 75 76 78 79
Small but excellent Cru Exceptionnel under the same direction as Ch. HAUT-BATAILLEY.

Coutet   Sauternes w. sw.   ★★★   **62 67 70'** 71' 75' 76 78 79
Rival to Ch. CLIMENS; 91 acres in Barsac. Said to be slightly less rich but certainly equally fine. "Cuvée Madame" is a selection of the very best (71, 75).

Couvent des Jacobins   St-Em. r. ★★★
Well-known vineyard of 20 acres adjacent to the town of St-Emilion on the east.

Le Crock   St-Est. r. ★★
Well-situated Cru Bourgeois of 80 acres in the same family as Ch. LÉOVILLE-POYFERRÉ.

La Croix Pomerol r. ✶✶ **70' 71' 73** 75' 76 78 79
    Well-reputed little property of 25+ acres. Old-fashioned tough wine; matures well.

La Croix de Gay Pomerol r. ✶✶✶ **70' 71'** 75' 76 78 79
    One of the larger Pomerol v'yds. 28 acres in the best part of the commune. Perhaps below full potential.

Croizet-Bages Pauillac r. ✶✶ **61 66 70' 71 73** 75' 76 78' 79'
    60-acre fifth-growth (lacking a ch.) owned by the same family as Ch. RAUZAN-GASSIES. Sound sturdy wines.

Croque-Michotte St-Em. r.✶✶ **66 70 72** 75 **76** 78 79
    Small but well-known classed-growth on the Pomerol border.

Curé-Bon-la-Madeleine St-Em. r. ✶✶✶ **66 70' 71'** 75 76' 78 79
    Small (12-acre) property among the best of the Côtes; between AUSONE and CANON. Managed by MOUEIX.

Dauzac Lab-Mar. r. ✶✶ **66 70 73** 75 **76** 78 79
    Substantial but somewhat neglected fifth-growth near the river s. of Margaux. In new hands since '79. 100 acres.

Why do the Châteaux of Bordeaux have such a large section of this book devoted to them? The reason is simple: collectively they form by far the largest supply of high-quality wine on earth. The quantities involved are very large.

    A single typical Médoc château with 150 acres (some have far more) makes approximately 26,000 dozen bottles of identifiable wine a year — the production of two or three Californian "boutique" wineries. The tendency over the last two decades has been for the better-known châteaux to buy more land. Many classed-growths have expanded considerably since they were classified.

Dillon Haut-Médoc r. ☐✶✶☐ **70 73** 75' 77 78' 79'
    Often very well-made wine. Run by local wine college of Blanquefort, just n. of Bordeaux. 73 acres.

Doisy-Daene Barsac w. sw. and dr. ☐✶✶✶☐ **70' 71'** 75 76' 78 79
    Forward-looking 50-acre estate making crisp dry white (incl. Riesling grapes) as well as traditional sweet Barsac.

Doisy-Dubroca Barsac w. sw. ☐✶✶☐ **71' 73** 75' 76 78' 79
    Tiny (8½-acre) Barsac classed-growth allied to Ch. CLIMENS.

Doisy-Védrines Sauternes w. sw. ☐✶✶✶☐ **67 70' 71** 75' 76' 78
    50-acre classed-growth at Barsac, near CLIMENS and COUTET and generally in the same high class.

Domaine de Chevalier Graves r. and w. dr. ✶✶✶✶ **61 64 66 67 70'** 71 72 **73** 74 75' 76 77 78' 79'
    Superb small estate of 36 acres at Léognan. The red is stern at first, richly subtle with age. The white is delicate but matures to rich flavours. (w. **70 71** 75 76 78 79)

Domaine de l'Eglise Pomerol r. ✶✶ **66 67 70 71** 75' 76 78 79'
    Small property: good wine distributed by BORIE-MANOUX.

La Dominique St-Em. r. ☐✶✶✶☐ **70 71 73** 75 76 78 79
    Fine 44-acre classed-growth next door to Ch. CHEVAL BLANC.

Ducru-Beaucaillou St-Jul. r. ☐✶✶✶☐ **61 62 64 66 67 70' 71** 74 75' 76 77 78' 79
    Outstanding second-growth; about 100 acres overlooking the river. The owner, M. Borie, makes classical long-lived but not harsh wines.

Duhart-Milon-Rothschild Pauillac r. ✶✶✶ **64 66 70' 71 73** 75' 76' 77 78 79'
    Fourth-growth neighbour of LAFITE under the same management. Wines tend to typical Pauillac toughness rather than Lafite's elegance. 100 acres.

Durfort-Vivens   Margaux r.   `***`   66 70 **71** 73 75′ 76 78′ 79′
Relatively small (46-acre) second-growth owned by M. Lurton of BRANE-CANTENAC and not far behind it in quality.

Dutruch-Grand-Poujeaux   Moulis r.   `**`   70 **71 73**′ 75 76 78′ 79
Rising star of Moulis, making typically hard tannic wines.

L'Eglise-Clinet   Pomerol r.   `***` 66 70 **71** 74 75 76 78 79
Highly ranked little property; typical, full, fleshy wine.

L'Enclos   Pomerol r.   `***`   64 67 70 71 **73 74** 75 76 78 79
Respected little property on the w. side of Pomerol, near CLOS-RENÉ. Big, well-made, long-flavoured wine.

L'Evangile   Pomerol r.   `***`   66 67 70′ **71**′ 73 74 75′ 76 78 79
30+ acres between PETRUS and CHEVAL BLANC. Impressive wines. In the same area and class as LA CONSEILLANTE.

Fargues   Sauternes w. sw.   `**`   70′ **71**′ 73 75′ 76′ 77 78 79
24-acre v'yd. in same ownership as Ch. YQUEM. Fruity and good but much lighter wines.

Ferrière   Margaux r.   `**` 66 70 75 78 79
Little-known third-growth of only 12 acres. The wine is made at Ch. LASCOMBES and sold to a chain of French hotels.

Feytit-Clinet   Pomerol r.   `**` 64 70′ 71′ **74** 75′ 76 78 79
Little property next to LATOUR-POMEROL. Has made some fine big strong wines. Managed by J-P MOUEIX.

Fieuzal   Graves r. and (w. dr.)   `***`   64 66 67 70′ **71** 74 75′ 76 78′ 79
53-acre classed-growth at Léognan. Changed hands in peak condition in 1973; now making some of the best GRAVES.

Figeac   St-Em. r.   `***`   61 62 64 66 67 70′ **71** 73 74 75′ 76 78 79
Famous first-growth neighbour of CHEVAL BLANC. Superb 70+ acre v'yd. gives one of Bordeaux's most attractive full-bodied wines maturing fairly quickly.

Filhot   Sauternes w. sw. and dr.   `***`   67 70 **71**′ 72 75 76′ 78 79′
Second-rank classed-growth with splendid ch., 140-acre v'yd Very good sweet wines, a little dry and red.

La Fleur   St-Em. r.   `**` 70 **73 74** 75 76 78 79
Very small but well-regarded Côtes estate.

La Fleur-Petrus   Pomerol r.   `***` 66 67 70 71′ **73 74** 75′ 76′ 78 79
18-acre v'yd. flanking PETRUS and under the same MOUEIX management. Very fine rich plummy wines.

Fombrauge   St-Em. r.   `**`   70′ **71** 75′ 76 77 78′ 79
Major property of St-Christophe-des-Bardes, e. of St-Emilion with 115 acres. Reliable classic St-Emilion, if never great.

Fonbadet   Pauillac r.   `**` 70 75 78 79
Well-known Cru Bourgeois with 70 acres next door to Ch PONTET-CANET. Same owner as Ch. GLANA.

Fonpiqueyre   See Ch. Liversan.

Fonplégade   St-Em. r.   `**` **71 73** 75 76 78 79
35-acre v'yd. on the Côtes w. of St. Emilion in another branch of the MOUEIX family.

Fonréaud   Listrac r.   `**` 70′ **71** 75′ **76** 77 78′ 79
One of the bigger (113 acres) and better Crus Bourgeois of its area, selling mainly in France and at the cellar door.

Fonroque   St-Em. r.   `***` 66 67 70 **71**′ **73 74** 75′ 76′ 78 79
50 acres on the plateau n. of St-Emilion, the property of another branch of the ubiquitous family MOUEIX. Big dark wine.

Les Forts de Latour   Pauillac r.   `***` 66 67 70 71 72 73 74
The second wine of Ch. Latour; well worthy of its big brother Unique in being bottle-aged at least three years before re-lease. Fetches the price of a second-growth Château.

Fourcas-Dupré   Listrac r.   `**` 70′ **71** 75 76 78′ 79
A top-class 100-acre Cru Bourgeois making consistent and elegant wine. To follow.

Fourcas-Hosten Listrac r. [**] **66** 70 **71 73'** 75 76 78' **79**
Reliable 96-acre Cru Bourgeois of the central Médoc.
Changed hands in '79. Rather hard wine is typical of Listrac.

Franc-Mayne St-Em. r. ** **70 71 73** 75 76 78 79
Small well-regarded v'yd. w. of St-Emilion.

La Gaffelière St-Em. r. [***] **61 66 67 70 71** 75' 76 **77** 78 79
Excellent though not always reliable 50-acre first-growth at
the foot of the Côtes below Ch. BEL-AIR.

La Garde Graves r. (w. dr.) ** **70' 71 74** 75' 76' 78 79
Substantial ESCHENAUER property making reliably sound red.
100 acres red; 12 acres white.

Le Gay Pomerol r. *** **70 71 74** 75' 76' 78 79
Well-known 14-acre v'yd. on the northern edge of Pomerol.

Gazin Pomerol r. *** **66 67 70' 71'** 75' 76 78 79
Large property (for Pomerol) with 77 acres. Not quite as
splendid as its position next to PETRUS.

Giscours Lab-Mar. r. [***] **66 67 70 71 73 74** 75' 76 78 79'
Splendid 190-acre third-growth s. of CANTENAC. Dynamically
run and making excellent wine for long maturing.

du Glana St-Jul. r. ** **66 70'** 75' 78 79
Big Cru Bourgeois in centre of St-Julien. Variable quality.

Gloria St-Jul. r. [***] **66 67 70' 71 73** 75' 76 78' 79'
Outstanding Cru Bourgeois making wine of vigour and
finesse, among good classed-growths in quality. 120
acres. Ch. Haut-Beychevelle-Gloria is the same property.

Grand-Barrail-Lamarzelle-Figeac St-Em. r. [**] **66 67 70 71 72
73** 75 76 78 79
Substantial property near FIGEAC. Well-reputed and popular.

Grand-Corbin-Despagne St-Em. r. [**] **70 71** 75 78 79
One of the larger classed-growths on the CORBIN plateau.

Grand-Pontet St-Em. r. **
Widely distributed 34-acre neighbour of Ch. BEAUSÉJOUR-
BÉCOT, now in the same hands. "Supple", smooth wine.

Grand-Puy-Ducasse Pauillac r. [**] **66 70** 75 76 77 78 79
Well-known little fifth-growth bought in '71, renovated and
enlarged to 70 acres under expert management.

Grand-Puy-Lacoste Pauillac r. [***] **66 70' 71 73** 75 76 78' 79'
Leading fifth-growth famous for fine full-bodied typical
Pauillac. 84 acres among the "Bages" ch'x. s. of the town,
recently bought by M. Borie of DUCRU-BEAUCAILLOU.

La Grave Trigant de Boisset Pom. r. [**] **70 71' 73** 75' 76' 78 79
Verdant ch. with small but first-class v'yd. owned by a
MOUEIX. One of the lighter Pomerols.

Gressier Grand Poujeaux Moulis r. [**] **66 70 71 73** 75' 76 78'
79
Good Cru Bourgeois. Fine firm wine.

Greysac Médoc r. ** **70' 71 74** 75' **76** 78 79'
Elegant 132-acre property whose wine is well-known in the
U.S.A., though scarcely exceptional.

Gruaud-Larose St-Jul. r. *** **62 66 70' 71 72 73** 75' 76 77 78 79
One of the biggest and best-known second-growths. 195 acres
making smooth rich stylish claret. Owned by CORDIER.

Guiraud Sauternes (r.) w. sw. (dr.) [***] **61 67 70' 71** 75' 76 78' 79
Large classed-growth of top quality. 170-acre v'yd. Excellent
sweet wine and a small amount of red and dry white.

La Gurgue Margaux r. **
Small well-placed property with fine typical Margaux recently bought by owners of Ch. CHASSE-SPLEEN. To watch.

Hanteillan Cissac r. [**] **73** 75' 76 79'
Large v'yd. renovated and enlarged since 1973. Ch. Tour du
Vatican is second-quality wine. See also Ch. LARRIVAUX-
HANTEILLAN.

Haut-Bages-Libéral Pauillac r. ★★ 75 76 78 79
> Lesser-known fifth-growth of 50 acres recently bought by the CRUSE family. Should improve.

Haut-Bages-Monpelou Pauillac r. ★★ 70 71′ 75′ 76 78 79
> 24-acre Cru Bourgeois stable-mate of CH. BATAILLEY. To watch.

Haut-Bailly Graves r. ★★★ 64 66 70′ 71 75 78′ 79
> 60-acre estate at Léognan. Potentially one of the best red Graves. New regime (since '79) will justify its reputation.

Haut-Batailley Pauillac r. ★★★ 64 66 70′ 71 73 75′ 76 77 78′ 79
> The smaller but currently better section of the fifth-growth Batailley estate: 43 acres owned by M. Borie of Ch. DUCRU-BEAUCAILLOU. One of the most reliable Pauillacs.

Haut-Brion Pessac, Graves r. (w.) ★★★★ 59 60 61 62 64 66 67 68 70′ 71 73 75′ 76 77 78′ 79
> The oldest great ch. of Bordeaux and the only non-Médoc first-growth of 1855. 100 acres. Splendid firm reds, particularly good since 1975. A little full dry white in 70 71 75 76 77 78 79. See also BAHANS-HAUT-BRION.

Haut-Marbuzet St-Estèphe r. ★★ 70′ 71 75′ 76 77 78′ 79
> One of the best of many St-Estèphe Crus Bourgeois. 100 acres.

Haut-Pontet St-Em. r. ★★ 70 71 73 75 78 79
> Well-regarded 12-acre v'yd. of the Côtes.

Houissant St-Estèphe r. ★★
> Typical robust well-balanced St-Estèphe Cru Bourgeois, well known in Denmark.

d'Issan Cant-Mar. r. ★★★ 66 70 71 72 73′ 75′ 76′ 78 79
> Beautifully restored moated ch. with 72-acre third-growth v'yd. well known for round and gentle wine.

Kirwan Cant-Mar. r. ★★ 70′ 71 75′ 76 78 79′
> Well-run 70-acre third-growth owned by SCHRÖDER & SCHŸLER. Recently much replanted: worth watching.

Labégorce Margaux r. ★★ 70′ 73 75′ 76 78′ 79
> Substantial 67-acre property north of Margaux with rather old-fashioned long-lived wines.

Labégorce-Zédé Margaux r. ★★ 70′ 71′ 72 73 75′ 76 78 79
> Reputable little Cru Bourgeois on the road n. from Margaux. 48 acres. Typical delicate wines. The same family as VIEUX-CHÂTEAU-CERTAN.

Lafaurie-Peyraguey Sauternes w. sw. ★★★ 67 70 71′ 75′ 76′ 77 78 79
> Fine classed-growth of only 40 acres at Bommes, belonging to CORDIER. Excellent wines, though not the richest.

Lafite-Rothschild Pauillac r. ★★★★ 61 62 66 70′ 75′ 76′ 78 79′
> First-growth of fabulous style and perfume in its great vintages, which keep for decades. Off-form for several years but resurgent since '76. 216+ acres.

Lafleur Pomerol r. ★★★ 66 67 70′ 71′ 73 75′ 76 78 79
> Tiny property of 13 acres just n. of PETRUS. Excellent wine of the finer, less "fleshy" kind.

Lafleur-Gazin Pomerol r. ★★ 70 71′ 73 74 75′ 76′ 78 79
> Distinguished small estate on the n.e. border of Pomerol.

Lafon-Rochet St-Est. r. ★★★ 61 64 66 67 70′ 71 75′ 76 78
> Fourth-growth neighbour of Ch. COS D'ESTOURNEL, restored to prominence in the '60s. 108 acres. Typical dark full-bodied St-Estèphe. Same owner as Ch. PONTET-CANET.

Lagrange Pomerol r. ★★ 66 67 70′ 71′ 75′ 76 78 79
> 20-acre v'yd. in the centre of Pomerol run by the ubiquitous house of MOUEIX.

Lagrange St-Jul. r. ★★★ 66 70′ 71 75′ 76 78 79′
> Rather run-down third-growth remote from most of St-Julien. 120 acres of the big estate are vines.

La Lagune Ludon r. ★★★ 62 66 70′ 71 72 73′ 74 75′ 76′ 77 78′ 79
Well-run ultra-modern 130-acre third-growth in the extreme s. of the Médoc. Attractively rich and fleshy wines.

Lamarque Lamarque (Haut-Médoc) r. ★★ 70′ 75′ 76 78 79
Splendid medieval fortress of the central Médoc with 113 acres giving admirable light wine.

"BREATHING IS FOR PEOPLE"

Fierce arguments take place between wine-lovers over whether it is a good thing or a bad to decant wine from its bottle into a carafe. The argument in favour is that it allows the wine to "breathe" and its bouquet to expand: against, that its precious breath is dissipated — or at the least that it makes no difference.

Two additional practical reasons in favour concern old wine which has deposited dregs, which can be left in the bottle by careful decanting, and young wine being consumed before it is fully developed: thorough aeration helps to create the illusion of maturity. An aesthetic one is that decanters are handsome on the table.

Decanting is done by pouring the wine into another container very steadily until any sediment reaches the shoulder of the bottle. To see the sediment clearly hold the bottle's neck over a light-bulb or a candle.

Lanessan Cussac (Haut-Médoc) r. ★★ 66 70′ 71 73 75′ 76 77 78′ 79
Well-known 108-acre Cru Bourgeois just s. of St-Julien. Same owner as PICHON-LONGUEVILLE-BARON.

Langoa-Barton St-Jul. r. ★★★ 66 67 70′ 71 73 74 75′ 76 78′
Fine 18th-century ch. housing the wine of third-growth Langoa (about 60 acres) as well as second-growth LÉOVILLE-BARTON. The wines are similar: Langoa slightly less fine.

Larcis-Ducasse St-Em. r. ★★★ 66 70′ 71′ 73 75′ 76 78 79
The top property of St-Laurent, eastern neighbour of St-Emilion, on the Côtes next to Ch. PAVIE. 24 acres. Rather heavy wine from largely Merlot v'yd.

Laroque St-Em. r. ★★ 70′ 71 73 74 75′ 76′ 78
Important 100-acre v'yd. with an impressive mansion on the St-Emilion côtes. MOUEIX property.

Larose-Trintaudon St-Lau. (Haut-Médoc) r. ★★ 70 75′ 76 78 79
The biggest v'yd. in the Médoc: nearly 400 acres. Modern methods and reliable full-flavoured Cru Bourgeois wine.

Laroze St-Em. r. ★★★ 70 71′ 75′ 76 78′ 79
Big v'yd. (70 acres) on the w. Côtes. Relatively light wines from sandy soil. Sometimes excellent.

Larrivaux-Hanteillan Cissac (Haut-Médoc) r. ★★
Ch. Larrivaux was bought and added to HANTEILLAN in 1979. The name is used for lighter wines from younger vines.

Larrivet-Haut-Brion Graves r. (w.) ★★ 70′ 71 75′ 76 79′
Reputable little property at Léognan.

Lascombes Margaux r. (p.) ★★★ 61 64 66 67 70′ 71′ 72 73 75′ 76 78 79
235-acre second-growth owned by the British brewers Bass-Charrington and recently lavishly restored. Good vintages are rich for a Margaux. Also a pleasant rosé from young vines.

Latour Pauillac r. ★★★★ 61 62 64 66 67 69 70′ 71 73 74 75′ 76′ 77 78′ 79
First-growth. The most consistent great wine in Bordeaux, in France and probably the world: rich, intense and almost immortal in great years, always classical and pleasing even in bad ones. British-owned. 140 acres. Second wine LES FORTS DE LATOUR.

Latour-Pomerol Pomerol r. `***` **66 67 70' 71' 73 74** 75' 76' 78 7
Top growth of 19 acres under MOUEIX management. Rich
fruity but firm wine for long maturing.

Laujac Médoc r. `**` **70' 71 73** 75' 76 78
Cru Bourgeois in the n. Médoc owned by the CRUSE family
Well known but scarcely outstanding. 72 acres.

Des Laurets St-Em. r. `**` **70' 71'** 75' 76 78 79
Major property of Puisseguin and Montagne-St-Emilion (t
the e.) with 115 acres on the Côtes.

Laville-Haut-Brion Graves w. dr. `***` **70 71 73 75 76 77 78** 79
A small production of one of the very best white Graves mad
at Ch. LA MISSION-HAUT-BRION.

Léoville-Barton St-Jul. r. `***` **61 62 64 66 67** 70' 71 74 75' 76 78
80-acre portion of the great second-growth Léoville v'yd. in
the Anglo-Irish hands of the Barton family for over 150 years
'Glorious classical claret, made by traditional methods at the
Bartons' third-growth Ch. LANGOA.

Léoville-Las Cases St-Jul. r. `****` **61 64 66 67 70' 71 73 74** 75
76 77 78' 79
The largest portion of the old Léoville estate, 180 acres, with
one of the highest reputations in Bordeaux. Elegant, neve
heavy wines. Second label Clos du Marquis.

Léoville-Poyferré St-Jul. r. `***` **66 67 70' 73** 75' 76 78' 79
At present the least outstanding of the Léovilles, though with
famous old vintages to its credit and some recent ones promis
ing well. 128+ acres. Second label Ch. Moulin-Riche.

Lestage Listrac r. `**` **75' 76** 78' 79
130-acre Cru Bourgeois in same hands as Ch. FONRÉAUL
Light, stylish wine.

Liot Barsac w. sw. `**` **70' 71 72** 75' 76 78
Consistently fine fairly light golden wines from 94 acres.

Liversan St-Sau. (Haut-Médoc) r. `**` **70' 71** 75' 76 78 79
100-acre Cru Bourgeois inland from Pauillac. Recently much
improved by its new German proprietor. Ch. Fonpiqueyre i
the same wine in certain markets.

Livran Médoc r. `**` 75 76' 77 78' 79
Big Cru Bourgeois at St-Germain in the n. Médoc. Consisten
round wines (half Merlot).

Loudenne St-Yzans (Médoc) r. `***` **70' 71** 75' 76 78' 79
Beautiful riverside ch. owned by Gilbeys since 1875. Well
made Cru Bourgeois red and a little excellent "modern-style
dry white from 90 acres.

La Louvière Graves r. and w. dr. `**` 75 76 77w. 78 79
Big estate at Léognan with the same director as Ch. COUHINS
Good dry white and agreeable red.

de Lussac St-Em. r. `**` **73 74** 75' 76 78' 79
One of the best estates in Lussac-St-Emilion (to the n.e.).

Lynch-Bages Pauillac r. `***` **61 66** 70' 71 75' 76 77 78' 79
One of the biggest and most popular fifth-growths. 178 acre
making old-style rich robust wine: delicious, if seldom great

Lynch-Moussas Pauillac r. `**` **71'** 75' 76 78 79
Neglected little fifth-growth bought by the director of Ch
BATAILLEY in 1969. Now 72 acres and new equipment are
making serious wine.

Magdelaine St-Em. r. `***` **66 67** 70' **71' 73** 75' 76 78 79
Leading first-growth of the Côtes, 25 acres next to AUSON
owned by J-P MOUEIX. Full-bodied wine. On top form.

Magence Graves r. w. dr. `**` (r.) **70 71' 75** 78 79' (w.) DYA
Go-ahead 75-acre property at St Pierre de Mons, in the s. o
the Graves, well known for distinctly SAUVIGNON-flavoured
very dry white and fruity red for early drinking.

Malartic-Lagravière Graves r. and (w. dr.) ★★★ (r.) **64 66** 70′ **71** **73** 75′ 76′ 78 79 (w.) **71′ 75 76** 79

Well-known Léognan classed-growth of 34 acres making excellent solid red for long maturing and a very little excellent fruity SAUVIGNON white.

Malescasse Lamarque (Haut-Médoc) r. ★★ 75 76 78 79′

Renovated Cru Bourgeois with 70 acres in a good situation recently bought by M. Tesseron of Ch. LAFON-ROCHET.

Malescot St-Exupéry Margaux r. ★★★ 61 64 **66 70′ 71** 75′ **76 77** 78′ 79′

Third-growth of 70 acres allied until 1979 with Ch. MARQUIS-D'ALESME. Rather hard, long maturing, eventually classically fragrant and stylish Margaux.

de Malle Sauternes r. w. sw./dr. ★★ **70 71** 75 76 78 79

Famous and beautiful ch. at Preignac. 90 acres. Good sweet and dry whites and red (Graves) Ch. de Cardaillan.

---

*Remember that vintage years generally ready for drinking in 1982 are printed in **bold type**. Those in light type will benefit from being kept. For an indication of how long they will improve consult the vintage charts on pages 24 and 25.*

---

de Marbuzet St-Est. r. ★★ **73** 75 76 78 79

The second label of Ch. COS D'ESTOURNEL. (The actual ch. overlooks the river from the hill n. of Cos.)

Margaux Margaux r. (w. dr.) ★★★★ 61 **66′ 67 70′ 71** 75′ 76 78′ 79

First-growth, the most delicate and finely perfumed of all in its best vintages. Changed hands in 1977 and much improved since. Noble ch. and estate with 160+ acres of vines. "Pavillon Blanc" is the best white wine of the Médoc.

Marquis-d'Alesme Margaux r. ★★ **70′ 71′ 72** 75′ 78 79

Tiny (17-acre) third-growth, formerly made with Ch. MALESCOT; independent since '79.

Marquis-de-Terme Margaux r. ★★★ **66** 70′ 75′ 76 77 78′ 79

Old-style fourth-growth making fine typical Margaux, tannic and harsh when young. 84 acres. Sells principally in France.

Martinens Margaux r. ★★ 75 **76** 78′ 79′

67-acre Cru Bourgeois at Cantenac, recently much improved.

Maucaillou Moulis r. ★★ **70′ 71 73** 75′ 76′ 78

120-acre Cru Bourgeois with high standards, property of DOURTHE FRÈRES. Full, fruity. "Franc Caillou" is second wine.

Meyney St-Est. r. ★★ **66 67** 70′ **71 74** 75′ 76 78′ 79

Big (130-acre) riverside property next door to Ch. MONTROSE, one of the best of many good Crus Bourgeois in St-Estèphe. Owned by CORDIER.

La Mission-Haut-Brion Graves r. ★★★★ **59 61** 64 66 70′ 71′ 75′ 76 77 78 79

Neighbour and rival to Ch. HAUT-BRION. Serious and grand old-style claret for long maturing. 62 acres. Ch. Latour-H-B is its second-quality wine.

Monbousquet St-Em. r. ★★ **70′ 71 74** 75 **76** 78′ 79′

Fine 70-acre estate in the Dordogne valley below St-Emilion. Attractive early-maturing wine from deep gravel soil.

Mondot

See Troplong-Mondot.

Montrose St-Est. r. ★★★ 61 **62** 64 66 70′ **71 72 73** 75′ 76 77 78 79

150-acre family-run second-growth well known for deeply coloured, forceful, old-style claret. Needs long ageing.

Moulin-à-Vent Moulis r. ★★ **70′ 71** 75′ **76** 78′ 79

55-acre property making efforts to improve its rather hard, typically Moulis wine.

Moulin des Carruades
>The second-quality wine of Ch. LAFITE

Moulin du Cadet St-Em. r. ⟦ ** ⟧ 70 71' 73 75' 76' 78 79
>First-class little v'yd. on the Côtes managed by J. P. MOUEIX.

Moulinet Pomerol r. *** 70 71 73 75 76 78 79
>One of Pomerol's bigger estates; 37 acres on lightish soil.

Mouton-Baronne-Philippe Pauillac r. *** 66 70' 71 75' 76 78' 79
>Substantial fifth-growth with the enormous advantage o
>belonging to Baron Philippe de Rothschild, 125 acres making
>gentler, less rich and tannic wine than Mouton.

Mouton-Rothschild Pauillac r. **** 61 66 67 70' 71 73 75' 76 78
>79
>Officially a first-growth since 1973, though for 20 years
>worthy of the title. 173 acres (87% CABERNET SAUVIGNON)
>making wine of majestic richness. Also the world's greates
>museum of works of art relating to wine.

Nairac Sauternes w. sw. ⟦ ** ⟧ 73 75 76 78
>Newly restored Barsac classed-growth.

Nenin Pomerol r. *** 66 67 70' 71' 75' 76 78
>Well-known 60-acre estate: good but not outstanding quality.

Olivier Graves r. and r. dr. *** (r.) 75' 76 78 79'
>80-acre classed-growth, run by the shipper ESCHENAUER, sur
>rounding a moated castle. Well-known, if not exciting, white
>less-known but serious red (42 acres).

Les Ormes-de-Pez St-Est. r. ⟦ ** ⟧ 66 70' 73 75' 76 77 78' 79
>Popular 72-acre Cru Bourgeois managed by Ch. LYNCH
>BAGES. Reliable full-flavoured St-Estèphe.

Padouen Barsac w. sw. (dr.) ** 76 78 79'
>Small Australian-owned property making classic rich Barsa
>and a fine dry white on sandy soil.

Palmer Cant-Mar. r. ⟦ **** ⟧ 59 61 66 69 70 71' 73 74 75' 76' 77 78
>79
>The star ch. of CANTENAC; a third-growth often on a level jus
>below the first-growths. Wine of power and delicacy. 10
>acres with Dutch, British and French owners.

Pape-Clément Graves r. and w. dr. ⟦ *** ⟧ 62 64 66 67 70 71 73 7
>75' 76 78' 79'
>Ancient v'yd. at Pessac, now 65 acres in fine condition makin
>one of the most attractive red Graves.

Patache d'Aux Bégadan (Médoc) r. ** 70 71 75' 76' 78 79'
>90-acre Cru Bourgeois of the n. Médoc. Well-made wine.

Pauillac, La Rose Pauillac r. **
>The wine of Pauillac's growers' co-op. Membership is dwin
>ling as small growers sell out to big. Generally good value.

Paveil-de Luze Margaux r. ⟦ ** ⟧ 70 71' 75' 76' 78 79
>Old family estate at Soussans. Small but highly regarded.

Pavie St-Em. r. ⟦ *** ⟧ 64' 66 67 70 71' 73 75' 76 78 79'
>Splendidly sited first-growth of 87 acres on the slope of th
>Côtes. Typically rich and tasty St-Em. consistently we
>made. The same family owns the smaller Ch. Pavie-Decess

Pavie-Macquin St-Em. r. ** 73 74 75 76 78 79
>Reliable small Côtes v'yd. e. of St-Emilion.

Pedesclaux Pauillac r. ** 70' 71 75' 76 78 79
>50-acre fifth-growth on the level of a good Cru Bourgeois.

Petit-Village Pomerol r. *** 66 67 70 71' 75' 76' 78 79
>One of the best-known little properties: 26 acres next
>VIEUX-CH.-CERTAN, same owner as Ch. COS D'ESTOURNE
>Powerful long-lasting wine.

Petrus Pomerol r. **** 61 62 66 67 70' 71' 73 75' 76' 78 79
>The great name of Pomerol. 28 acres of gravelly clay givi
>the world's most massively rich and concentrated wine. 95
>Merlot wines. '71 is considered the best of the decade.

Peyrabon St. Sauveur r. ⟦******⟧ 75 76 77 78 79
 Serious 90-acre Cru Bourgeois popular in the Low Countries.

de Pez St-Est. r. ⟦*******⟧ 66 67 **70**′ 71′ 73 75′ 76 78′ 79
 Outstanding Cru Bourgeois of 60 acres. As reliable as any of
 the classed growths of the village. Needs long storage.

Phélan-Ségur St-Est. r. ⟦******⟧ 66 **70**′ 71 75′ 76′ 78 79
 Big and important Cru Bourgeois (125 acres) with the same
 director as Ch. LÉOVILLE-POYFERRÉ.

Pichon-Longueville-Baron Pauillac r. ******* 66 **70**′ **71 73** 75 76 78′
 79′
 74-acre second-growth usually making fine sturdy Pauillac.

Pichon-Longueville, Comtesse de Lalande Pauillac r. ⟦*******⟧ 61
 64 66 **70**′ **71 73** 75′ 76 77 78′ 79′
 Second-growth neighbour to Ch. LATOUR. 144 acres. Recently
 among the top performers; classic long-lived wine.

Pindefleurs St-Em. r. ****** 75 76 78 79
 Up and coming 20-acre v'yd. on the St-Emilion plateau.

de Pitray Castillon r. ****** 75 76′ 78 79
 Substantial (62 acre) v'yd. on the Côtes de Castillon e. of
 St-Emilion. Good lightish wines.

THE COLOUR OF AGE

*One very easy way of gauging the maturity of a red wine without
opening the bottle is simply to hold the neck of the bottle up to a bright
light. If the colour of the wine in the neck is deep red the wine is almost
certainly still young and vigorous. If it appears a light orange colour,
the wine is fully mature and there is nothing to gain by keeping it
longer. If possible, compare a very fine Bordeaux and a simple one at,
say, ten years old to see the difference: the better wine will look much
darker.*

Plince Pomerol r. ****** 75
 Reputable 20-acre property on the outskirts of Libourne.
 Relatively hard and short wines.

La Pointe Pomerol r. ******* 66 **70**′ 71′ 75′ 76 78 79
 Prominent 53-acre estate for typically fat fruity Pomerol. Ch.
 LA SERRE is in the same hands.

Pontet-Canet Pauillac r. ******* 61 66 67 **70 71** 75′ 76 78′ 79′
 One of the biggest classed-growths with about 170 acres,
 neighbour to MOUTON and potentially far better than its
 official rank of fifth-growth. Belonged to the CRUSE family for
 many years, now to M. Tesseron of Ch. LAFON-ROCHET.

Potensac Potensac (Médoc) r. ⟦******⟧ 66 **70 71 73** 75′ **76 77** 78′ 79
 The best-known Cru Bourgeois of Ordonnac-et-Potensac in
 the n. Médoc. The neighbouring Ch'x. Lassalle and Gallais-
 Bellevue belong to the same family, the Delons, owners of Ch.
 LÉOVILLE–LASCASES.

Pouget Margaux ⟦******⟧ **70**′ 71 75 76 78
 19-acre v'yd. attached to Ch. BOYD-CANTENAC. Similar, rather
 lighter, wines.

Poujeaux-Theil Moulis r. ****** **70**′ 71 75′ 76 78 79′
 Family-run Cru Exceptionnel of 108 acres selling its rather
 hard wine direct to an appreciative French public.

Prieuré-Lichine Cant-Mar. r. ⟦*******⟧ 66 67 70 71 **73** 74 75 76 78′
 79′
 130-acre fourth-growth brought to the fore by Alexis Lichine
 since 1952. Excellent finely fragrant Margaux.

Puy Blanquet St-Em. r ****** 71′ **73** 75′ 76 78 79
 The major property of St-Etienne-de-Lisse, e. of St-Emilion,
 with over 60 acres. Typical full St-Em., if below the top class.

Puy-Razac St-Em. r. **★★ 75 76** 78 79

> Small property at the foot of the Côtes near Ch. PAVI
> connected with the well-known Ch. MONBOUSQUET.

Rabaud-Promis Sauternes w. sw. **★★★ 67 70 71** 75 76 78

> Classed-growth of 70 acres at Bommes. Good, not brilliant.

Rahoul Graves r. and w. dr. ★★ **75 76** 78' 79

> Australian-owned 34-acre v'yd. at Portets making partic
> larly good wine from young vines; 80% red.

Ramage-la-Batisse Haut-Médoc r. ★★ **70' 71' 75' 76** 78 79

> Outstanding Cru Bourgeois of 118 acres at St-Sauveur, we
> of Pauillac. To watch.

Rausan-Ségla Margaux r. **★★★ 61 66 70' 71' 75' 76 77** 78 79

> 100-acre second-growth; famous for its fragrance; a grea
> Médoc name, but recently below par. Owned by ESCHENAUE

Rauzan-Gassies Margaux r. **★★★ 61 66** 70 75' 76 78' 79'

> 72-acre second-growth neighbour of the last with a poo
> record in the '60s. Looking up recently.

Raymond-Lafon Sauternes w. sw. ★★ 75 76 78

> Serious Sauternes estate run by the manager of Ch. YQUEM.

de Rayne-Vigneau Sauternes w. sw. **★★★ 67 70 71' 73** 75' 76' 78

> 180-acre classed-growth at Bommes with rich golden wine
> Brand new equipment in 1980.

Respide Graves (r.) w. dr. ★★ **76 78** 79

> One of the better white-wine ch'x. of s. Graves, at St Pierre d
> Mons. Full-flavoured wines.

Reysson Vertheuil Haut-Médoc r. ★★

> Recently replanted, up-and-coming Cru Bourgeois with th
> same owners as Ch. CHASSE-SPLEEN.

Rieussec Sauternes w. sw. ★★★ **66 67 69 70 71' 75' 76' 78** 79

> Worthy neighbour of Ch. D'YQUEM with 144 acres in Fargue
> Not the sweetest, but can be exquisitely fine.

Ripeau St-Em. r. ★★ 75 78

> Above-average classed-growth in the centre of the plateau.

Rouget Pomerol r. **★★ 67 70 71 74** 75' 76' 78 79

> Attractive old estate on the n. edge of Pomerol. Full roun
> wines, maturing well. Popular in smart Paris restaurants.

Royal St-Emilion

> Brand name of the important growers' co-operative.

St-André Corbin St-Emilion r. ★★ **64 66 71** 75' 76' 78 79

> Considerable 50-acre property in Montagne-St-Emilion wit
> a long record of above-average wines.

St-Estèphe, Marquis de St-Est. r. ★ **70 71 73** 75 76 78 79

> The growers' co-operative; over 200 members. Good value.

St-Georges St-Geo., St-Em. r. ★★ **70 75 76** 78 79

> Noble 18th-century ch. overlooking the St-Emilion platea
> from the hill to the n. 120 acres; wine sold direct to the public.

St-Pierre-Sevaistre St-Jul. r. ★★★ **70' 71 73** 75' 76' 78 79

> Well-run small (40-acre) fourth-growth in Belgian owner
> ship. Attractively ripe and fruity wines.

St-Pierre Graves (r.) w. dr. ★★ **76 78** 79

> Estate at St Pierre de Mons making old-style Graves c
> notable character and flavour.

de Sales Pomerol r. **★★★ 66 67 70' 71** 75' 76' 78' 79'

> The biggest v'yd. of Pomerol (114 acres), attached to th
> grandest ch. Not poetry but excellent prose.

Sénéjac Haut-Médoc r. ★★ **70' 74'** 75 76' 78 79

> 43-acre Cru Bourgeois in S. Médoc. Skilful production.

La Serre St-Em. r. ★★ 70 75' 78 79

> Small property with typical soft St-Emilion.

Sigalas-Rabaud Sauternes w. sw. ★★ **67 70 71' 72 73** 75' 76'

> The lesser part of the former Rabaud estate: 34 acres i
> Bommes, making first-class sweet wine.

Siran Lab-Mar. r. ⭐⭐ **61 66** 70 **71' 75' 78'** 79
74-acre Cru Bourgeois of distinguished quality. Elegant, long-lived wines (and Bordeaux's first anti-nuclear cellar).

Smith-Haut-Lafitte Graves r. and (w. dr.) ⭐⭐⭐ **70' 71' 74** 75' 76 78 79
Run-down old classed-growth at Martillac restored by ESCHENAUER in the '60s. Now 120 acres (14 of white). The white wine is light and fruity; the red dry and interesting.

Soutard St-Em. r. ⭐⭐ **66 67 70' 71 74 75' 76 78'** 79
Reliable 50-acre classed-growth n. of the town. Wine "generous" rather than "fine".

Suduiraut Sauternes w. sw. ⭐⭐⭐ **67 70 71 75** 76' 78
One of the best Sauternes: of glorious creamy richness. Over 200 acres of the top class, under promising new management.

Taillefer Pomerol r. ⭐⭐ **67 70 73** 75 76 78
24-acre property on the edge of Pomerol owned by another branch of the MOUEIX family.

Talbot St-Jul. r. (w.) ⭐⭐⭐ **62 66 70' 71 73** 75' 76 77 78' 79
Important 215-acre fourth-growth, sister-ch. to GRUAUD-LAROSE, with similarly attractive rich and satisfying wine. A little white is called "Caillou Blanc".

du Tertre Ar-Mar. r. ⭐⭐ **66 70' 71 72 73** 75 76 78 79
Underestimated fifth-growth isolated s. of Margaux. Thoroughly well-made claret matures admirably.

Tertre-Daugay St-Em. r. ⭐⭐ 78 79
Small classed-growth in a spectacular situation on the brow of the Côtes. Same owner as LA GAFFELIÈRE.

La Tour-Blanche Sauternes w. sw. (r.) ⭐⭐⭐ **67 70 71** 75' 76 78' 79'
Top-rank 72-acre estate at Bommes with a state wine-growing school. Not among the leaders recently.

Several readers have asked what decides when a vintage is "mature" enough to qualify for bold type in this book. The answer is not simple, principally because tastes vary. The French, for example, generally prefer all their wines much younger than the British. Financial pressure also urges merchants and (particularly) restaurants to offer for present drinking wines with the potential to improve for years. In an ideal world the red Bordeaux vintages to drink in 1982 would be 1961, '62, '64, the lighter, more "forward" wines of '66 and '70, most '71s and many '73s.

La Tour-Carnet St-Lau. r. ⭐⭐ **66 70'** 75' 76 78 79
Fourth-growth reborn from total neglect in the '60s. Medieval tower with 100+ acres just w. of St-Julien.

La Tour de By Bégadan (Médoc) r. ⭐⭐ **70 71** 75' 76 77 78' 79'
Very well-run 144-acre Cru Bourgeois in the n. Médoc increasing its reputation for powerful, long-maturing wine.

La Tour-de-Mons Sou-Mar. r. ⭐⭐⭐ **66 70' 71 73** 74 75' 78 79
Distinguished Cru Bourgeois of 60+ acres, three centuries in the same family. Sometimes excellent claret with a long life.

La Tour-du-Pin-Figeac St-Em. r. ⭐⭐
20-acre classed-growth, once part of LA TOUR-FIGEAC. Off form recently.

La Tour-du-Pin-Figeac-Moueix St-Em. r. ⭐⭐ **66 70 74** 75 76 78 79
Another 20-acre section of the same old property, owned by one of the famous MOUEIX family.

La Tour-Figeac St-Em. r. ⭐⭐ **70** 75 78
40-acre classed-growth between Ch. FIGEAC and Pomerol. Well run by a German proprietor.

La Tour-Haut-Brion　Graves r. ** **66** **70** **74** 75 76 78 79

The second label of Ch. LA MISSION-HAUT-BRION. A plainer smaller-scale wine.

La Tour-Martillac　Graves r. and w. dr. 　**★★**　 **70'** **71** **74** 75' 77 7 79'

Small but serious property at Martillac. 10 acres of white grapes; 50 of black. Quantity is sacrificed for quality.

La Tour St-Bonnet　Médoc r. 　**★★**　 **70'** **71** **73** 75' 76 78' 79

Consistently well-made and typical n. Médoc from St Christoly. 100 acres.

La Tour du Haut Moulin　Cussac (Haut-Médoc) r. 　**★★**　 **70** 75' 76 78 79

Little-known 70-acre property; classic old-style claret.

Tournefeuille　Lalande de Pomerol r. 　**★★**　 **67** **70** **71'** **74** 75' 76' 78 79

The star of Néac, overlooking Pomerol from the n. A small property (43 acres), but excellent long-lived wine.

des Tours　Moutagne-St-Em. r. ** **70** **71'** 75' **76** 78 79

Spectacular ch. with modern 170-acre v'yd. Sound commercial wine.

Tronquoy-Lalande　St-Est. r. 　**★★**　 **70** **71** **73** 75 76 78 79

50-acre Cru Bourgeois making typical St-Estèphe. Distributed by DOURTHE.

Troplong-Mondot　St-Em. r. 　**★★**　 **66** **70'** **71'** 75' 76 78 79

One of the bigger classed-growths of St-Emilion. 70+ acres well sited on the Côtes above Ch. PAVIE.

Trotanoy　Pomerol r. 　**★★★**　 **61** **67** **70** **71'** **73** **74** 75' 76' 78 79

One of the top Pomerols. Only 20 acres but a splendid fleshy, 'perfumed wine (the '73 is famous). Managed by J-P MOUEIX.

Trottevieille　St-Em. r. **★★★** **66** **67** **70** **71** 75' 76 78 79

Small but highly reputed first-growth of 25 acres on the Côtes e. of the town. Attractive full wines.

Le Tuquet　Graves r. and w. dr. ** **76** 78 79

Substantial estate at Beautiran making light fruity wines the white better.

Vieux-Château-Certan　Pomerol r. **★★★** **61** **66** **67** **70'** **71'** **74** 75' 76 78 79

Potentially the second ch. of Pomerol, just s. of PETRUS, the first. 30+ acres, Belgian owned.

Vieux-Château-St-André　St-Emilion r. ** **71** 75' 76' 78 79'

Small v'yd. in Montagne-St-Emilion newly acquired by a leading wine-maker of Libourne. To watch.

Villegeorge　Avensan r. ** **73'** 75' 76 78' 79

24-acre Cru Exceptionnel to the n. of Margaux with the same owner as Ch. BRANE-CANTENAC. Excellent full-bodied wine.

Villemaurine　St-Em. r. ** **70'** **71** 75' 76 78' 79

Good classed-growth well sited on the Côtes by the town.

Vraye-Croix-de-Gay　Pomerol 　**★★★**　 **70'** **71'** **73** **74** 75' 76 78 79

Very small ideally situated v'yd. in the best part of Pomerol.

d'Yquem　Sauternes w. sw. (dr.) **★★★★** **59** **62** **66** **67'** **68** **69** **70'** **71'** **73** 75' 76' 77 78 79

The world's most famous sweet-wine estate. 240 acres making only 500 bottles per acre of very strong, intense, luscious wine. Good vintages need a decade of maturity.

More Bordeaux châteaux are listed under Côtes Canon-Fronsac, Côtes de Bourg, Cubzac, Côtes de Fronsac.

Switzerland

Switzerland has some of the world's most efficient and productive vineyards. Costs are high and nothing less is viable. All the most important are lined along the south-facing slopes of the upper Rhône valley and Lake Geneva, respectively the Valais and the Vaud. Wines are known both by place-names, grape-names, and legally controlled type-names. All three, with those of leading growers and merchants, appear in the following list. On the whole, D.Y.A.

Aigle Vaud w. dr. ★★
Principal town of CHABLAIS, between La. Geneva and the VALAIS. Dry whites of appropriately transitional style: at best strong and well balanced.

Amigne
Traditional white grape of the VALAIS. Heavy but tasty wine, usually made dry.

Arvine
Another old VALAIS white grape, similar to the last; perhaps better. Makes good dessert wine. Petite Arvine is similar.

Auvernier Neuchâtel r. p. w. dr. (sp.) ★★
Village s. of NEUCHÂTEL known for PINOT NOIR, CHASSELAS and OEIL DE PERDRIX.

Blauburgunder
One of the names given to the form of PINOT NOIR grown in German Switzerland.

Bonvin
Old-established growers and merchants at SION.

Chablais Vaud (r.) w. dr. ★★
The district between Montreux on La. Geneva and Martigny where the Rhône leaves the VALAIS. Good DORIN wines. Best villages: AIGLE, YVORNE, Bex.

Chasselas
The principal white grape of Switzerland, neutral in flavour but taking local character. Known as FENDANT in VALAIS, DORIN in VAUD and PERLAN round Geneva.

Clevner (or Klevner)
Another name for BLAUBURGUNDER.

Cortaillod Neuchâtel r. (p. w.) ★★
Village near NEUCHÂTEL specializing in light PINOT NOIR reds.

Côte, La
The n. shore of La. Geneva between Geneva and Lausanne. Pleasant DORIN and SALVAGNIN. Best villages incl. Féchy and Rolle.

Dézaley Vaud w. dr. ★★★

Best-known village of LAVAUX, between Lausanne and Montreux. Steep s. slopes to the lake make fine fruity DORIN. Dézaley-Marsens is equally good.

Dôle Valais r. ★★

Term for red VALAIS wine of PINOT NOIR or GAMAY or both grapes, reaching a statutory level of strength and quality.

Domaine Château Lichten

Property making first-class VALAIS wines at Loèche Ville.

Dorin Vaud w. dr. ★→★★

The name for CHASSELAS wine in the VAUD, the equivalent of FENDANT from the VALAIS.

Epesses Vaud w. dr. ★★

Well-known lakeside village of LAVAUX. Good dry DORIN.

Ermitage

VALAIS name for white wine from MARSANNE grapes. Rich, concentrated and heavy; usually dry.

Fendant Valais w. dr. ★→★★★

The name for CHASSELAS wine in the VALAIS, where it reaches its ripest and strongest. SION is the centre.

Flétri

Withered grapes for making sweet wine, often MALVOISIE.

Glacier, Vin du

Almost legendary long-matured white stored at high altitudes. Virtually extinct today.

Goron Valais r. ★

Red VALAIS wine that fails to reach the DÔLE standard.

Herrschaft Grisons r. (w. sw.) ★→★★★

District near the border of Austria and Liechtenstein. Small amount of light PINOT NOIR reds and a few sweet whites.

Humagne

Old VALAIS grape. Some red Humagne is sold: decent country wine. The strong white is a local speciality.

Johannisberg

The Valais name for SYLVANER, which makes pleasant soft dry wine here.

Lavaux Vaud r. w. dr. ★→★★★

The n. shore of La. Geneva between Lausanne and Montreux. The e. half of the VAUD. Best villages incl. DÉZALEY, EPESSES, Villette, Lutry, ST-SAPHORIN.

Légèrement doux

Most Swiss wines are dry. Any with measurable sugar must be labelled thus or as "avec sucre résiduel".

Malvoisie

VALAIS name for PINOT GRIS.

Mandement Geneva r. (p.) w. dr. ★

Wine district just w. of Geneva, (see Vin-Union-Genève). Very light reds, chiefly GAMAY, and whites (PERLAN).

Marsanne

The white grape of Hermitage on the French Rhône, used in the VALAIS to make ERMITAGE.

Merlot

Bordeaux red grape (see Grapes for red wine) used to make the better wine of Italian Switzerland (TICINO). See also Viti.

Mont d'Or, Domaine du Valais w. dr. sw. ★★★★

The best wine estate of Switzerland: 60 acres of steep hillside near SION. Good FENDANT, JOHANNISBERG, AMIGNE, etc., and real Riesling. Very rich concentrated wines.

Neuchâtel Neuchâtel r. p. w. dr. sp. ★→★★★

City of n.w. Switzerland and the wine from the n. shore of its lake. Pleasant light PINOT NOIR and attractive sometimes sparkling CHASSELAS.

Nostrano

Word meaning "ours" applied to the lesser red wine of the TICINO, made from a mixture of native and Italian grapes, in contrast to MERLOT from Bordeaux.

Oeil de Perdrix

Pale rosé of PINOT NOIR.

Orsat

Important and popular wine firm at Martigny, VALAIS.

Perlan Geneva w. dr. ★

The MANDEMENT name for the ubiquitous CHASSELAS, here at its palest, driest and least impressive.

Premier Cru

Any wine from the maker's own estate can call itself this.

Provins

One of the best-known producers of VALAIS wine.

Rèze

The grape, now rare, used for VIN DU GLACIER.

Rivaz Vaud r. w. dr. ★★

Well-known village of LAVAUX.

St-Saphorin Vaud w. dr. ★★

One of the principal villages of LAVAUX: wines drier and more austere than DÉZALEY or EPESSES.

Salvagnin Vaud r. ★→★★

Red VAUD wine of tested quality: the equivalent of DÔLE.

Savagnin

Swiss name for the TRAMINER, called Païen in the VALAIS.

Schafiser Bern (r.) w. dr. ★→★★

The n. shore of La. Bienne (Bielersee) is well known for light CHASSELAS sold as either Schafiser or Twanner.

Sion Valais w. dr. ★→★★★

Centre of the VALAIS wine region, famous for its FENDANT.

Spätburgunder

PINOT NOIR: by far the commonest grape of German Switzerland, making very light wines.

Testuz

Well-known growers and merchants at Cully, LAVAUX.

Ticino

Italian-speaking s. Switzerland. See Merlot, Viti, Nostrano.

Twanner

See Schafiser

Valais

The Rhône valley between Brig and Martigny. Its n. side is an admirable dry sunny and sheltered v'yd., planted mainly, alas, to the second-rate CHASSELAS grape, which here makes its best wine.

Vaud

The region of La. Geneva. Its n. shore is Switzerland's biggest v'yd. and in places as good as any. DORIN and SALVAGNIN are the main wines.

Vétroz Valais (r.) w. dr. ★★

Village near SION in the best part of the VALAIS.

Vevey

Town near Montreux with a famous wine festival once every 30-odd years. The last was in 1977.

Vin-Union-Genève

Big growers' co-operative at Satigny in the MANDEMENT. Light reds and white PERLAN are Geneva's local wine.

Viti Ticino r. ★★

Legal designation of better-quality TICINO red, made of MERLOT and with at least 12% alcohol.

Yvorne

Village near AIGLE with some of the best CHABLAIS v'yds.

Germany

Germany has the most complicated labelling system in the world—a fact that has put most people off tackling it seriously and driven them to settle for pleasantly innocuous blended wines: Liebfraumilch and the like.

Yet those who funk its complications will never experience the real beauty of the style of wine which is Germany's unique contribution.

The secret of the style is the balance of sweetness against fruity acidity. A great vintage in Germany is one in which the autumn weather allows the late-ripening Riesling—the grape which makes virtually all the great German wines—to develop a high sugar content. What is so special about the Riesling is that as it ripens it also develops a concentration of fragrant acids and essences to balance the increasing sweetness. The resulting wine is tense and thrilling with this sugar/acid balance.

It smells and tastes extraordinarily flowery, lively and refreshing while it is young. But because of its internal equilibrium it also has the ability to live and mature for a remarkable length of time. As good Riesling matures all sorts of subtle scents and flavours emerge. Straight sweetness gives way to oily richness. Suggestions of countless flowers and fruits, herbs and spices develop.

These are the rewards for anyone who can be bothered to master the small print. They lead into realms of sensation where Liebfraumilch (with all the respect due to a perfectly decent drink) can never follow. The great German growers make wine for wine's sake. Food is irrelevant, except in so far as it gets in the way.

The Labels and the Law

German wine law is based on the ripeness of the grapes at harvest time. Recent vintages have been exceptionally kind to growers, but as a general rule most German wine needs sugar added to make up for the missing warmth and sunshine of one of the world's northernmost vineyards.

The exceptional wine, from grapes ripe enough not to need sugar, is kept apart as Qualitätswein mit Prädikat or QmP. Within this top category its natural sugar-content is expressed by traditional terms—in ascending order of ripeness: Kabinett, Spätlese, Auslese, Beerenauslese, Trockenbeerenauslese.

But reasonably good wine is also made in good vineyards from grapes that fail to reach the natural sugar-content required for a QmP label. The authorities allow this, within fairly strict controls, to be called Qualitätswein as well, but with the different qualification of bestimmter Anbaugebiete (i.e. QbA) instead of mit Prädikat. mP is therefore a vitally important ingredient of a fine-wine label.

Both levels are officially checked, tested and tasted at every bottling. Each batch is given an identifying test ("prüfungs") number. No other country has quality control approaching this. It can't make dull wine exciting, but it can and does make all "quality" wine a safe bet.

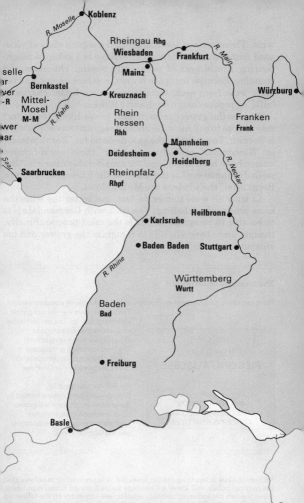

The third level, Tafelwein, has no pretensions to quality and is not allowed to give itself airs beyond the name of the village or the general region it comes from.

Though there is very much more detail in the laws this is the gist of the quality grading. Where it differs completely from the French system is in ignoring geographical difference. There are no Grands Crus, no VDQS. In theory all any German vineyard has to do to make the best wine is to grow the ripest grapes.

The law distinguishes only between degrees of geographical exactness. In labelling quality wine the grower or merchant is given a choice. He can (and always will) label the relatively small quantities of his best wine with the name of the precise vineyard or Einzellage where it was grown. Germany has about 3,000 Einzellage names. Obviously only particularly good ones are famous enough to help sell the wine. Therefore the law has created a second class of vineyard name: the Grosslage. A Grosslage is a group of neighbouring Einzellages of supposedly similar character and standing. Because there are fewer Grosslage names, and far more wine from each, Grosslages have a better chance of building reputations, brand-name fashion.*

Thirdly the grower or merchant (more likely the latter) may choose to sell his wine under a regional name: the word is Bereich. To cope with the vast demand for "Bernkasteler" or "Niersteiner" or "Johannisberger" these world-famous names have been made legal for considerable districts. "Bereich Johannisberg" is the whole of the Rheingau; "Bereich Bernkastel" the whole of the Mittel-Mosel.

As with all wine names, in fact, the better the wine the more precise the labelling. The trick with German labels is to be able to recognize which is the most precise. Finally, though, and above all, it is to recognize the grower and his vineyard.

The basic German label

The order of wording on German quality wine labels follows a standard pattern.

> **TRIERER**
> **ABSTBERG**
> **RIESLING AUSLESE**
>
> QmP
> A.P. NR. 12345678
> ERZEUGERABFÜLLUNG
> WINZERVEREIN TRIER

The first name is the town or parish, with the suffix -er. The second is the vineyard (either Einzellage or Grosslage—see introduction). The third (optional) is the grape variety. The fourth is the quality in terms of ripeness. For QmP see page 86.
For A.P. Nr. see page 78.
Erzeugerabfüllung means bottled by the grower, in this case the grower's co-operative of Trier. For other words appearing on German labels see the Germany A–Z.

---

*Where the law is less than candid, however, is in pretending to believe that the general public will know a Grosslage name from an Einzellage name, when the two are indistinguishably similar (see any entry on the following pages). It is actually against the law to indicate on the label whether the name in question is that of a particular plot or a wider grouping. The names of all relevant Grosslages are given in this book. Note that Grosslage wines are very rarely of the stature of Einzellage wines.

N.B. on vintage notes opposite

Vintage notes after entries in the German section are given in a different form from those elsewhere, to show the style of the vintage as well as its quality.
Three styles are indicated:
The classic, super-ripe vintage with a high proportion of natural (QmP) wines, including Spätleses and Ausleses. Three of the six vintages shown, an unprecedented proportion, come into this category.
Example: **76**
The "normal" successful vintage with plenty of good wine but no great preponderance of sweeter wines. Example: 79
The cool vintage with generally poor ripeness but a fair proportion of reasonably successful wines, tending to be over-acid. Such wines sometimes mature better than expected. Example: *80*
Where no mention is made the vintage is generally not recommended, or most of its wines have passed maturity.

Recent Vintages

Mosel/Saar/Ruwer

Mosels (including Saar and Ruwer wines) are so attractive young that their keeping qualities are not often enough explored, and wines older than seven years or so are unusual. But well-made wines of Kabinett class gain from two or three years in bottle, Spätleses by a little longer, and Ausleses and Beerenausleses by anything from 10 to 20 years, depending on the vintage.

As a rule, in poor years the Saar and Ruwer fare worse than the Middle Mosel and make sharp, thin wines, but in the best years they can surpass the whole of Germany for elegance and "breed".

1980	A terrible summer. Some pleasant wines but little more.
1979	A patchy vintage after bad winter damage. But several excellent Kabinetts and better. Light but well-balanced wines to keep up to 3–4 years.
1978	A similar vintage to '77, though very late and rather small. Very few sweet wines but many with good balance.
1977	Big vintage of serviceable quality, mostly QbA. Drink up.
1976	Very good small vintage, with some superlative sweet wines and almost no dry. Most wines now ready; the best will keep 5 years.
1975	Very good; many Spätleses and Ausleses. Most have now matured.
1974	Most wine needed sugaring; few Kabinetts, but some well-balanced wines which have kept well. Drink now.
1973	Very large, attractive, but low acid and extract have meant a short life. Good eiswein. Drink now.
1972	Large; medium to poor; few late-picked wines, many with unripe flavour. Should be drunk by now.
1971	Superb, with perfect balance. Many top wines will still improve.
1970	Large; good to average. Quite soft, not for keeping.
1969	Some very fine wines; most merely good. Best in the Saar and Ruwer. Now mature.

Older fine vintages: '67, '64, '59, '53, '49, '45.

Rhine/Nahe/Palatinate

Even the best wines can be drunk with pleasure after two or three years, but Kabinett, Spätlese and Auslese wines of good vintages gain enormously in character and complexity by keeping for longer. Rheingau wines tend to be longest-lived, often improving for 10 years or more, but wines from the Nahe and the Palatinate can last nearly as long. Rheinhessen wines usually mature sooner, and dry Franconian wines are best young.

The Riesling, predominant in the Rheingau, benefits most from hot summers; Palatinate wines can taste almost overripe.

1980	Bad weather from spring to autumn. Only passable wines.
1979	Uneven and reduced in size. Few great wines but many typical and good. The best will keep 3–4 years.
1978	Satisfactory vintage saved by late autumn. 25% QmP, but very few Spätleses. Some excellent wines in the south. Drink soon.
1977	Big and useful; few Kabinett wines or better. Not to keep. Rheinpfalz best.
1976	The richest vintage since 1921 in places. Very few dry wines. Balance less consistent than 1975. Maturing well.
1975	A splendid Riesling year, a high percentage of Kabinetts and Spätleses. Should be drunk fairly soon.
1974	Variable; the best fruity and good; many Kabinetts. Drink now.
1973	Very large, consistent and attractive, but not for keeping.
1972	Excess acidity was the problem; no exciting wines, but some presentable. Should be drunk now.
1971	A superlative vintage with perfect balance. The finest are still improving.
1970	Very pleasant wines, but no more. Huge crop. Not for keeping.
1969	All above average; the best great. Nahe and Palatinate specially good. Now mature.
1967	Marvellous; the best of the '60s; Rheinhessen made great wines.

Older fine vintages: '66, '64, '59, '57, '53, '49, '45.

Achkarren   Bad. (r.) w. ★→★★

Well-known wine village of the KAISERSTUHL.

Adelmann, Graf

Famous grower with 125 acres at Kleinbottwar, WÜRTTEM-BERG. Uses the name Brussele. Light reds; good RIESLINGS.

Ahr   Ahr-r. ★→★★★ 71 75 76 7779 80

Germany's best-known red-wine area, s. of Bonn. Very light pale SPÄTBURGUNDERS.

Amtliche Prüfungsnummer

See Prüfungsnummer

Anbaugebiet

Wine-region. See QbA.

Anheuser

Name of two distinguished growers of the NAHE.

Annaberg   Rhpf. w. ★★★ 71 75 76 77 78 79 80

Thirty-two-acre estate at DÜRKHEIM famous for sweet and pungent wines, esp. SCHEUREBE.

A.P.Nr.

Abbreviation of AMTLICHE PRÜFUNGSNUMMER.

Assmannshausen   Rhg. r. ★→★★★ 71 75 76 77 7879 80

RHEINGAU village known for its pale reds. Top v'yd.: Höllenberg. Grosslage: Steil.

The German Wine Academy runs regular courses of wine-instruction at all levels for both amateurs and professionals, in German and English. The Academy is based at the glorious 12th-century Cistercian monastery of Kloster Eberbach in the Rheingau. The course normally includes tasting-tours of Germany's wine regions. Particulars can be obtained from the Academy, P. O. Box 1705, D-6500 Mainz, West Germany.

Auslese

Late-gathered wine with high natural sugar content.

Avelsbach   M-S-R (Ruwer) w. ★★★ 71 75 76 77 7879 80

Village near TRIER. Supremely delicate wines. Growers: Staatliche Weinbaudomäne (see Staatsweingut), BISCHÖF-LICHE WEINGÜTER. Grosslage: Trierer Römerlay.

Ayl   M-S-R (Saar) w. ★★★ 71 75 76 77 7879 80

One of the best villages of the SAAR. Top v'yds.: Kupp, Herrenberger. Grosslage: Scharzberg.

Bacchus

Modern highly perfumed grape variety.

Bacharach (Bereich)

District name for the s. Mittelrhein v'yds. downstream from the RHEINGAU. No great or famous wines; some pleasant.

Baden

Huge area of scattered wine-growing. Few classic wines: most are heavy or soft. Best areas are KAISERSTUHL and ORTENAU.

Badische Bergstrasse/Kraichgau (Bereich)

Principal district name of n. BADEN.

Bad Dürkheim

See Dürkheim

Badisches Frankenland (Bereich)

Minor district name of n. BADEN.

Bad Kreuznach   Na. w. ★★→★★★ 71 75 76 77 78 79 80

Main town of the NAHE with some of its best wines. Many fine v'yds., incl. Brückes, St. Martin, Kauzenberg. Grosslage: Kronenberg.

Balbach Erben

One of the best growers of NIERSTEIN.

Basserman-Jordan

100-acre MITTEL-HAARDT family estate with many of the best v'yds. in DEIDESHEIM, FORST, RUPPERTSBERG, etc.

Beerenauslese

Extremely sweet and luscious wine from very late-gathered individual bunches.

Bereich

District within a Gebiet (region). See under Bereich names, e.g. Bernkastel (Bereich).

Bergzabern, Bad   Rhpf. (r.) w. ✶→✶✶ 75 76 77 78 79 *80*

Town of SÜDLICHE-WEINSTRASSE. Pleasant sweetish wines. Grosslage: Liebfrauenberg.

Bernkastel   M-M w. ✶✶→✶✶✶✶ 71 75 76 77 78 79 *80*

Top wine-town of the Mosel; the epitome of RIESLING. Best v'yds.: Doktor, Bratenhöfchen, etc. Grosslages: Badstube (✶✶✶) and Kurfürstlay (✶✶).

Bernkastel (Bereich)

Wide area of mixed quality but decided flowery character. Includes all the Mittel-Mosel.

Bingen   Rhh. w. ✶✶→✶✶✶ 71 75 76 77 78 79 *80*

Town on Rhine and Nahe with fine v'yds., incl. Scharlachberg. Grosslage: Sankt Rochuskapelle.

Bingen (Bereich)

District name for w. Rheinhessen.

Bischöfliche Weingüter

Outstanding M-S-R estate at TRIER, a union of the Cathedral properties with two famous charities. 230 acres of top v'yds. in AVELSBACH, WILTINGEN, SCHARZHOFBERG, AYL, KASEL, EITELSBACH, PIESPORT, TRITTENHEIM, ÜRZIG, etc.

Blue Nun

The best-selling brand of LIEBFRAUMILCH, from SICHEL.

Bodensee (Bereich)

Minor district of s. BADEN, on Lake Constance.

Boxbeutel

Flask-shaped bottle used for FRANKEN wines.

Brauneberg   M-M w.   ✶✶✶   71 75 76 77 78 79 *80*

Village near BERNKASTEL with 100 acres. Excellent full-flavoured wine. Best v'yd.: Juffer. Grosslage: Kurfürstlay.

Breisgau (Bereich)

Minor district of BADEN, just n. of KAISERSTUHL.

Brentano, von

20-acre old family estate in WINKEL, Rheingau.

Bühl, von

Great RHEINPFALZ family estate. 200+ acres in DEIDESHEIM, FORST, RUPPERTSBERG, etc. In the very top class.

Bullay   M-S-R ✶→   ✶✶   76 77 78 79 *80*

Lower Mosel village. Good light wine to drink young.

Bundesweinprämierung

The top German Wine Award: a gold, silver or bronze medal on bottles of remarkable wines.

Burgerspital zum Heiligen Geist

Ancient charitable estate at WÜRZBURG. 185 acres in WÜRZBURG, RANDERSACKER, etc., make rich dry wines.

Bürklin-Wolf

Great RHEINPFALZ family estate. 222 acres in WACHENHEIM, FORST, DEIDESHEIM and RUPPERTSBERG, with rarely a dull, let alone poor, wine.

Castell'sches, Fürstlich Domäne

110-acre princely estate in STEIGERWALD. Good typical FRANKEN wines: Sylvaner, Müller-Thürgau. Also SEKT.

Crown of Crowns

Popular brand of LIEBFRAUMILCH from LANGENBACH & CO.

Deidesheim \ Rhpf. w. (r.) ****** →**** 71 74 75 76 77 78 79 80
    Biggest top-quality wine-village of RHEINPFALZ with 1,000 acres. Rich, high-flavoured, lively wines. V'yds. incl. Hohenmorgen, Kieselberg, Grainhübel, Leinhöhle, Herrgottsacker, etc. Grosslages: Hofstück, Mariengarten.

Deinhard
    Famous old Koblenz merchants and growers in Rheingau (see Wegeler), Mittel-Mosel (27 acres in Bernkastel, incl. part of Doktor v'yd., and Graach) and Rheinpfalz.

Deutscher Tafelwein
    TAFELWEIN from Germany (only).

Deutsches Weinsiegel
    A quality "seal" (i.e. neck label) for wines which have passed a stiff tasting test.

DLG (Deutsche Landwirtshaft Gesellschaft)
    The German Agricultural Society. The body that awards national medals for quality.

Dhron
    See Neumagen-Dhron.

Diabetiker Wein
    Wine with minimal residual sugar (less than 4gms/litre). Suitable for diabetics—or those who like very dry wine.

Dienheim Rhh. w. **→*** 78 79 80
    Southern neighbour of OPPENHEIM. Mainly run-of-the-mill wines. Top v'yds.: Kreuz, Herrenberg, Schloss. Grosslages: Guldenmorgen, Krötenbrunnen.

Remember that vintage information about German wines is given in a different form from the ready/not ready distinction applying to other countries. Read the explanation on page 76.

Dom German for Cathedral. Wines from the famous TRIER Cathedral properties have "Dom" before the v'yd. name.

Domäne
    German for "domain" or "estate". Sometimes used alone to mean the "State domain" (Staatliche Weinbaudomäne).

Durbach Baden w. (r.) *→*** 75 76 77 78 79 80
    150 acres of the best v'yds. of BADEN. Top growers: Schloss Staufenberg, Wolf-Metternich, von Neveu. Choose their RIESLINGS and KLEVNERS, esp. D. Kochberg.

Dürkheim, Bad Rhpf. w. or (r.) ****** →*** 75 76 77 78 79 80
    Main town of the MITTEL-HAARDT. Top v'yds.: Hochbenn, Michelsberg. Grosslages: Feuerberg, Schenkenböhl.

Edel Means "noble". Edelfäule means "noble rot": the condition which gives the greatest sweet wines (see p. 47).

Edenkoben Rhpf. w.(r.) *→ ****** 75 76 77 78 79 80
    Important village of n. SÜDLICHE WEINSTRASSE Grosslage: Ludwigshöhe.

Egon Müller-Scharzhof
    Top Saar estate of 24 acres at WILTINGEN. SCHARZHOFBERGERS are supreme in top years.

Eiswein
    Wine made from frozen grapes with the ice (e.g. water content) rejected, thus very concentrated in flavour and sugar. Rare and expensive. Sometimes produced as late as the January or February following the vintage.

Eitelsbach Ruwer w. **→**** 71 75 76 77 78 79 80
    RUWER village now part of TRIER, incl. superb Karthäuserhofberg estate. Grosslage: Trierer Römerlay.

Elbling
    Inferior grape widely grown on upper Mosel.

Eltville Rhg. w. ⭐⭐ →⭐⭐⭐ 71 75 76 77 78 79 *80*

Major wine-town with cellars of the Rheingau State domain, SCHLOSS ELTZ and VON SIMMERN estates. Excellent wines. Top v'yds.: Sonnenberg, Taubenberg. Grosslage: Heiligenstock.

Eltz, Schloss

Former Rheingau estate now divided. The name and a small portion are connected with PIEROTH.

Enkirch M-M w. ⭐⭐→ ⭐⭐⭐ 71 75 76 77 78 79 *80*

Minor middle-Mosel village, often overlooked but with lovely light tasty wine. Grosslage: Schwarzlay.

Erbach Rhg. w. ⭐⭐⭐→⭐⭐⭐⭐ 71 75 76 77 78 79 *80*

One of the best parts of the Rheingau with powerful, perfumed wines, incl. the great MARCOBRUNN; other top v'yds.: Schlossberg, Siegelsberg, Hönigberg, Michelmark. Grosslage: Mehrhölzchen. Major estates: SCHLOSS REINHARTSHAUSEN, VON SCHÖNBORN.

Erden M-M w. ⭐⭐→⭐⭐⭐ 71 75 76 77 78 79 *80*

Village between Urzig and Kröv with full-flavoured vigorous wine. Top v'yds.: Prälat, Treppchen. Leading grower: Beeres. Grosslage: Schwarzlay.

Erzeugerabfüllung

Bottled by the grower.

Escherndorf Franc. w. ⭐⭐→⭐⭐⭐ 71 75 76 77 78 79 *80*

Important wine-town near WÜRZBURG. Similar tasty dry wine. Top v'yds.: Lump, Berg. Grosslage: Kirchberg.

Feine, feinste, hochfeinste

Terms formerly used to distinguish a good grower's best barrels. Now, unfortunately, illegal.

Forst Rhpf. w. ⭐⭐→⭐⭐⭐⭐ 71 75 76 77 78 79 *80*

MITTEL-HAARDT village with 500 acres of Germany's best v'yds. Ripe, richly fragrant but subtle wines. Top v'yds.: Kirchenstück, Jesuitengarten, Ungeheuer, etc. Grosslages: Mariengarten, Schnepfenflüg.

Franken

Franconia: region of excellent distinctive dry wines. The centre is WÜRZBURG. BEREICH names: MAINVIERECK, MAINDREIECK, STEIGERWALD.

Freiburg Baden w. (r.) ⭐→⭐⭐ D.Y.A.

Centre of MARKGRÄFLERLAND. Good GUTEDEL.

Friedrich Wilhelm Gymnasium

Superb 104-acre charitable estate with v'yds. in BERNKASTEL, ZELTINGEN, GRAACH, TRITTENHEIM, OCKFEN, etc., all M-S-R.

Geisenheim Rhg. w. ⭐⭐→⭐⭐⭐ 71 75 76 77 78 79 *80*

Village famous for Germany's leading wine-school. Best v'yds. incl. Rothenberg, Kläuserweg. Grosslage: Burgweg.

Gemeinde

A commune or parish.

Gewürztraminer

Spicy grape of Alsace, used a little in s. Germany, esp. Rheinpfalz.

Gimmeldingen Rhpf. w. ⭐→ ⭐⭐ 75 76 77 78 79 *80*

Village just s. of MITTEL-HAARDT. Similar wines. Grosslage: Meerspinne.

Goldener Oktober

Popular Rhine-wine and Mosel blend from ST. URSULA.

Graach M-M w. ⭐⭐→ ⭐⭐⭐ 71 75 76 77 78 79 *80*

Small village between BERNKASTEL and WEHLEN. Top v'yds.: Himmelreich, Domprobst, Abstberg, Josephshöfer. Grosslage: Münzlay.

Grosslage

See Introduction, p. 76

Guntersblum Rhh. w. ★→★★ 75 76 77 78 79 80
Big wine-town s. of OPPENHEIM. Grosslages: Krötenbrunnen, Vogelsgarten.

Guntrum, Louis
Fine 130-acre family estate in NIERSTEIN, OPPENHEIM, etc.

Gutedel
German for the Chasselas grape, used in s. BADEN.

Halbtrocken
"Half-dry". Containing less than 18 grams per litre unfermented sugar. A rather vague category of wine intended for meal-times, often better-balanced than "TROCKEN".

Hallgarten Rhg. w. ★★→★★★ 71 75 76 77 78 79 80
Important little wine-town behind HATTENHEIM. Robust full-bodied wines. Top v'yds. incl. Schönhell, Jungfer. Grosslage: Mehrhölzchen.

Hallgarten, House of
Well-known London-based wine-merchant.

Hanns Christof
Top brand of LIEBFRAUMILCH from DEINHARD'S.

Hattenheim Rhg. w. ★★→★★★★ 71 75 76 77 78 79 80
Superlative 500-acre wine-town. V'yds. incl. STEINBERG, MARCOBRUNN, Nüssbrunnen, Mannberg, etc. Grosslage: Deutelsberg.

Heilbronn Württ. w. r. ★→★★ 75 76 77 78 79 80
Wine-town with many small growers and a big co-op. Seat of DLG competition.

Hessische Bergstrasse Rhh. w. ★★→★★★ 75 76 77 78 79 80
Minor (700-acre) region s. of Frankfurt. Pleasant Riesling from State domain v'yds. in Heppenheim and Bensheim.

Hessische Forschungsanstalt für Wein- Obst- & Gartenbau
Germany's top wine-school and research establishment, at GEISENHEIM.

Heyl zu Herrnsheim
Fine 50-acre estate at NIERSTEIN.

Hochfeinste
"Very finest." Traditional label-term, now illegal.

Hochheim Rhg. w. ★★→★★★ 71 75 76 77 78 79 80
500-acre wine-town 15 miles e. of RHEINGAU. Similar fine wines. Top v'yds.: Domdechaney, Kirchenstück, Hölle, Königin Viktoria Berg. Grosslage: Daubhaus.

Hock English term for Rhine-wine, derived from HOCHHEIM.

Huxelrebe
Modern very fruity grape variety.

Ihringen Bad. (r.) w. ★→★★ 75 76 77 78 79 80
One of the best villages of the KAISERSTUHL, BADEN. Heavy dryish wines.

Ilbesheim Rhpf. w. ★→ ★★ 75 76 77 78 79 80
Base of important growers' co-operative of SÜDLICHE WEIN STRASSE. See also Schweigen.

Ingelheim Rhh. r. or w. ★ 76 77 79 80
Village on Rhine known for red wine.

Iphofen Franc. w. ★★→ ★★★ 71 75 76 77 78 79 80
Village e. of WÜRZBURG. Top v'yd.: Julius-Echter-Berg. Grosslage: Burgweg.

Jesuitengarten
V'yd. in FORST. One of Germany's best.

Johannisberg Rhg. w. ★★→★★★★ 71 75 76 77 78 79 80
260-acre village with superlative subtle wine. Top v'yds. incl. SCHLOSS JOHANNISBERG, Hölle, Klaus, etc. Grosslage: Erntebringer.

Johannisberg (Bereich)
District name of the entire RHEINGAU.

Josephshöfer

Fine v'yd. at GRAACH, the property of von KESSELSTATT.

Juliusspital

Ancient charity at WÜRZBURG with top FRANKEN v'yds.

Kabinett

The term for the driest and least expensive natural unsugared (QmP) wines.

Kaiserstuhl-Tuniberg (Bereich)

Best v'yd. area of BADEN. Villages incl. IHRINGEN, ACHKARREN.

Kallstadt Rhpf. w. (r.) ★★→★★★ 71 75 76 77 78 79 *80*

Village just n. of MITTEL-HAARDT. Fine rich wines. Top v'yd.: ANNABERG. Grosslages: Kobnert, Feuerberg.

Kanzem M-S-R (Saar) w. ★★→★★★ 71 75 76 77 78 79 *80*

Small but excellent neighbour of WILTINGEN. Top v'yds.: Sonnenberg, Altenberg. Grosslage: Scharzberg.

Kasel M-S-R (Ruwer) w. ★★ 71 75 76 77 78 79 *80*

Village with attractive light wines. Best v'yd.: Nieschen. Grosslage: Römerlay.

Keller

Wine-cellar or winery.

Kerner

Modern very flowery grape variety.

Kesselstatt, von

The biggest private Mosel Estate, 600 years old. 150 acres in GRAACH, PIESPORT, KASEL, MENNIG, WILTINGEN, etc. making light and fruity typical Mosels.

Kesten M-W w. ★→★★★ 71 75 76 77 78 79 *80*

Neighbour of BRAUNEBERG. Best wines (from Paulinshofberg v'yd.) similar. Grosslage: Kurfürstlay.

Kiedrich Rhg. w. ★★→★★★★ 71 75 76 77 78 79 *80*

Neighbour of RAUENTHAL; almost as splendid and high flavoured. Top v'yds.: Gräfenberg, Wasseros, Sandgrub. Grosslage: Heiligenstock.

Klevner (or Clevner)

Term for the PINOT BLANC grape used in BADEN-WÜRTTEMBERG. Red Klevner is supposedly Italian Chiavenna, an early-ripening black Pinot.

Klingelberger

BADEN term for the RIESLING.

Kloster Eberbach

Glorious 12th-century Abbey at HATTENHEIM, Rheingau, now State domain property and H.Q. of the German Wine Academy. See panel, p. 78.

Klüsserath M-M w. ★★→ ★★★ 71 75 76 78 79 *80*

Minor Mosel village worth trying in good vintages. Best v'yds.: Brüderschaft, Königsberg. Grosslage: St. Michael.

Kreuznach (Bereich)

District name for the entire northern NAHE. See also Bad Kreuznach.

Kröv M-M w. ★→★★★ 75 76 78 79 *80*

Popular tourist resort famous for its Grosslage name: Nacktarsch, meaning "bare bottom".

Landespreismünze

Prizes for quality at state, rather than national, level. Considered by some more discriminating than DLG medals.

Landgräflich Hessisches Weingut

75-acre estate in JOHANNISBERG, WINKEL, etc.

Langenbach & Co.

Well-known merchants of London and WORMS.

Lauerburg

One of the three owners of the famous Doktor v'yd. in BERNKASTEL, with THANISCH and DEINHARD.

Liebfrauenstift

26-acre v'yd. in the city of WORMS, said to be the origin of the name LIEBFRAUMILCH.

Liebfraumilch

Legally defined as a QbA "of pleasant character" from RHEINHESSEN, RHEINPFALZ, NAHE or RHEINGAU, blended from RIESLING, SYLVANER or MÜLLER-THURGAU. Most is mild semi-sweet wine from Rheinhessen and Rheinpfalz.

Lieser M-M w. ∗→ [∗∗] 71 75 76 77 78 79 80

Little-known neighbour of BERNKASTEL. Grosslages: Beerenlay, Kurfürstlay.

Lorch Rhg. w. (r.) ∗→∗∗ 71 76 78 79 80

At extreme w. end of Rheingau. Secondary quality. Best grower: von Kanitz.

Löwenstein, Fürst

70-acre FRANKEN estate: classic dry wines.

Maikammer Rhpf. w. (r.) ∗→ [∗∗] 75 76 77 78 79 80

Village of n. SÜDLICHE WEINSTRASSE. Very pleasant wines incl. those from co-op at Rietburg. Grosslage: Mandelhöhe.

Maindreieck (Bereich)

District name for central part of FRANKEN, incl. WÜRZBURG.

Mainviereck (Bereich)

District name for minor w. part of FRANKEN.

Marcobrunn

See Erbach

Markgräflerland (Bereich)

Minor district s. of Freiburg (BADEN). GUTEDEL wine. Drink very young.

Martinsthal Rhg. w. ∗∗→ [∗∗∗] 71 75 76 77 78 79 80

Little-known neighbour of RAUENTHAL. Top v'yds.: Langenberg, Wildsau. Grosslage: Steinmacher.

Matuschka-Greiffenclau, Graf

Owner of the ancient SCHLOSS VOLLRADS estate.

Maximin Grünhaus M-S-R (Ruwer) w. ∗∗∗∗ 71 75 76 77 78 79 80

Supreme RUWER estate of 52 acres at Mertesdorf.

Mennig M-S-R (Saar) w. [∗∗] 71 75 76 77 78 79 80

Village between TRIER and the SAAR. Its Falkensteiner v'yd. is famous.

Mertesdorf

See Maximin Grünhaus

Mittelheim Rhg. w. ∗∗→ [∗∗∗] 71 75 76 77 78 79 80

Minor village between WINKEL and OESTRICH. Top grower: WEGELER. Grosslage: Honigberg.

Mittel-Haardt

The northern, best part, of RHEINPFALZ, incl. FORST, DEIDESHEIM, WACHENHEIM, etc.

Mittel-Mosel

The central and best part of the Mosel, incl. BERNKASTEL, PIESPORT, etc.

Mittelrhein

Northern Rhine area of secondary quality, incl. BACHARACH.

Morio Muskat

Stridently aromatic grape variety.

Moselblümchen

The "LIEBFRAUMILCH" of the Mosel, but on a lower quality level: TAFELWEIN not QbA.

Mosel-Saar-Ruwer

Huge wine area, incl. MITTEL-MOSEL, SAAR, RUWER and lesser areas.

Müller, Felix

Fine small SAAR estate with delicate SCHARZHOFBERGER.

Müller-Thurgau

Fruity, low-acid grape variety; the commonest in RHEINPFALZ and RHEINHESSEN, but increasingly planted in all areas.

Mumm, von

111-acre estate in JOHANNISBERG, RUDESHEIM, etc.

Munster Nahe w. ★→★★★ 71 75 76 77 78 79 80

Best village of n. NAHE, with fine delicate wines. Top grower: State Domain. Grosslage: Schlosskapelle.

Nackenheim Rhh. w. ★→★★★ 71 75 76 77 78 79 80

Neighbour of NIERSTEIN; best wines (Engelsberg, Rothenberg) similar. Grosslages: Spiegelberg, Gutes Domtal.

Nahe

Tributary of the Rhine and quality wine region. Balanced, fresh and clean but full-flavoured wines. Two Bereiche: KREUZNACH and SCHLOSS BÖCKELHEIM.

Neef M-S-R w. ★→ ★★ 71 75 76 78 79 80

Village of lower Mosel with one fine v'yd.: Frauenberg.

Neipperg, Graf

62-acre top WÜRTTEMBERG estate at Schwaigern.

Nell, von

40-acre family estate at TRIER and AYL, etc.

Neumagen-Dhron M-M w. ★★→★★★ 71 75 76 77 78 79 80

Neighbour of PIESPORT. Top v'yd.: Hofberger. Grosslage: Michelsberg.

Every wine district has its own favourite pattern of glass for bringing out the character of the local product. For practical purposes at home, however, three shapes/sizes are enough. These three were designed by Professor Lord Queensberry of the Royal College of Art and the author for Ravenhead Glass as ideal glasses for, respectively, sherry/port, fine red wines, white wine/general purpose.

Neustadt

Central city of Rheinpfalz, with famous wine school.

Niederhausen Na. w. ★★→ ★★★★ 71 75 76 77 78 79 80

Neighbour of SCHLOSS BÖCKELHEIM and H.Q. of Nahe State Domain. Wines of grace and power. Top v'yds. incl. Hermannshöhle, Steinberg. Grosslage: Burgweg.

Niedermennig

See Mennig

Niederwalluf

See Walluf

Nierstein (Bereich)

Large e. RHEINHESSEN district of very mixed quality.

Nierstein Rhh. w. ★→★★★ 71 75 76 77 78 79 80

Famous but treacherous name. 1,300 acres incl. superb v'yds.: Hipping, Orbel, Pettenthal, etc., and their Grosslages Rehbach, Spiegelberg, Auflangen: ripe, racy wines. But beware Grosslage Gutes Domtal: no guarantee of anything.

Nobling

Promising new grape variety in BADEN.

Norheim Nahe w. ★→★★★ 71 75 76 77 78 79 80

Neighbour of NIEDERHAUSEN. Top v'yds.: Klosterberg, Kafels, Kirschheck. Grosslage: Burgweg.

Oberemmel M-S-R (Saar) w. ★★→★★★ 71 75 76 77 78 79 80
Next village to WILTINGEN. Very fine wines from Rosenberg Hütte, etc. Grosslage: Scharzberg.

Obermosel (Bereich)
District name for the upper Mosel above TRIER. Generally poor wines from the Elbling grape.

Ockfen M-S-R (Saar) w. ★★→★★★ 71 75 76 77 78 79 80
200-acre hill with superb fragrant austere wines. Top v'yds.: Bockstein, Herrenberg. Grosslage: Scharzberg.

Oechsle
Scale for sugar-content of grape-juice (see page 21).

Oestrich Rhg. w. ★★→★★★ 71 75 76 77 78 79 80
Big village; good but rarely top grade. V'yds. incl. Doosberg, Lenchen. Grosslage: Gottesthal.

Oppenheim Rhh. w. ★→★★★ 71 75 76 77 78 79 80
Town s. of NIERSTEIN, best wines (Kreuz, Sackträger) similar. Grosslages: Guldenmorgen (★★★) Krotenbrunnen (★★).

Originalabfüllung
Bottled by the grower. An obsolete term.

Ortenau (Bereich)
District just s. of Baden-Baden. Soft wines to drink young. Best village DURBACH.

Othegraven, Von
Excellent 12-acre estate at KANZEM.

Palatinate
English for RHEINPFALZ.

Perlwein
Semi-sparkling wine.

Pfalz See Rheinpfalz

Pieroth
Major wine-sales company; also has small vineyard holdings.

Piesport M-M w. ★★→★★★★ 71 75 76 77 78 79 80
Tiny village with famous amphitheatre of vines giving fine gentle fruity wine. Top v'yds.: Goldtröpfchen, Gunterslay, Falkenberg. Treppchen is on flatter land and inferior. Grosslage: Michelsberg.

Plettenberg, von
Fine 100-acre Nahe estate at BAD KREUZNACH.

Pokalwein
Café wine. A pokal is a big glass.

Portugieser
Second-rate red-wine grape.

Prädikat
Special attributes or qualities. See QmP.

Prüfungsnummer
The official identifying test-number of a quality wine.

Prüm, J. J.
Superlative 35-acre Mosel estate in WEHLEN, GRAACH, BERNKASTEL. Rich, long-lived wines.

Qualitätswein bestimmter Anbaugebiete (QbA)
The middle quality of German wine, with added sugar but strictly controlled as to grape areas, etc.

Qualitätswein mit Prädikat (QmP)
Top category, incl. all wines ripe enough to be unsugared, from KABINETT to TROCKENBEERENAUSLESE.

Randersacker Franc. w. ★★→★★★ 71 75 76 77 78 79 80
Leading village for distinctive dry wine. Top v'yds. incl. Teufelskeller. Grosslage: Ewig Leben.

Rauenthal Rhg. w. ★★★ →★★★★ 71 75 76 77 78 79 80
Supreme village for powerful spicy wine. Top v'yds. incl. Baiken, Gehrn, Wulfen. Grosslage: Steinmacher. The State Domain is an important grower.

Rautenstrauch Erben

Owners of the splendid Karthäuserhof, EITELSBACH.

Rheinard Erben

Distinguished 23-acre Mosel estate at Longuich, near TRIER.

Rheinburgengau (Bereich)

District name for the v'yds. of the MITTELRHEIN round the famous Rhine gorge. Moderate quality only.

Rheingau

The best v'yd. region of the Rhine, near Wiesbaden. 5,000 acres. Classic, subtle but substantial RIESLING. Bereich name, JOHANNISBERG.

Rheinhessen

Vast region (30,000 acres of v'yds.) between Mainz and the NAHE, mostly second-rate, but incl. NIERSTEIN, OPPENHEIM, etc.

Rheinpfalz

Even vaster 35,000-acre v'yd. region s. of Rheinhessen. Wines inclined to sweetness. (See Mittel-Haardt and Südliche Weinstrasse.) This and the last are the chief sources of LIEBFRAUMILCH.

Rhodt

Village of SÜDLICHE WEINSTRASSE with well-known co-operative. Agreeable fruity wines. Grosslage: Ordensgut.

Rieslaner

Cross between RIESLING and SYLVANER; a good grape in FRANCONIA and BADEN.

Riesling

The best German grape: fine, fragrant, fruity, long-lived.

Ritter zu Groenesteyn, Baron

Fine 37-acre estate in KIEDRICH and RÜDESHEIM.

Roseewein

Rosé wine.

Rotenfelser Bastei

See Traisen

Rotwein

Red wine.

Rüdesheim Rhg. w. ** → *** 71 75 76 79 *80*

Rhine resort with 650 acres of excellent v'yds.; the three best called Berg. . . . Full-bodied wines. Grosslage: Burgweg.

Rüdesheimer Rosengarten

Rüdesheim is also the name of a NAHE village near BAD KREUZNACH. Do not be misled by the ubiquitous blend going by this name. It has nothing to do with Rheingau RÜDESHEIM.

Ruländer

The PINOT GRIS: grape giving soft heavy wine. Best in BADEN.

Ruppertsberg Rhpf. w. ** → ★★★ 71 75 76 77 78 79 80

Southern village of MITTEL-HAARDT. Top v'yds. incl. Gaisbohl, Hoheburg. Grosslage: Hofstück.

Ruwer

Tributary of Mosel near TRIER. Very fine delicate wines. Villages incl. EITELSBACH, MERTESDORF, KASEL.

Saar   Tributary of Mosel s. of RUWER. Brilliant austere wines. Villages incl. WILTINGEN, AYL, OCKFEN, SERRIG.

Saar-Ruwer (Bereich)

District incl. the two above.

Salem, Schloss

113-acre estate of Margrave of Baden on L. Constance in S. Germany. MÜLLER-THURGAU and WEISSHERBST.

St. Ursula

Well-known merchants at BINGEN.

Scharzberger

Grosslage name of WILTINGEN and neighbours.

Scharzhofberger Saar w. **** 71 75 76 77 78 79 80
> Superlative 30-acre SAAR v'yd.: austerely beautiful wines, the perfection of RIESLING. Do not confuse with the last.

Schaumwein
> Sparkling wine.

Scheurebe
> Fruity aromatic grape used in RHEINPFALZ.

Schillerwein
> Light red or rosé QbA, speciality of WÜRTTEMBERG.

Schlossabzug
> Bottled at the Schloss (castle).

Schloss Böckelheim Nahe w. **→→**** 71 75 76 77 78 79 80
> Village with the best NAHE v'yds., incl. Kupfergrübe, Felsenberg. Firm yet delicate wine. Grosslage: Burgweg.

Schloss Böckelheim (Bereich)
> District name for the whole S. NAHE.

Schloss Johannisberg
> Famous RHEINGAU estate of 66 acres belonging to the Oetke family and now run in conjunction with VON MUMM. Polished, elegant wine.

Schloss Reinhartshausen
> Fine 99-acre estate in ERBACH, HATTENHEIM, etc. much improved since 1976.

Schloss Vollrads Rhg. w. ***→**** 71 75 76 77 78 79 80
> Great estate at WINKEL, since 1300. 81 acres producing classical RHEINGAU RIESLING esp. since 1977. TROCKEN wines a speciality.

Schmitt, Gustav Adolf
> Fine old 124-acre family estate at NIERSTEIN.

Schmitt, Franz Karl
> Even older 74-acre ditto.

Schönborn, Graf von
> One of the biggest and best Rheingau estates, based at HATTENHEIM. Full-blooded wines. Also very good SEKT.

Schoppenwein
> Café wine: i.e. wine by the glass.

Schorlemer, Freiherr von
> Important MOSEL estate at LIESER, known for crisp, delicate wines.

Schubert, von
> Owner of MAXIMIN GRÜNHAUS.

Schweigen Rhpf. w. *→ ☐☐ 75 76 77 78 79 80
> Southernmost Rheinpfalz village with big co-operative, Deutsches WEINTOR. Grosslage: Guttenberg.

Sekt
> German (QbA) sparkling wine.

Serrig M-S-R (Saar) w. **→→**** 71 75 76 77 78 79 80
> Village known for "steely" wine, excellent in hot years. Top growers: VEREINIGTE HOSPITIEN and State Domain. Grosslage: Scharzberg.

Sichel H., Söhne
> Famous wine-merchants of London and Mainz.

Silvaner
> Common German white grape, best in FRANKEN.

Simmern, von
> 94-acre family estate at HATTENHEIM since 1464 and in ELTVILLE, RAUENTHAL, etc. Fine, relatively light wines.

Sonnenuhr
> "Sun-dial." Name of several famous v'yds., esp. one at WEHLEN.

Spätburgunder
> PINOT NOIR: the best red-wine grape in Germany.

Spätlese
"Late gathered." One better (stronger/sweeter) than KABINETT.

Spindler
Fine 33-acre family estate at FORST, Rheinpfalz.

Staatsweingut (or Staatliche Weinbaudomäne)
The State wine estate or domain.

Staufenberg, Schloss
65-acre DURBACH estate of the Margrave of Baden. Fine "Klingelberger" (RIESLING).

Steigerwald (Bereich)
District name for e. part of FRANKEN.

Süss-reserve and rest-süsse are terms commonly heard in relation to German wine. Süss is sweetness. Rest-süsse is the sweetness left in a wine after fermentation has either stopped naturally at a high alcoholic degree or been artificially stopped at a lower one. The latter used to be common practice in German wine-making, to arrive at a pleasant balance of sweet-and-sour. The same effect is more often achieved today by completing the fermentation to total dryness, then adding back some unfermented (sweet) juice of the same or similar grapes, known as süss-reserve. Thus the wine-maker has exact control of the wine's sweetness and can make dry (trocken), half-dry (halbtrocken) and rather sweet versions of the same wine. The technique is only made possible by sterile filtration, which removes every particle of yeast. If any were left the wine could re-ferment.

Steinberg Rhg. w. ***→**** 71 75 76 77 78 79 80
Famous 62-acre v'yd. at HATTENHEIM walled by Cistercians 700 yrs. ago. Now property of the State.

Steinwein
Wine from WÜRZBURG's best v'yd., Stein. Loosely used for all Franconian wine.

Stuttgart
Chief city of WÜRTTEMBERG, producer of some pleasant wines, recently beginning to be exported.

Südliche Weinstrasse (Bereich)
District name for the s. RHEINPFALZ.

Tafelwein
"Table wine." The vin ordinaire of Germany. Can be blended with other EEC wines. But Deutscher Tafelwein must come from Germany alone.

Thanisch, Dr.
32-acre BERNKASTEL family estate of top quality, incl. part of Doktor v'yd.

Traben-Trarbach M-W w. ** 75 76 78 79 80
Secondary wine-town, some good light wines. Top v'yds. incl. Schlossberg, Ungsberg. Grosslage: Schwarzlay.

Traisen Na. w. ***
Small village incl. superlative Bastei v'yd., making wine of great concentration and class.

Traminer
See Gewürztraminer

Trier M-S-R w. **→****
Important wine city of Roman origin, on the Mosel, adjacent to RUWER, now incl. AVELSBACH and EITELSBACH. Grosslage: Römerlay.

Trittenheim M-M w. ** →*** 71 75 76 77 78 79 80
Attractive light wines. Top v'yds. Apotheke, Altärchen, Grosslage: Michelsberg.

Trocken

Dry. On labels Trocken *alone* means with a statutory maximum of unfermented sugar (9 grams per litre). But see next entry. See also Halbtrocken.

Trockenbeerenauslese

The sweetest and most expensive category of wine, made from selected withered grapes. See also Edelfäule.

Trollinger

Common red grape of WÜRTTEMBERG: locally very popular.

Ungstein Rhpf. w. **★★→** ★★★ 71 75 76 77 78 79 *80*

MITTEL-HAARDT village with fine harmonious wines. Top v'yd. Herrenberg. Top grower Führmann (weingut Pfeffingen). Grosslage Hönigsackel.

Ürzig M-M w. ★★★ 71 75 76 77 78 79 *80*

Village famous for lively spicy wine. Top v'yd.: Würzgarten. Grosslage: Schwarzlay.

Vereinigte Hospitien

"United Hospitals." Ancient charity with large holdings in SERRIG, WILTINGEN, TRIER, PIESPORT, etc.

Verwaltung

Property.

Villa Sachsen

75-acre BINGEN estate belonging to ST. URSULA Weingut.

Wachenheim Rhpf. w. ★★★ →★★★★ 71 75 76 77 78 79 *80*

840 acres, incl. exceptionally fine Rieslings. V'yds. incl. Gerümpel, Böhlig, Rechbächel. Top grower: Bürklin-Wolf. Grosslages: Schenkenbohl, Schnepfenflug, Mariengarten.

Waldrach M-S-R (Ruwer) w. ★★ 75 76 77 78 79 *80*

Some charming light wines. Grosslage: (Trierer) Römerlay.

Walluf Rhg. w. ★★ 73 75 76 77 79 *80*

Neighbour of ELTVILLE; formerly Nieder- and Ober-Walluf. Good but not top wines. Grosslage: Steinmacher.

Walporzheim-Ahrtal (Bereich)

District name for the whole AHR valley.

Wawern M-S-R (Saar) w. ★★→★★★ 71 75 76 77 78 79 *80*

Small village with fine Rieslings. Grosslage: Scharzberg.

Wegeler Erben

138-acre Rheingau estate owned by DEINHARD'S. V'yds. in OESTRICH, MITTELHEIM, WINKEL, GEISENHEIM, RÜDESHEIM, etc.

Wehlen M-M w. ★★★ →★★★★ 71 75 76 77 78 79 *80*

Neighbour of BERNKASTEL with equally fine, somewhat richer, wine. Best v'yd.: Sonnenuhr. Top growers: Prüm family. Grosslage: Münzlay.

Weil, Dr.

45-acre private estate at KIEDRICH. Very fine wines.

Weingut

Wine estate. Can only be used by estates that grow all their own grapes.

Weinkellerei

Wine cellars or winery.

Weinstrasse

"Wine road." Scenic route through v'yds. Germany has several, the most famous in RHEINPFALZ.

Weintor, Deutsches

See Schweigen

Weissenheim-am-Sand Rhpf. w. (r.) ★→★★ 75 76 77 78 79 *80*

Big northern Pfalz village on sandy soil. Light wines.

Weissherbst

Rosé of QbA standard or above, even occasionally BEERENAUSLESE, the speciality of BADEN and WÜRTTEMBERG.

Werner, Domdechant

Fine 32-acre family estate at HOCHHEIM.

Wiltingen Saar w. ★★→★★★★

The centre of the Saar. 330 acres. Beautiful subtle austere wine. Top v'yds. incl. SCHARZHOFBERG, Braune Kupp, Braunfels, Klosterberg. Grosslage (for the whole Saar): Scharzberg.

Winkel Rhg. w. ★★★→★★★★ 71 75 76 77 78 79 *80*

Village famous for fragrant wine, incl. SCH. VOLLRADS. V'yds. incl. Hasensprung, Jesuitengarten. Grosslage: Hönigberg.

Wintrich M-M w. ★★→★★★ 71 75 76 77 78 79 *80*

Neighbour of PIESPORT; similar wines. Top v'yds.: Grosser Herrgott, Ohligsberg, Sonnenseite. Grosslage: Kurfürstlay.

Winzergenossenschaft

Wine-growers' co-operative, often making good and reasonably priced wine.

Winzerverein

The same as the last.

Wonnegau (Bereich)

District name for S. RHEINHESSEN.

Worms Rhh. w. ★★

City with the famous LIEBFRAUENSTIFT v'yd.

Württemberg

Vast s. area little known for wine outside Germany. Some good RIESLINGS, esp. from Neckar valley. Also TROLLINGER.

Würzburg Frank. ★★→★★★★ 71 75 76 77 78 79 *80*

Great baroque city on the Main, centre of Franconian (FRANKEN) wine: fine, full-bodied and dry. Top v'yds.: Stein, Leiste, Schlossberg. No Grosslage. See also Maindreieck.

ZBW (Zentralkellerei Baden-Württemberg)

Germany's (and Europe's) biggest ultra-modern co-operative, at Breisach, BADEN with 23,000 grower-members, producing 80 per cent of Baden's wine.

Zell M-S-R w. ★→★★ 75 76 77 78 79 *80*

Lower Mosel village famous for its Grosslage name Schwarze Katze ("Black Cat"). No fine wines.

Zell (Bereich)

District name for the whole lower Mosel from Zell to Koblenz.

Zeltingen-Rachtig M-M w. ★★ →★★★★ 71 75 76 77 78 79 *80*

Important Mosel village next to WEHLEN. Typically lively but full-bodied wine. Top v'yds.: Sonnenuhr, Schlossberg. Grosslage: Münzlay.

THE STRENGTH OF WINE *The alcoholic strength of wine varies considerably. Alcohol provides much of the feeling of "body" in strong wines, but needs to be balanced by the flavouring elements: sugar, acidity, tannin and assorted "extract". Without this richness of flavour it would be fierce and unpleasant.*
Typical alcoholic strengths (% by volume), as found in a laboratory analysing commercial samples, are:

German Tafelwein 8–11 *German Kabinett* 8–9
German Auslese 10–10.5 *German Beerenauslese* 12.8–14
French vin de table 9–12 *Red Bordeaux* 10.5–13
Bordeaux cru classé 11–16 *Beaujolais-Villages* 10–10.5
Muscadet 12 *Alsace Riesling* 10.5–11.5
Chablis Premier Cru 10.5–12.7 *Beaune* 11–14 *Chambertin* 12.4
Châteauneuf-du-Pape 12.6+ *Montrachet* 12.6
California Zinfandel 12–16 *California Chardonnay* 10.5–13.5
California Cabernet 11.44 *Australian Cabernet/Shiraz* 13.8
Barolo 12–14 *Chianti* 12–13 *Valpolicella* 11.7
Rioja reserva 12.5 *Sauternes* 12–15 *Château Yquem* 13.5–16
Fino sherry 18–20 *Oloroso sherry* 18–20 *Vintage port* 19–20

Italy

Italy is the world's biggest wine producer with the bigges
per capita consumption: 130 bottles a year. She is so at hom
with wine that she can seem alarmingly casual about it. .
sense of humour is as important as a corkscrew to anyon
who steps off the well-beaten track.

The chief clue to Italian wine is the DOC system, a
approximate equivalent of France's Appellations Co
trolées, which has been taking shape since the 1960s. Most
Italy's worthwhile wines now have defined areas and sta
dards under the new system. A few, like Chianti Classico,
must be said, had them long before. A few, however, hav
not—and DOCs have been granted to many areas of onl
local interest: so the mere existence of a DOC proves littl
The entries in this book ignore a score of unimportant DOC
and include considerably more non-DOCs. They also includ
a large number of grape-name entries.

Italian wines are named in a variety of ways: some ge
graphical like French wines, some historical, some foll
lorical, and many of the best from their grapes. Thes
include old "native" grapes such as Barbera and Sangioves
and more and more imported "international" grapes fro
France and Germany. Many of the DOCs, particularly in th
north-east, are area names applying to widely differer
wines from as many as a dozen different varieties. N
overall comment on the quality of such a diversity is reall
possible, except to say that general standards are risin
steadily and a small number of producers are emerging a
outstanding by international standards.

Another rather disconcerting aspect of Italian wine
clear from the following pages: in many cases the same nam
applies to wine which can be red or white or in betwee
sweet or dry or in between, still or sparkling or in betwee
This must be taken into account when interpreting th
necessarily cryptic grades of quality and vintage note
Vintage notes are given when specific information has bee
available. Where there is no comment the best plan is to ai
for the youngest available white wine and experiment wit
the oldest available red . . . within reason.

Trentino-Alto
-Adige **Tr-Aad**
● **Bolzano**
● **Trento**
rdy

Friuli-
Venezia
-Giulia
Fr-Vg
● **Trieste**

● **Verona**
Veneto Ven
● **Venice**

-Romagna

● **Bologna**

ce

any **Tusc**
na

Marches
● **Perugia** **Mar**

Umbria
Umbr

R. Tiber

Abruzzi Abr

● **Rome**
Latium
Lat

Molise M

Campania Camp
● **Naples**

Apulia Apu

Bari ●

ghero

Sardinia
Sard

Basilicata
Bas

Calabria
Cal

Cagliari ●

● **Palermo**
Marsala

Mt Etna ▲
Sicily Sic

he map is the key to the pro-
nce names used for locating
ch entry.

bbreviations of province
ames shown in bold type are
ed in the text.

The following abbreviations are
used in the Italian section
Pa.   passito
Pr.   Province
Com.   commune
f.   fortified
See also key to symbols opposite
Contents

Abboccato

Semi-sweet.

Aglianico del Vulture Bas. DOC r. (s/sw. sp.) ⋆⋆⋆ **75 77 78**

Among the best wines of s. Italy. Ages well. Called Vecch
after 3 yrs., Riserva after 5 yrs.

Alba

Major wine-centre of PIEMONTE.

Albana di Romagna Em-Ro. DOC w. dr. s/sw. (sp.) ⋆⋆ **77 78 79 8**

Produced for several centuries in Romagna from Alba
grapes. The dry slightly tannic, the semi-sweet fruity.

Alcamo Sic. DOC w. dr. ⋆

Soft neutral whites from western Sicily. Rapitalia is the be
brand.

Aleatico

Red muscat-flavoured grape.

Aleatico di Gradoli Lat. DOC r. sw. or f. ⋆⋆

Aromatic, fresh, fruity, alcohol 12–15%, made in Viterbo.

Aleatico di Puglia Apu. DOC r. sw. or f. ⋆⋆

Aleatico grapes make good dessert wine over a large are
14% alcohol or more, aromatic and full.

Allegrini

Well-known producer of Veronese wines, incl. VALPOLICELL

Alto Adige Tr-AAd. DOC r. p. w. dr. sw. sp. ⋆⋆

A DOC covering some 17 different wines named after the
grape varieties in 33 villages round Bolzano.

Amabile

Semi-sweet, but usually sweeter than ABBOCCATO.

Amaro

Bitter.

Amarone

See Recioto

Antinori

A long-established Tuscan house of repute producing fir
rate, if not truly typical, CHIANTI and ORVIETO.

Asti Major wine-centre of PIEMONTE.

Asti Spumante Piem. DOC w. sp. ⸤⋆⋆⋆⸥ NV

Sweet and very fruity muscat sparkling wine. Low in alcoh

Attems, Count

Leading producer and Consorzio president of COLLIO. Go
PINOT GRIGIO, MERLOT, etc.

Badia a Coltibuono **71 73 75 77 78**

Fine Chianti-maker at Gaiole with a restaurant and remar
able collection of old vintages.

Banfi, Villa

Major American importers of Italian wine, esp. LAMBRUSCO

Barbacarlo (Oltrepo' Pavese) Lomb. DOC r. dr. or sw. ⋆⋆ **77 78**

Delicately flavoured with bitter after-taste, made in the Co
of Broni in the Pr. of Pavia.

Barbaresco Piem. DOCG r. dr. ⋆⋆⋆ **70 71 74 76** 78 79

Neighbour of BAROLO from the same grapes but light
ageing sooner. At best subtle and fine. At 3 yrs. becor
Riserva. Best producers incl. GAJA.

Barbera

Dark acidic red grape, a speciality of Piemonte also used
Lombardy, Veneto, Friuli and other n. provinces. Its b
wines are:

Barbera d'Alba Piem. DOC r. dr. ⋆⋆ **74 78** 79

Round ALBA NEBBIOLO is sometimes added. Clean, tasty, fr
rant red improves for 3–4 yrs.

Barbera d'Asti Piem. DOC r. dr. (s/sw.) ⸤⋆⋆⸥ **74 78** 79

Reputedly the best of the Barberas; all Barbera grapes; da
grapy and appetizing. Ages up to 7–8 yrs.

Barbera del Monferrato   Piem. DOC r. dr. (s/sw.) ✶ 76 77 78 79
From a large area in the Pr. of Alessandria and ASTI. Pleasant, slightly fizzy, sometimes sweetish.

Bardolino   Ven. DOC r. dr. (p.) ✶✶ D.Y.A.
Pale, light, slightly bitter red from e. shore of La Garda. Bardolino Chiaretto is even paler and lighter.

Barolo   Piem. DOCG r. dr. ✸✸✸ 68 70 71 74 76 78 79
Small area s. of Turin with one of the best Italian red wines, dark, rich, alcoholic (minimum 12°), dry but deep in flavour. From NEBBIOLO grapes. Ages for up to 15 yrs.

Bell 'Agio
Brand of sweet white MOSCATO from BANFI.

Bertani
Well-known producers of quality Veronese wines (VALPOLICELLA, SOAVE, etc.).

Bertolli, Francesco
Among the best-known producers of CHIANTI CLASSICO. Cellars at Castellina in Chianti, n. of Siena. Ambra is their standard branded range.

Bianco
White.

Bianco di Pitigliano   Tusc. DOC w. dr ✶ D.Y.A.
A soft, fruity, lively wine made near Grosseto.

Bigi   Famous producers of ORVIETO and other wines of Umbria and Tuscany.

Biondi-Santi
One of the leading producers of BRUNELLO with cellars in Montalcino (Siena).

Boca   Piem. DOC r. dr. ✶✶ 70 71 74 75 76 78 79
From same grape as BAROLO in n. of PIEMONTE, Pr. of Novara.

Bolla
Famous Veronese firm producing VALPOLICELLA, SOAVE, etc.

Bonarda
Minor red grape widely grown in PIEMONTE and Lombardy.

Bonarda (Oltrepo' Pavese)   Lomb. DOC r. dr. ✶✶ 75 76 77 78 79
Soft, fresh, pleasant red from s. of Pavia.

Bosca
Wine-producers from PIEMONTE known for their ASTI SPUMANTE and Vermouths.

Botticino   Lomb. DOC r. dr. ✶ 73 74 76 77 78 79
Strong, full-bodied rather sweet red from Brescia.

Brachetto d'Acqui   Piem. DOC r. sw. (sp.) ✶ 76 78 79
Sweet sparkling red with pleasant muscat aroma.

Bricco Manzoni   Piem. r. ✸✸✸ 76 78 79
Excellent red of blended BARBERA and NEBBIOLO from Monforte d'Alba.

Brolio
The oldest (c. 1200) and most famous CHIANTI CLASSICO estate now owned by Seagrams. Good whites as well as red.

Brunello di Montalcino   Tusc. DOCG r. dr. ✶✶✶✶ 66 70 73 75 77 78 79
Italy's most expensive wine. Strong, full-bodied, high-flavoured and long-lived. After 5 yrs. is called Riserva. Produced for over a century 15 miles s. of Siena.

Cabernet
Bordeaux grape much used in n.e. Italy and increasingly in Tuscany and the south. See place names, e.g.:

Cabernet di Pramaggiore   Ven. DOC r. dr. ✶✶ 75 77 78 79
Good, herb-scented, rather tannic, middle-weight red. Riserva after 3 yrs.

Cacciano, Castello di
First-rate CHIANTI CLASSICO estate at Gaiole, owned by RICASOLI.

Calcinaia

First-class CHIANTI CLASSICO estate for centuries in the Caponi family.

Caldaro or Lago di Caldaro Tr–AAd. DOC r. dr. ★★ 75 76 77 78

Light, soft, slightly bitter-almond red. Classico from a smaller area is better. From s. of Bolzano.

Calissano

A long-established House of PIEMONTE producing ASTI SPUMANTE, Vermouths and red wines of that region.

Caluso Passito Piem. DOC w. sw. (f.) ★★ 70 71 74 75 78

Made from selected Erbaluce grapes left to partly dry; delicate scent, velvety taste. From a large area in the Pr. of Turin and Vercelli.

Cannonau di Sardegna Sard. DOC r. dr. or s/sw. (f.) ★★ 74 76 77 78

One of the good wines of the island capable of ageing.

Cantina

1. Cellar or winery. 2. Cantina Sociale = growers' co-op.

Capena Lat. DOC w. dr. s/sw ★ D.Y.A.

A sound wine for daily drinking from n. of Rome.

Capri

Widely abused name of the famous island in the Bay of Naples. No guarantee of quality.

Carema Piem. DOC r. dr. ★★ 71 73 74 75 78 79

Old speciality of Val d'Aosta. NEBBIOLO grapes traditionally fermented Beaujolais-style before crushing. (See France: Macération carbonique.) More conventional today.

Carmignano Tusc. DOC r. dr. ★★→ ⸢★★★⸣ 75 78 79

Section of CHIANTI using CABERNET to make good wine.

Casa fondata nel ...

Firm founded in ...

Castel del Monte Apu. DOC r. p. w. dr. ★★ 73 74 75 76 77 78 79

Dry, fresh, well-balanced southern wines. The red becomes Riserva after 3 yrs.

Castel San Michele

A good red made of Cabernet and Merlot grapes by the Trentino Agricultural College near Trento.

CAVIT

CAntina VITicultori, a co-operative of co-operatives near Trento, producing large quantities of table wine.

Cellatica Lomb. DOC r. dr. ★★ 75 76 77 78 79

Light red with slightly bitter after-taste of Schiava grapes, from Brescia.

Ceretto

High-quality grower of BARBARESCO, BAROLO, etc.

Ceretto, Castello di

CHIANTI CLASSICO estate owned by Emilio Pucci.

Cerveteri Lat. DOC w. dr. ★

Sound wines produced n.w. of Rome between Lake Bracciano and the Tyrrhenian Sea.

Chianti Tusc. DOC r. dr. ⸢★★⸣ 71 75 77 78 79

The lively local wine of Florence. Fresh but warmly fruity when young, usually sold in straw-covered flasks. Ages moderately. Montalbano, Rufina and Colli Fiorentini, Senesi, Aretini, Colline Pisane are sub-districts.

Chianti Classico Tusc. DOC r. dr. ⸢★★★⸣ 70 71 75 77 78 79

Senior Chianti from the central area. Many estates make fine powerful scented wine. Riservas (after 3 yrs.) often have the bouquet of age in oak.

Chianti Putto

Often high-quality Chianti from a league of producers outside the Classico zone. Designated by a neck-label of a pink and white cherub.

Chiaretto

Very light reds, almost rosé (the word means "claret") produced around Lake Garda. See Riviera de Garda.

Cinque Terre   Lig. DOC w. dr. or sw. or pa. ★★★

Fragrant, fruity white made for centuries near La Spezia. The PASSITO is known as Sciacchetra.

Cinzano

Major Vermouth company also known for its ASTI SPUMANTE from PIEMONTE.

Cirò   Cal. DOC r. (p. w.) dr. ★★ 73 74 75 77 78 79

The wine of the ancient Olympic games. Very strong red, fruity white (to drink young).

Classico

Term for wines from a restricted, usually central, area within the limits of a DOC. By implication, and often in practice, the best of the region.

Clastidio   Lomb. r. (p.) w. dr. ★★ 74 75 76 77 78 79

Pleasant, sour touch to the white. The red full, slightly tannic.

Collavini, Cantina

High-quality producers of GRAVE DEL FRIULI wines: PINOT GRIGIO, RIESLING, MERLOT, PINOT NERO, etc.

THE BEST-KNOWN ITALIAN WINES, REGION BY REGION, ARE:

Piemonte: Barolo, Barbaresco, Barbera, Dolcetto, Nebbiolo, Asti Spumante.
Liguria: Cinqueterre, Dolceacqua.
Trentino-Alto Adige: Teroldego, Caldaro, Santa Maddalena, Merlot, Pinot Bianco, etc.
Veneto: Soave, Valpolicella, Recioto, Colli Euganei, Prosecco, etc.
Friuli-Venezia-Giulia: Collio, Pinot Grigio, Merlot, etc.
Emilia-Romagna: Albana, Lambrusco.
Tuscany: Chianti, Brunello, Vino Nobile di Montepulciano.
Umbria: Orvieto, Rubesco di Torgiano.
Marches: Verdicchio, Rosso Conero.
Latium: Frascati, Marino.
Abruzzi/Molise: Montepulciano.
Campania: Lacryma Christi, Taurasi.
Apulia: Castel del Monte.
Basilicata: Aglianico del Vulture.
Calabria: Ciro.
Sicily: Marsala, Corvo, Etna.
Sardinia: Nuraghus, Cannonau, Monica.

Colli   Means "hills" in many wine-names.

Colli Albani   Lat. DOC w. dr. or s/sw. (sp.) ★★ 77 78 79

Soft fruity wine of the Roman hills.

Colli Bolognesi   Em-Ro. DOC r.p. w. dr. ★ D.Y.A.

From the hills s.w. of Bologna.

Colli Euganei   Ven. DOC r. w. dr. or s/sw. (sp.) ⌐★⌐ 77 78 79

A DOC applicable to 3 wines produced s.w. of Padua. The red is scarcely memorable, the white soft and pleasant. The table wine of Venice.

Colli Orientali del Friuli   Fr-VG. DOC r. w. dr. or sw. ★ 77 78 79

12 different wines are produced under this DOC on the hills e. of Udine and named after their grapes.

Collio (Goriziano)   Fr-VG. DOC r. w. dr. ⌐★★⌐ 76 77 78 79

Ten different wines named after their grapes from a small area between Udine and Gorizia nr. the Yugoslav border. Top grower: ATTEMS.

Conterno, Aldo

Highly regarded grower of BAROLO, etc.

Contratto
>Piemonte firm known for BAROLO, ASTI SPUMANTE, etc.

Cora
>A leading House producing ASTI SPUMANTE and Vermouth from PIEMONTE.

Cori Lat DOC w. r. dr./sw. ★
>Soft and well-balanced wines made 30 miles s. of Rome.

Cortese di Gavi Piem. DOC w. dr. (sp.) ★★ D.Y.A.
>Delicate fresh white from between Alessandria and Genoa.

Cortese (Oltrepo' Pavese) Lomb. DOC w. dr. ★ D.Y.A.
>The same from w. Lombardy.

Corvo Sic. r. w. dr. ★★
>Popular Sicilian wines. Sound dry red, pleasant soft white.

D'Ambra
>Well-known producer of ELBA and other wines of that island.

Dolce Sweet.

Dolceacqua
>See Rossese di Dolceacqua

Dolcetto
>Common low-acid red grape of PIEMONTE, giving its name to:

Dolcetto d'Acqui Piem. DOC r. dr. ★ D.Y.A.
>Good standard table wine from s. of ASTI.

Dolcetto d'Alba Piem. DOC r. dr. ★★ 78 79
>Among the best Dolcetti, with a trace of bitter-almond.

Dolcetto d'Asti Piem. DOC r. dr. ★ D.Y.A.

Donnaz Vd'A. DOC r. dr. ★★ 76 78 79
>A mountain NEBBIOLO, fragrant, pale and faintly bitter. Aged for a statutory 3 yrs.

Donnici Cal. DOC r. (p.) dr. ★
>Middle-weight southern red from Cosenza.

Elba Tusc. r. w. dr. (sp.) ★ 78 79
>The island's white is better: admirable with fish.

Enfer d'Arvier Vd'A. DOC r. dr. ★★
>An Alpine speciality: pale, pleasantly bitter, light red.

Enoteca
>Italian for "wine library", of which there are many in the country, the most comprehensive being the Enoteca Italica Permanente di Siena. Chianti has one at Greve

Erbaluce di Caluso Piem. DOC w. dr. ★ 76 78 79
>Pleasant fresh hot-weather wine.

Est! Est!! Est!!! Lat. DOC w. dr. or s/sw. ★★ D.Y.A.
>Famous soft fruity white from La. Bolsena, n. of Rome. The name is more remarkable than the wine.

Etna Sic. DOC r. p. w. dr. ★★ 73 74 75 77 78 79
>Wine from the volcanic slopes. The red is warm, full, balanced and ages well; the white is distinctly grapy.

Falerio dei Colli Ascolani Mar. DOC w. dr. ★ D.Y.A.
>Made in the Pr. of Ascoli Piceno. Pleasant, fresh, fruity; a wine for the summer.

Falerno Camp. r. w. dr. ★
>One of the best-known wines of ancient times, but nothing special today. Strong red, fruity white.

Fara Piem. DOC r. dr. ★★ 71 74 75 76 77 79
>Good NEBBIOLO wine from Novara, n. PIEMONTE. Fragrant; worth ageing. Small production.

Faro Sic. r. dr. ★★ 75 77 78 79
>Sound strong Sicilian red, made in sight of the Straits of Messina.

Favonio Apu. r. w. dr. ★★★
>Revolutionary estate e. of Foggia using CABERNET, CHARDONNAY and PINOT BIANCO.

Fazi-Battaglia

Well-known producer of VERDICCHIO, etc.

Ferrari

Firm making Italy's best dry sparkling wine by the champagne method nr. Trento, Trentino-Alto Adige.

Fiorano Lat. r. ∗∗

Interesting reds of Cabernet Sauvignon and Merlot.

Florio

The major producer of Marsala, owning several brands, controlled by CINZANO.

Folonari

Leading producers of quality Veronese wines as well as other table wines from various parts of Italy.

Fontana Candida

One of the biggest producers of FRASCATI.

Fontanafredda

Leading producer of Piemontese wines, incl. BAROLO.

Fonterutoli

High-quality CHIANTI CLASSICO estate at Castellina.

Fracia Lomb. DOC r. dr. ∗∗ 73 75 76 78 79

Good light but fragrant red from VALTELLINA.

Franciacorta Pinot Lomb. DOC w. dr. (sp.) ∗∗

Agreeable soft white and good sparkling wines made of PINOT BIANCO.

Franciacorta Rosso Lomb. DOC r. dr. ∗∗ 76 77 78 79

Lightish red of mixed CABERNET and BARBERA from Brescia.

Franco Fiorina

Highly regarded producer of BAROLO, BARBARESCO, etc.

Frascati Lat. DOC w. dr. s/sw. sw. (sp.) ∗→ ∗∗ 76 79

Best-known wine of the Roman hills: soft, ripe, golden, tasting of whole grapes. Most is pasteurized and neutral today: look for dated wines from small producers (e.g. Colli di Catone). The sweet is known as Cannellino.

Frecciarossa Lomb. r. w. dr. ∗∗ 73 76 77 78 79

Sound wines produced nr. Casteggio in the Oltrepo' Pavese; the white is better known.

Freisa d'Asti Piem. DOC r. s/sw. or sw. (sp.) ∗∗ 73 74 78 79

Sweet, often sparkling red, said to taste of raspberries and roses.

Frescobaldi

Leading pioneers of CHIANTI PUTTO at Nippozano, e. of Florence. Also elegant white POMINO.

Friuli-Venezia Giulia

The north-eastern province on the Yugoslav border. Many wines, esp. COLLIO.

Frizzante

Semi-sparkling or "pétillant", a word used to describe wines such as LAMBRUSCO.

Gaja Old family firm at BARBARESCO. Top-quality Piemonte wines. Pioneer with carbonic maceration to make VINÒT.

Gambellara Ven. DOC w. dr. or s/sw. (sp.) ∗ 76 77 78 79

Neighbour of SOAVE. Dry wine similar. Sweet (known as RECIOTO DI GAMBELLARA), agreeably fruity.

Gancia

Famous ASTI SPUMANTE house from Piemonte, also produces vermouth.

Garganega

The principal white grape of SOAVE.

Gattinara Piem. DOC r. dr. ∗∗∗ 69 70 74 75 76 78 79

Excellent big-scale BAROLO-type red from n. PIEMONTE. Made from NEBBIOLO, locally known as Spanna.

Gavi Piem. w. dr. **✭✭→ ✭✭✭**

At best almost burgundian dry white. Gavi dei Gavi from Rovereto di Gavi Ligure is best. Needs two or three years ageing.

Geografico, Chianti

Good-quality Chianti Classico from a major growers' cooperative near Gaiole.

Ghemme Piem. DOC r. dr. ⬚**✭✭** 70 71 73 74 78 79

Neighbour of GATTINARA, capable of Bordeaux-style finesse.

Giacobazzi

Well-known producers of Lambrusco wines with cellars in Nonantola and Sorbara, near Modena.

Giacosa, Bruno

Old family business making excellent Barolo and other Piemonte wines at Neive (Cuneo).

Gradi

Degrees (of alcohol) i.e. percent by volume.

Grave del Friuli Fr-VG. DOC r. w. dr. **✭✭** 75 76 77 78 79

A DOC covering 7 different wines named after their grapes, from near the Yugoslav border. Good MERLOT and light CABERNET, esp. from Duca Badoglio.

Greco di Tufo Camp. DOC w. dr. s/sw. **✭✭** 76 77 78 79

One of the best whites of the south, fruity and slightly bitter.

Grignolino d'Asti Piem. DOC r. dr. **✭** 74 76 78 79

Pleasant lively standard wine of PIEMONTE.

Grumello Lomb. DOC r. dr. **✭✭** 71 73 75 76 78 79

NEBBIOLO wine from Valtellina, can be delicate and fine.

Gutturnio dei Colli Piacentini Em-Ro. DOC r. dr. (s/sw.) **✭✭** 74 77 78 79

Full-bodied wine of character from the hills of Piacenza. Named after a large Roman drinking cup.

Inferno Lomb. DOC r. dr. ⬚**✭✭** 70 73 75 76 78 79

Similar to GRUMELLO and like it classified as VALTELLINA Superiore.

Ischia Camp. DOC (r.) w. dr. **✭** 77 78 79

The wine of the island off Naples. The slightly sharp white is best; ideal with fish.

Isonzo Fr-VG. DOC r. w. dr. **✭**

DOC covering 10 varietal wines in the extreme north-east.

Kalterersee

German name for Lago di CALDARO.

Kretzer

German term for rosé used in the Italian Tyrol.

Lacrima Cristi del Vesuvio Camp. r. p. w. (f.) dr. (sw.) **✭**

Famous but frankly ordinary wines in great variety from the slopes of Mount Vesuvius.

Lago di Caldaro

See Caldaro

Lagrein del Trentino Tr-AAd. DOC r. dr. **✭✭** 76 78 79

Lagrein is a Tyrolean grape with a bitter twist. Good fruity light wine.

Lamberti

Producers of SOAVE, VALPOLICELLA and BARDOLINO at Lazise on the e. shore of La. Garda.

Lambrusco DOC (or not) r. p. (w.) s/sw. **✭** D.Y.A.

Bizarre but popular fizzy red, generally drunk secco (dry) in Italy but a smash hit in its amabile (sweet) version in the USA.

Lambrusco di Sorbara Em-Ro. DOC r. (w.) dr. or s/sw. sp. **✭✭✭** 78 79

The best of the Lambruscos. From near Modena.

Lambrusco Grasparossa di Castelvetro Em-Ro. DOC r. dr. or s/sw. sp. ★★ 78 79
> Similar to above. Highly scented, pleasantly acidic; often drunk with rich food.

Lambrusco Salamino di Santa Croce Em-Ro. DOC r. dr. or s/sw. sp. ★ 78 79
> Similar to above. Fruity smell, high acidity and a thick "head".

Langhe
> The hills of central PIEMONTE.

Latisana Fr-VG. DOC r. w. dr. ★★
> DOC for 7 varietal wines from some 50 miles n.e. of Venice.

Lessona Piem. DOC r. d. ★★ 74 78 79
> Soft, dry, claret-like wine produced in the province of Vercelli from Nebbiolo grapes.

Liquoroso
> Strong and usually sweet, e.g. like Tuscan Vinsanto.

Locorotondo Apu. DOC w. dr. ★ D.Y.A.
> A pleasantly fresh southern white.

Lugana Lomb. DOC w. dr. ★★★ 78 79
> One of the best white wines of s. La. Garda: fragrant and delicate.

Lungarotti
> Leading producer of TORGIANO wine, with cellars and an outstanding Wine Museum near Perugia.

Most Italian wines have a simple name, in contrast to the combination village and vineyard names of France and Germany.

SOAVE
CLASSICO

VINO A DENOMINAZIONE DI ORIGINE CONTROLLATA

IMBOTTIGLIATO DAL PRODUTTORE ALL 'ORIGINE
CANTINA SOCIALE DI SOAVE

Soave is the name of this wine. It is qualified only by the word Classico, a legal term for the central (normally the best) part of many long-established wine regions. "Denominazione di Origine Controllata" is the official guarantee of authenticity. Imbottigliato . . . all origine means bottled by the producer. Cantina Sociale di Soave means the growers' co-operative of Soave.

Malfatti Apu. DOC r. p. w. dr. ★★ 78 79
> Recent go-ahead estate with modern methods, near Lecce, Apulia.

Malvasia
> Important white or red grape for luscious wines, incl. Madeira's Malmsey. Used all over Italy.

Malvasia di Bosa Sard. DOC w. dr. sw. or f. ★★
> A wine of character. Strong and aromatic with a slightly bitter after-taste. A liquoroso (fortified) version is best.

Malvasia di Cagliari Sard. DOC w. dr. s/sw. or sw. (f. dr. s.) ★★
> Interesting strong Sardinian wine, fragrant and slightly bitter.

Malvasia di Casorzo d'Asti Piem. DOC r. p. sw. sp. ★★ 74 76 78 79
> Fragrant grapy sweet red, sometimes sparkling.

Malvasia di Castelnuovo Don Bosco Piem. DOC r. sw. (sp.) ★★
> Peculiar method of interrupted fermentation gives very sweet aromatic red.

Malvasia delle Lipari Sic. DOC w. sw. (pa. f.) ★★★ 76 77 78 79
> Among the very best Malvasias, aromatic and rich, produced on the Lipari or Aeolian Islands n. of Sicily.

Malvasia di Nus Vd'A. w. dr. ★★★
> Rare Alpine white, with a deep bouquet of honey.
> Small production and high reputation. Can age
> remarkably well.

Mamertino Sic. w. s/sw. ★★ **74 75 76 77** 78 79
> Made near Messina since Roman times. Sweet-scented, rich
> in glycerine. Mentioned several times by Caesar in *De Bello
> Gallico*.

Manduria (Primitivo di) Apu. DOC r. s/sw. (f. dr. or sw.) ★★
> Heady red, naturally strong but often fortified. From nr.
> Taranto. Primitivo is a southern grape.

Mantonico Cal. w. sw. f. ★★
> Fruity deep amber dessert wine from Reggio Calabria.
> Can age remarkably well. Named from the Greek for
> "prophetic".

Marino Lat. DOC w. dr. or s/sw. ⌈★⌋ **78 79**
> A neighbour of FRASCATI with similar wine, often a better buy.

Marsala Sic. DOC br. dr. s/sw. or sw. f. ★★★ NV
> Dark sherry-type wine invented by the Woodhouse Brothers
> from Liverpool in 1773; excellent apéritif or for dessert. The
> dry ("virgin"), sometimes made by the solera system, must be
> 5 years old.

Marsala Speciali
> These are Marsalas with added flavours of egg, almond,
> strawberry, etc.

Martinafranca Apu. DOC w. dr. ★ D.Y.A.
> Agreeable but rather neutral southern white.

Martini & Rossi
> Well-known vermouth House also famous for its fine wine
> museum in Pessione, PIEMONTE.

Marzemino (del Trentino) Tr.-AAd. DOC r. dr. ★ **75 76 77 78** 79
> Pleasant local red of Trento. Fruity fragrance; slightly bitter
> taste. Mozart's Don Giovanni liked it.

Masi, Cantina
> Well-known specialist producers of VALPOLICELLA, RECIOTO,
> SOAVE, etc., incl. fine red Campo Fiorin.

Mastroberardino
> Leading wine-producer of Campania, incl. TAURASI and LACRI-
> MA CRISTI DEL VESUVIO.

Melini
> Long-established important producers of CHIANTI CLASSICO at
> Pontassieve. Inventors of standard *fiasco*, or litre flask.

Melissa Cal. r. dr. ★★ **74 75 77 78** 79
> Mostly made from Gaglioppo grapes in the Pr. of Catanzaro.
> Delicate, balanced, ages rather well.

Meranese di Collina Tr.-AAd. DOC r. dr. ★ **76 77 78** 79
> Light red of Merano, known in German as Meraner.

Merlot
> Adaptable red Bordeaux grape widely grown in n.e. Italy and
> elsewhere.

Merlot di Aprilia Lat. DOC r. dr. ★ **77 78** 79
> Harsh at first, softer after 2–3 yrs.

Merlot Colli Berici Ven. DOC r. dr. ★ D.Y.A.
> Pleasantly light and soft.

Merlot Colli Orientali del Friuli Fr-VG. DOC r. dr. ★
> Pleasant herby character, best at 2–3 yrs.

Merlot Collio Goriziano Fr-VG. DOC r. dr. ★
> Grassy scent, slightly bitter taste. Best at 2–3 yrs.

Merlot Grave del Friuli Fr-VG. DOC r. dr. ★
> Pleasant light wine, best at 1–2 yrs.

Merlot (Isonzo) Fr-VG. DOC r. dr. ★
> A DOC in Gorizia. Dry, herby, agreeable wine.

Merlot del Piave Ven. DOC r. dr. ✶✶ 75 77 78 79
> Sound tasty red, best at 2–3 yrs.

Merlot di Pramaggiore Ven. DOC r. dr. ✶✶ 76 77 78 79
> A cut above other Merlots; improves in bottle. Riserva after 3 yrs.

Merlot (del Trentino) Tr-AAd. DOC r. dr. ⋆ 78 79
> Full flavour, slightly grassy scent, improves for 2–3 yrs.

Monica di Cagliari Sard. DOC r. dr. or sw. (f. dr. or sw.) ✶✶ 77 78 79
> Strong spicy red, often fortified and comparable with Spanish MALAGA. Monica is a Sardinian grape.

Monica di Sardegna Sard. DOC r. sw. ⋆ NV
> Commoner form of above, not fortified.

Moniga (del Garda)
> Village at s.w. end of Lake Garda, known for good fresh CHIARETTO (D.Y.A.).

Montecarlo Tusc. DOC w. dr. ✶✶
> One of Tuscany's best whites, smooth and delicate, achieving a Graves-like style after 3–4 years. From near Lucca.

Montecompatri-Colonna Lat. DOC w. dr. or s/sw. ⋆
> A neighbour of FRASCATI. Similar wine.

Montepaldi
> Well-known producers and merchants of CHIANTI CLASSICO at San Casciano Val di Pesa. Owned by the Corsini family.

Montepulciano, Vino Nobile di
> See Vino Nobile di Montepulciano.

Montepulciano d'Abruzzo (or Molise) Abr&M. DOC r. p. dr. ⋆⋆⋆ 74 75 77 78 79
> One of Italy's best reds, from Adriatic coast round Pescara. Soft, slightly tannic, reminiscent of MARSALA when aged. Best from Francavilla al Mare, Sulmona, Pratola Peligna.

Monterosso (Val d'Arda) Em-Ro. DOC w. dr. or sw. (sp.) ⋆ D.Y.A.
> Agreeable and fresh minor white from Piacenza.

Moscato
> Fruitily fragrant grape grown all over Italy.

Moscato d'Asti Piem. DOC w. sw. sp. ⋆ NV
> Low-strength sweet fruity sparkler made in bulk. ASTI SPUMANTE is the superior version.

Moscato dei Colli Euganei Ven. DOC w. sw. (sp.) ✶✶ 78 79
> Golden wine, fruity and smooth, from nr. Padua.

Moscato Naturale d'Asti Piem. DOC w. sw. ⋆ D.Y.A.
> The light and fruity base wine for Moscato d'Asti.

Moscato di Noto Sic. DOC w. s/sw. or sw. or sp. or f. ⋆ NV
> Light sweet still and sparkling versions, or strong Liquoroso. Noto is near Siracuse.

Moscato (Oltrepo' Pavese) Lomb. DOC w. sw. (sp.) ✶✶79
> The Lombardy equivalent of Moscato d'Asti.

Moscato di Pantelleria Sic. DOC w. sw. (sp.) (f. pa.) ✶✶✶
> Italy's best muscat, from the island of Pantelleria close to the Tunisian coast; rich, fruity and aromatic. Ages well.

Moscato di Siracusa Sic. DOC w. sw. ⋆⋆ NV
> Strong amber dessert wine from Siracuse. Can be superb.

Moscato di Sorso Sennori Sard. DOC w. sw. (f.) ⋆
> Strong golden dessert wine from Sassari, n. Sardinia.

Moscato di Trani Apu. DOC w. sw. or f. ⋆ 74 76 77 79
> Another strong golden dessert wine, sometimes fortified, with "bouquet of faded roses".

Moscato (Trentino) Tr-AAd. DOC w. sw. ⋆
> Typical muscat: high strength for the north.

Nasco di Cagliari Sard. DOC w. dr. or sw. (f. dr. or sw.) ⋆ 73 74
> Sardinian speciality, light bitter taste, high alcoholic content.

Nebbiolo
> The best red grape of PIEMONTE and Lombardy.

Nebbiolo d'Alba Piem. DOC r. dr. s/sw. (sp.) ⁂ **74 76 77 78** 79
> Like light-weight BAROLO; often good. Barolo that fails to reach the statutory 12° alcohol is sold under this name. Some prefer it so.

Negri, Nino
> Producer of VALTELLINA known for his above-average reds.

Nipozzano, Castello di
> The most important CHIANTI producer outside the Classico zone, to the n. near Florence. Owned by FRESCOBALDI.

Nozzole
> Famous estate in the heart of CHIANTI CLASSICO n. of Greve.

Nuraghe Majore Sard. w. dr. ✶✶ D.Y.A.
> Sardinian white: delicate, fresh, among the island's best.

Nuragus di Cagliari Sard. DOC w. dr. ✶ **78 79**
> Lively Sardinian white, not too strong.

Oliena Sard. r. dr. ✶✶
> Interesting strong fragrant red; a touch bitter.

Oltrepò Pavese Lomb. DOC r. w. dr. sw. sp. ✶→✶✶
> DOC applicable to 7 wines produced in the Pr. of Pavia, named after their grapes.

Orvieto Umb. DOC w. dr. or s/sw. ✶✶→✶✶✶ **77 78 79**
> The classical Umbrian golden-white, smooth and substantial, though the dry version is sometimes flat and rather dull. O. Classico is superior.

Ostuni Apu. DOC w. dr. ✶✶
> Rather delicate, dry, balanced; produced in the Pr. of Brindisi.

Parrina Tusc. r. or w. dr. ✶✶ D.Y.A.
> Light red and fresh appetizing white from n. Tuscany.

Passito
> Strong sweet wine from grapes dried either in the sun or indoors.

Per' e' Palummo Camp. r. dr. ✶✶
> Excellent red produced on the island of Ischia; delicate, slightly grassy, a bit tannic, balanced.

Pian d'Albola
> Renowned old CHIANTI CLASSICO estate.

Piave Ven. DOC r. or w. dr. ✶✶ **75 76 78 79**
> DOC covering 4 wines, 2 red and 2 white, named after their grapes.

Picolit (Colli Orientali del Friuli) Fr-VG. DOC w. s/sw. or sw. ✶✶✶✶ **64 69 71 72 73 74 75 77** 78 79
> Known as Italy's Château d'Yquem. Delicate bouquet, well balanced, high alcoholic content. Ages very well.

Piemonte
> The most important Italian region for quality wine. Turin is the capital, Asti the wine-centre. See Barolo, Barbera, Grignolino, Moscato, etc.

Pieropan
> Outstanding producers of SOAVE.

Pinocchio Tusc. r. w. ✶
> Long-established brand notable for its variable nose.

Pinot Bianco
> Rather neutral grape popular in n.e., good for sparkling wine.

Pinot Bianco (dei Colli Berici) Ven. DOC w. dr. ✶✶
> Straight satisfying dry white.

Pinot Bianco (Colli Orientali del Friuli) Fr-VG. DOC w. dr. ✶✶ **75 76 77 78** 79
> Good white; smooth rather than showy.

Pinot Bianco (Collio Goriziano) Fr-VG. DOC w. dr. ✶✶ **77 78 79**
> Similar to the above.

Pinot Bianco (Grave del Friuli) Fr-VG. DOC w. dr. ✶✶
> Same again.

Pinot Grigio

Tasty, low-acid white grape popular in n.e.

Pinot Grigio (Collio Goriziano) Fr-VG. DOC w. dr. ** 76 77 78 79

Fruity, soft, agreeable dry white. The best age well.

Pinot Grigio (Grave del Friuli) Fr-VG. DOC w. dr. ** 76 77 78 79

Hardly distinguishable from the above.

Pinot Grigio (Oltrepo' Pavese) Lomb. DOC w. dr. (sp.) ** 74 75 77 78 79

Lombardy's P.G. is considered best.

Pinot Nero Trentino Tr-AAd. DOC r. dr. ** 75 76 77 78 79

Pinot Nero (Noir) gives lively burgundy-scented light wine in much of n.e. Italy, incl. Trentino.

Pio Cesare

A producer of quality red wines of PIEMONTE, incl. outstanding BAROLO.

Poggio al Sole

Up-and-coming CHIANTI CLASSICO estate.

Pomino

Fine Tuscan white, partly Chardonnay, from FRESCOBALDI.

Primitivo di Apulia Apu. r. dr. **

One of the best southern reds. Fruity when young, soft and full-flavoured with age. (See also Manduria.)

Prosecco di Conegliano Ven. DOC w. dr. or s/sw. (sp.) ***

Popular sparkling wine of the n.e. Slight fruity bouquet, the dry pleasantly bitter, the sw. fruity; the best are known as Superiore di Cartizze. Best producer: Carpene-Malvolti.

Raboso del Piave Ven. r. dr. ** 71 73 74 75 76 78 79

Powerful but sharp country red; needs age.

Ramandolo

See Verduzzo Colli Orientali del Friuli.

Ravello Camp. r. p. w. dr. **

Among the best wines of Campania: full dry red, fresh clean white. Caruso is the best-known brand.

Recioto

Wine made of half-dried grapes. Speciality of Veneto.

The 1980 vintage was generally disappointing throughout Italy. A late spring and a cold October meant a late harvest with poor ripeness. The north suffered most; Tuscany and Umbria made some good wine. The overall quantity was high.

Recioto di Gambellara Ven. DOC w. s/sw. sp. *

Sweetish golden wine, often half-sparkling.

Recioto di Soave Ven. DOC w. s/sw. (sp.) **

Soave made from selected half-dried grapes; sweet, fruity, fresh, slightly almondy: high alcohol.

Recioto della Valpolicella Ven. DOC r.s/sw. sp. ** 74 77 78 79

Strong rather sweet red, sometimes sparkling.

Recioto Amarone della Valpolicella Ven. DOC r. dr. **** 64 66 68 70 74 77 78 79

Dry version of the above; strong concentrated flavour, rather bitter. Impressive and expensive.

Refosco (Colli Orientali del Friuli) Fr-VG. DOC r. dr. ** 75 77 78

Full-bodied dry red; Riserva after 2 yrs. Refosco is said to be the same grape as the MONDEUSE of Savoie (France).

Refosco (Grave del Friuli) Fr-VG. DOC r. dr. **

Similar to above but slightly lighter.

Regaleali Sic. w. r. p. *

Among the better Sicilian table wines, produced between Caltanissetta and Palermo.

Ribolla (Colli Orientali del Friuli) Fr-VG. DOC w. dr. ★ D.Y.A.
> Clean and fruity n.e. white.

Ricasoli
> Famous Tuscan family, "inventors" of CHIANTI, whose Chianti is named after their BROLIO estate and castle.

Riecine Tusc. **75 77** 78
> First-class CHIANTI CLASSICO estate at Gaiole started by an Englishman. First wine 1975.

Riesling
> Normally refers to Italian (R. Italico). German Riesling, uncommon, is R. Renano.

Riesling Italico (Collio Goriziano) Fr-VG. DOC w. dr. ★★ 77 78 79
> Pleasantly fruity, fairly full-bodied n.e. white.

Riesling (Oltrepo' Pavese) Lomb. DOC w. dr. (sp.) ★★
> The Lombardy version, quite light and fresh. Occasionally sparkling. Keeps well.

Riesling (Trentino) Tr-AAd. DOC w. dr. ★★ D.Y.A.
> Delicate, slightly acid, very fruity.

Riserva
> Wine aged for a statutory period in barrels.

Riunite
> Cantine Sociali, a Co-operative cellar near Reggio Emilia producing large quantities of LAMBRUSCO.

Rivera
> Important and reliable wine-makers at Andria, near Bari, with good red and CASTEL DEL MONTE rosé.

Riviera Rosso Stravecchio Apu. r. dr. ★★ 67 70 73 74 75 76 78 79
> Good dry full-bodied red from Castel del Monte. Ages well.

Riviera del Garda Chiaretto Ven. DOC p. dr. ★★ D.Y.A.
> Charming cherry-pink, fresh and slightly bitter, from s.w. Garda esp. round Moniga del Garda.

Riviera del Garda Rosso Ven. DOC r. dr. ★★ 75 76 77 78 79
> Red version of the above; ages surprisingly well.

Rosato
> Rosé.

Rosato del Salento Apu. DOC p. dr. ★ D.Y.A.
> Strong but refreshing southern rosé from round Brindisi.

Rossese di Dolceacqua Lig. DOC r. dr. ★★ 75 76 78 79
> Well-known fragrant light red of the Riviera with typical touch of bitterness. Superiore is stronger.

Rosso
> Red.

Rosso delle Colline Lucchesi Tusc. DOC r. dr. ★★ 77 78 79
> Produced round Lucca but not greatly different from CHIANTI.

Rosso Conero Mar. DOC r. dr. ★★ 77 78 79
> Substantial CHIANTI-style wine from the Adriatic coast.

Rosso Piceno Mar. DOC r. dr. ★ 77 78 79
> Unremarkable Adriatic red.

Rubesco
> See Torgiano

Rubino di Cantavenna Piem. DOC r. dr. ★★
> Lively red, principally BARBERA, from a well-known co-operative s.e. of Turin.

Rufina
> A sub-region of CHIANTI in the hills e. of Florence.

Ruffino
> Well-known CHIANTI merchants.

Runchet (Valtellina) Lomb. DOC r. dr. ★★
> Small production, soft bouquet, slightly tannic, drink relatively young.

Sangiovese
> Principal red grape of CHIANTI, used alone for:

Sangiovese d'Aprilia Lat. DOC p. dr. ★ **77 78 79**
Strong dry rosé from s. of Rome.

Sangiovese di Romagna Em-Ro. DOC r. dr. ★★ **75 78 79**
Pleasant standard red; gains character with a little age.

Sangue di Giuda (Oltrepo' Pavese) Lomb. DOC r. dr. ★★
"Judas' blood". Strong rather tannic red of w. Lombardy.

San Severo Apu. DOC r. p. w. dr. ★ **75 77 78** 79
Sound neutral southern wine; not particularly strong.

Santa Maddalena Tr-AAd. DOC r. dr. ⟦★★⟧ **73 75 78** 79
Perhaps the best Tyrolean red. Round and warm, slightly almondy. From Bolzano.

Sassella
A CHIANTI CLASSICO estate of Melini producing an excellent single-vineyard wine.

Sassella (Valtellina) Lomb. DOC r. dr. ★★★ **71 73 75** 78 79
Considerable NEBBIOLO wine, tough when young. Known since Roman times, mentioned by Leonardo da Vinci.

Sassicaia Tusc. r. dr. ⟦★★★★⟧ **75** 76 78
Perhaps Italy's best red wine, produced from CABERNET grapes in the Tenuta San Guido of the Incisa family, at Bolgheri near Livorno since 1968 and cellared by ANTINORI. Tiny production.

Sauvignon
The Sauvignon Blanc: excellent white grape used in n.e.

Sauvignon (Colli Berici) Ven. DOC w. dr. ★★ D.Y.A.
Delicate, slightly aromatic, fresh white from near Vicenza.

Sauvignon (Colli Orientali del Friuli) Fr-VG. DOC w. dr. ★★ **75 77 78 79**
Full, smooth, freshly aromatic n.e. white.

Sauvignon (Collio Goriziano) Fr-VG. DOC w. dr. ★★ **77 78 79**
Very similar to the last; slightly higher alcohol.

Savuto Cal. DOC r. p. dr. ★★
The ancient Savuto produced in the Pr. of Cosenza and Catanzaro. Big juicy wine.

A new top category, DOCG, Denominazione Controllata e Garantita, is gradually being added to the Italian wine classification. It is awarded only to certain wines from top-quality zones which have been bottled and sealed with a government seal by the producer. The first four areas to be "guaranteed" are Barolo, Barbaresco, Brunello di Montalcino and Vino Nobile di Montepulciano. Albana di Romagna has apparently applied to be the first white. But it should be remembered that several of Italy's best wines are not covered by the DOC system. Examples are Sassicaia, Tignanello, Venegazzú, Bricco Manzoni.

Schiava
Good red grape of Trentino-Alto Adige with characteristic bitter after-taste.

Sciacchetra
See Cinque Terre

Secco Dry.

Sella & Mosca
Major Sardinian growers and merchants at Alghero.

Settesoli
Sicilian growers' co-operative with range of adequate table wines.

Sforzato (Valtellina) Lomb. DOC r. dr. ★★★ **67 68 70 71 75** 78 79
Valtellina equivalent of RECIOTO AMARONE made with partly dried grapes. Velvety, strong, ages remarkably well. Also called Sfursat.

Sfursat
>See Sforzato.

Sizzano Piem. DOC r. dr. ** 71 74 75 76 78 79
>Attractive full-bodied red produced at Sizzano in the Pr. of Novara, mostly from NEBBIOLO.

Soave Ven. DOC w. dr. *** D.Y.A.
>Famous, if not very characterful, Veronese white. Fresh with attractive texture. Classico is more restricted and better.

Solopaca Camp. DOC r. w. dr. *
>Comes from nr. Benevento, rather sharp when young, the white soft and fruity.

Sorni Tr-AAd. r. w. dr. ** 78 79
>Made in the Pr. of Trento. Light, fresh and soft. Drink young.

Spanna
>See Gattinara.

Spumante
>Sparkling.

Squinzano Apu. r. p. dr. *
>Strong southern red from Lecce.

Stravecchio
>Very old.

Sylvaner
>German white grape successful in ALTO ADIGE and elsewhere.

Sylvaner (Alto Adige) Tr-AAd. DOC w. dr. ** 77 78 79
>Pleasant grapy well-balanced white.

Sylvaner (Terlano) Tr-AAd. DOC w. dr. [**] 78 79
>Attractive lively and delicate wines.

Sylvaner (Valle Isarco) Tr-AAd. DOC w. dr. **
>Similar to the last.

Taurasi Camp. DOC r. dr. [**] 71 73 75 77 78 79
>The best Campanian red, from Avellino. Bouquet of cherries. Harsh when young, improves with age. Riserva after 4 yrs.

Terlano Tr-AAd. DOC w. dr. [**] 77 78 79
>A DOC applicable to 6 white wines from the Pr. of Bolzano, named after their grapes. Terlaner in German.

Termeno Tr-AAd. r. w. dr. **
>Village nr. Bolzano. Tramin in German, reputedly the origin of the TRAMINER. Its red is light and slightly bitter.

Teroldego Rotaliano Tr-AAd. DOC r. dr. ** 75 76 77 78 79
>The attractive local red of Trento. Blackberry-scented, slight bitter after-taste, ages moderately.

Tignanello Tusc. r. dr. [***] 71 75 77 78
>One of the new style of Bordeaux-inspired Tuscan reds, made by ANTINORI. Small production.

Tocai
>North-east Italian white grape; no relation of Hungarian but possibly related to Alsace Tokay.

Tocai di Lison Ven. DOC w. dr. ** 76 77
>From Treviso, delicate smoky/fruity scent, fruity taste. Classico is better.

Tocai (Colli Berici) Ven. DOC w. dr. *
>Less character than the last.

Tocai (Grave del Friuli) Fr-VG. DOC w. dr. **
>Similar to TOCAI DI LISON, generally rather milder.

Tocai di S. Martino della Battaglia Lomb. DOC w. dr. ** D.Y.A.
>Small production s. of La. Garda. Light, slightly bitter.

Torbato Sard. w. dr. (pa.) **
>Good n. Sardinian table wine, also PASSITO of high quality.

Torgiano, Rubesco di Umb. DOC r. w. dr. [***] 70 71 73 75 77 78
>Excellent red from near Perugia comparable with CHIANTI CLASSICO. Small production. White Torre di Giano also good, but not as outstanding as the red.

Torricella

Remarkable aged dry white from BROLIO.

Traminer Aromatico (Trentino) Tr-AAd. DOC w. dr. ★★ D.Y.A.

Delicate, aromatic, rather soft Traminer.

Trebbiano

The principal white grape of Tuscany and most of central Italy. Ugni Blanc in French.

Trebbiano d'Abruzzo Abr&M. DOC w. dr. ★ D.Y.A.

Gentle, rather neutral, slightly tannic. From round Pescara.

Trebbiano d'Aprilia Lat. DOC w. dr. ★ D.Y.A.

Heady, mild-flavoured, rather yellow. From s. of Rome.

Trebbiano di Romagna Em-Ro. DOC w. dr. or s/sw. (sp.) ★ D.Y.A.

Clean, pleasant white from near Bologna.

Trentino Tr-AAd. DOC r. w. dr. or sw. ★→★★

DOC applicable to 10 wines named after their grapes.

Uzzano, Castello di

Fine old estate at Greve. First-class CHIANTI CLASSICO.

Valcalepio Lomb. DOC r. w. dr. ★ 74 77 78 79

From nr. Bergamo. Pleasant red; lightly scented, fresh white.

Valdadige Tr-AAd. DOC r. w. dr. or s/sw. ★

Name for the ordinary table wines of the Adige valley—in German Etschtal.

Valgella (Valtellina) Lomb. DOC r. dr. ★★ 73 74 75 76 78 79

One of the VALTELLINA NEBBIOLOS: good dry red growing nutty with age. Riserva at 4 yrs.

Valle Isarco Tr-AAd. DOC w. dr. ★→★★

A DOC applicable to 5 varietal wines made n.e. of Bolzano.

Italian bottle shapes

1 Orvieto 2 Chianti 3 Verdicchio 4 Barolo

Valpolicella Ven. DOC r. dr. ★★★ 78 79

Attractive light red from nr. Verona; most attractive when young. Delicate nutty scent, slightly bitter taste. Classico more restricted; Superiore has 12% alcohol and 1 yr. of age.

Valtellina Lomb. DOC r. dr. ★★→★★★

A DOC applicable to wines made principally from Chiavennasca (NEBBIOLO) grapes in the Pr. of Sondrio, n. Lombardy. V. Superiore is better.

Velletri Lat. DOC r. w. dr. or s/sw. ★★

Agreeable Roman dry red and smooth white. Drink young.

Vendemmia

Vintage.

Venegazzù Fr-VG. r. dr. ★★★ 72 74 78

Remarkable rustic Bordeaux-style red produced from CABERNET grapes nr. Treviso. Rich bouquet, soft, warm taste, 13.5% alcohol, ages well.

Verdicchio dei Castelli di Jesi Mar. DOC w. dr. (sp.) ★★★ D.Y.A.

Ancient, famous and very pleasant fresh pale white from nr. Ancona. Goes back to the Etruscans. Classico is more restricted. Comes in amphora-shaped bottles.

Verdicchio di Matelica Mar. DOC w. dr. (sp.) ★★

Similar to the last, though less well known.

Verdiso

Native white grape of n.e., used for PROSECCO.

Verduzzo (Colli Orientali del Friuli) Fr-VG. DOC w. dr. s/sw or sw. ★★

Full-bodied white from a native grape. The sweet is called Ramandolo.

Verduzzo (Del Piave) Ven. DOC w. dr. ★★

Similar to the last but dry.

Vermentino Lig. w. dr. ★★ D.Y.A.

The best dry white of the Riviera: good clean seafood wine made at Pietra Ligure and San Remo.

Vermentino di Gallura Sard. DOC w. dr. ★★

Soft, dry, rather strong white from n. Sardinia.

Vernaccia di Oristano Sard. DOC w. dr. (f.) ★★★ 74 75 76 77 78

Sardinian speciality, like light sherry, a touch bitter, full bodied and interesting. Superiore with 15.5% alcohol and 3 yrs. of age.

Vernaccia di San Gimignano Tosc. DOC w. dr. (f.) ★★ 78 79

Distinctive strong high-flavoured wine from nr. Siena Michelangelo's favourite.

Vernaccia di Serrapetrona Mar. DOC r. dr. s/sw. sw. sp. ★★

Comes from the Pr. of Macerata; aromatic bouquet pleasantly bitter after-taste.

Vicchiomaggio

Important CHIANTI CLASSICO estate near Greve.

Vignamaggio

Historic and beautiful CHIANTI CLASSICO estate near Greve.

Villa Ronche

Reputable producer of GRAVE DEL FRIULI, esp. for CABERNET MERLOT, REFOSCO.

Villa Terciona

Important CHIANTI CLASSICO estate controlled by ANTINORI.

Vino da arrosto

"Wine for roast meat", i.e. good dry red.

Vino da pasto

Table wine: i.e. nothing special.

Vino Nobile di Montepulciano Tusc. DOCG r. dr. ★★★ 67 70 73 7 78 79

Impressive traditional Tuscan red with bouquet and styl Aged for 3 yrs. Riserva; for 4 yrs. Riserva Speciale. Be estate: Boscarelli.

Vinòt

Italy's first "new wine", inspired by Beaujolais Nouveau From GAJA.

V.I.D.E.

An association of better-class producers for marketing the wines.

Vinsanto

Term for certain strong sweet wines esp. in Tuscany: usual PASSITI.

Vinsanto di Gambellara Ven. DOC w. sw. ★★

Powerful, velvety, golden: made near Vicenza and Verona.

Vinsanto Toscano Tusc. w. s/sw. ★★

Made in the Pr. of Siena. Aromatic bouquet, rich and smooth Aged in very small barrels known as Carratelli.

VQPRD

Often found on the labels of DOC wines to signify "Vini Qualita Prodotti in Regioni Delimitate", or quality wir from restricted areas in accordance with E.E.C. regulation

Zagarolo Lat. DOC w. dr. or s/sw. ★★

Neighbour of FRASCATI, similar wine.

Spain & Portugal

Abbreviations of regional names shown in bold type are used in the text.

The following additional abbreviations are used in the Spanish section (see p. 104):

R'a.A. Rioja Alta
R'a.Al. Rioja Alavesa
Res. Reserva
g. see Vino generoso

The very finest wines of Spain and Portugal are respectively sherry and port and madeira, which have a section to themselves on pages 122 to 127.

Spain's table wines divide naturally into those from the Mediterranean climate of the centre, south and east and those from the Atlantic climate of the north and west. The former are strong and with rare exceptions dull. The latter include the very good wines of Rioja, certainly, with the Penedès in Catalonia, the most important quality table-wine region of the peninsula.

Rainy north-west Spain and northern Portugal make their very similar "green" wines. Central Portugal has an excellent climate for wines like full-bodied Bordeaux.

The old and outdated Portuguese system of controlled appellation is being progressively overhauled; it includes areas of dwindling interest and excludes several good new areas. The Spanish system dates from the post-war era and, although much amended in recent years, is for the moment over-optimistic, delimiting some areas of purely domestic interest.

The listing here includes the best and most interesting types and regions of each country, whether legally delimited or not. Geographical references (see map) are to the traditional division of Spain into the old kingdoms, and the major provinces of Portugal.

Spain

Alavesas, Bodegas R'a. Al. r. (w. dr.) res. ∗∗→∗∗∗ 68 70 73
> The pale orange-red Solar de Samaniego is one of the most delicate of the soft, fast-maturing Alavesa wines.

Albariño del Palacio Gal. w. dr. ∗∗
> Flowery "green wine" from FEFIÑANES near Cambados, made with the Albariño grape, the best of the region.

Alella Cat. r. (p.) w. dr. or sw. ∗∗
> Small demarcated region just n. of Barcelona. Makes pleasantly fresh and fruity wines in limited amounts. (See Marfil.)

Alicante Lev. r. (w.) ∗
> Demarcated region. Its wines tend to be "earthy", high in alcohol and heavy.

Almansa Lev. r. ∗
> Demarcated region w. of ALICANTE, producing heavy wines high in alcohol.

Aloque N. Cas. r. ∗
> A light (though not in alcohol) variety of VALDEPEÑAS, made by fermenting together red and white grapes.

Almendralejo Ext. r. w. ∗
> Commercial wine centre of the Extremadura. Much of its produce is distilled to make the spirit for fortifying sherry.

Ampurdán
> See Perelada.

Año
> 4° Año (or Años) means 4 years old when bottled.

Banda Azul R'a. a. r. ∗∗ 75
> Big-selling wine from Bodegas Paternina, S.A., much improved over recent years.

Benicarló Lev. r. ∗
> Town on the Mediterranean. Its strong red wines were formerly used for adding colour and body to Bordeaux.

Berberana, Bodegas R'a.A. r. (w. dr.) res. ∗→∗∗∗ 66 70 72 74 75
> Best are the fruity, full-bodied reds: the 3° año Carta de Plata, the 5° año Carta de Oro and the smooth velvety reservas.

Bilbainas, Bodegas R'a.A. r. (p.) w. dr. sw. or sp. res. ∗∗ →∗∗∗ 66 69 70 72 73
> Large bodega in HARO, making a wide range of reliable wines including Viña Pomal, Viña Zaco, Vendimia Especial Reserves and "Royal Carlton" by the champagne method.

Blanco
> White.

Bodega
> 1. a wineshop; 2. a concern occupied in the making, blending and/or shipping of wine.

Campanas, Las Nav. r. (w.) ∗∗
> Small wine area near Pamplona. Clarete Campanas is a sturdy red. Mature 5° año Castillo de Tiebas is like a heavy RIOJA Reserva.

Campo Viejo, Bodegas R'a.A. r. (w. dr.) res. ∗ →∗∗∗ 64 66 70 71 78
> Branch of Savin s.a., one of Spain's largest wine companies. Makes the popular 2° año San Asensio and some big, fruity red reservas.

Cañamero Ext. w. ∗
> Remote village near Guadalupe whose wines grow FLOR and acquire a sherry-like taste. ∗∗

Caralt, Cavas Conde de Cat. sp. ∗∗
> Sparkling wines from SAN SADURNÍ DE NOYA, made by the champagne method.

Cariñena Ara. r. (p.w.) ∗
> Demarcated region and large-scale supplier of strong wine for everyday drinking.

Casar de Valdaigo O.Cas. r. w. dr. ★★

Best is the light, bone-dry clarete from the famous district of El Bierzo n. of León.

Castillo Ygay

See Marqués de Murrieta.

Cava

1. an establishment making sparkling wines by the champagne method; 2. a Spanish name for such wines.

Cenicero

Wine township in the RIOJA ALTA.

Cepa

Wine or grape variety.

Chacolí Gui. (r.) w. ★

Alarmingly sharp "GREEN WINE" from the Basque coast, containing only 8% to 9% alcohol.

Champaña

"Champagne": i.e. Spanish sparkling wine.

Cheste Lev. r. w. ★

Demarcated region inland of VALENCIA. Blackstrap wines with 13% to 15% alcohol.

Clarete

Light red wine (occasionally dark rosé).

Codorníu, S.A. Cat. sp. ★★★

Largest and best known of the firms in SAN SADURNI DE NOYA making good wines by the champagne method. Ask for the extra dry Non Plus Ultra, and better still the vintage version.

Compañía Vinicola del Norte de España (C.V.N.E.) R'a.A r. (p.) w. dr. or sw. res. ★★→★★★ 66 70 73 74 75 78

The 3° año is among the best of young red Riojas and Monopol one of the best dry whites. Excellent red Imperial and Viña Real reservas.

Consejo Regulador

Official organization for the defence, control and promotion of a DENOMINACIÓN DE ORIGEN.

Cosecha

Crop or vintage.

Criado y embotellado por . . .

Grown and bottled by . . .

Crianza

The "nursery" where the wine is brought up. New or unaged wine in "sin crianza".

Cumbrero

See Montecillo, Bodegas.

Domecq Domain R'a.A. r. ★★ 73 74

A reliable red Rioja made by Pedro Domecq in their new bodega near Laguardia.

Denominación de origen

Officially regulated wine region. (See introduction p. 111.)

Dulce Sweet.

Elaborado y añejado por . . .

Made and aged by . . .

Elciego

Village in the Rioja Alavesa surrounded by vineyards.

Espumoso

Sparkling.

Faustino Martínez, S.A. R'a.Al. r. w. dr. (p.) res. ★★ →★★★

Good red wines and the dry, light, fruity new-style white Faustino V.

Fefiñanes Palacio Gal. w. res. ★★★

Best of all the ALBARIÑO wines, though hardly "green", since it is aged for 2–6 years.

Ferrer, José L. Mallorca r. res. ✶

His wines, made in Binisalem, are the only ones of any distinction from Mallorca.

Flor

A wine yeast peculiar to sherry and certain other wines that oxidize slowly and tastily under its influence.

Franco-Españolas, Bodegas R'a.A. r. w. dr. or sw. res. ✶→✶✶ **64 7:**

Reliable wines from LOGROÑO. Bordon is a fruity red. The sweet white Diamante is a favourite in Spain.

Freixenet, S.A., Cavas Cat. sp. ✶✶→✶✶✶

Cava, next in size to CODORNIU, making a range of good sparkling wines by the champagne method.

Fuenmayor

Wine township in the RIOJA ALTA.

Gaseoso

A cheap sparkler made by pumping carbon dioxide into wine.

Gonzalez y Dubosc, S.A., Cavas Cat. sp. ✶✶→ ✶✶✶

Its pleasant sparkling wines, sold in the UK as JEAN PERICO are made in the cavas of Vinda Seguras.

Gran Vas

Pressurized tanks (*cuves closes*) for making inexpensive sparkling wines; also used to describe this type of wine.

Green Wines

See under Portugal, p. 119.

Haro

The wine centre of the RIOJA ALTA.

Huelva And. r. w. br. ✶→✶✶

Demarcated region w. of Cadiz. The best of its wine is not or sale, since it goes to JEREZ for blending.

Jean Perico

See Gonzalez y Dubosc

Jerez de la Frontera

The city of sherry. (See p. 122.)

Jumilla Lev. r. ✶ (w. dr. p.) ✶

Demarcated region in the mountains north of MURCIA. It full-bodied wines approaching 18% of alcohol are now being lightened by selection of the grapes and improved methods o fermentation.

La Bastida, Cooperativa Vinícola de R'a.Al. r. res ✶✶→ ✶✶✶ 66 70 75 78

Very drinkable Manuel Quintano and fruity, well-balanced Montebuena, Gastrijo and Castillo Labastida reservas and gran reservas.

Laguardia

Picturesque walled town at the centre of the wine-growing district of LA RIOJA ALAVESA.

Lan, Bodegas R'a.A. r. (p.w.) ✶✶→✶✶✶ **70 73 75**

A huge new bodega, lavishly equipped and making red Rioja of quality.

La Rioja Alta, Bodegas R'a.A. r. (p.) w. dr. (or sw.) res. ✶✶→✶✶✶ 6 68 70 73 76 78

Excellent wines, esp. the red 3° año Viña Alberdi, the velvet 5° año Ardanza, the lighter 6° año Arana, the fruity Reserva 904 and dry white Metropol Extra.

León O.Cas. r. p. w. ✶→✶✶

Northern region becoming better known. Its wines, particu larly those from the unfortunately named V.I.L.E. (e.g. Re León, the young Coyanza and Don Suero reserva), are light dry and refreshing.

Logroño

Principal town of the RIOJA region.

López de Heredia, S.A.   R'a.A. r. (p.) w. dr. or sw. res. ★★→ ★★★
68 70 73 76 78

> Old established bodega in HARO with typical and good dry red Viña Tondonia of 6° año or more. Its wines are exceptionally long-lasting, and the Tondonia whites are also impressive, like old-fashioned Graves.

Malaga   And. br. sw. ★★→★★★

> Demarcated region around the city of Malaga. At their best, its dessert wines yield nothing to tawny port.

Mallorca

> No wine of interest except from José FERRER.

Mancha/Manchuela   N.Cas. r. w. ★

> Large demarcated region n. and n.e. of VALDEPEÑAS, but wines without the light and fresh flavour of the latter.

Marqués de Caceres, Bodegas   R'a.A. r. w. dr. ★★→★★★ 70 71
73 78

> Good red Riojas of various ages made by French methods and also a surprisingly light and fragrant white.

Marqués de Monistrol, Bodegas   Cat. w. r. (dr. or sw.) sp. res.
★★→★★★

> A family firm, just taken over by Martini and Rossi. Refreshing whites, esp. the Vin Nature, a good red and an odd sweet red wine.

Marqués de Murrieta, S.A.   R'a.A. r. w. dr. res. ★★→ ★★★ 64 68
70 74 78

> Highly reputed bodega near LOGROÑO. Makes 4° año Etiqueta Blanca, superb red Castillo Ygay and a dry fruity white.

Marqués de Riscal, S.A.   R'a.Al. r. (p. and w. dr.) res. ★→★★★ 64 65
68 71 73 75 78

> The best-known bodega of the RIOJA ALAVESA. Its red wines are relatively light and dry. Recently disappointing.

RIOJA VINTAGES

Thanks to a more consistent climate and the blending of a proportion of wine from better vintages in poor years, Riojas do not vary to the same extent as the red wines from Bordeaux and Burgundy. The 71 and 77 vintages were a disaster, owing to high rainfall and the onset of rot and oidium. Of other recent years, the best were: 52 55 58 64 66 68 70 73 76 and 78. (Those in bold type were outstanding.)

Riojas are put on the market when they are ready to drink. The best reservas of the best vintages, however, have very long lives and improve with more bottle age. Certain '64s, for example (even white wines) are still improving.

Mascaró, Cavas   Cat. sp. (w. dr. r.) ★★→ ★★★

> Maker of some of the best Spanish brandy, good sparkling wine and a refreshing dry white Viña Franca.

Masía Bach   Cat. r. p. w. dr. or sw. ★★ →★★★ 70 74 78

> Extrisimo Bach from SAN SADURNÍ DE NOYA, luscious and oaky, is one of the best sweet white wines of Spain.

Marfíl   Cat. r. (p.) w. ★★

> Brand name of Alella Vinicola (Bodegas Cooperativas), best known of the producers in ALELLA. Means "ivory".

Méntrida   N.Cas. r. w. ★

> Demarcated region w. of Madrid, supplying everyday wine to the capital.

Monopole

> See Compania Vinicola del Norte de España.

Montánchez   Ext. r. g. ★

> Village near Mérida, interesting because its red wines grow FLOR yeast like FINO sherry.

Montecillo, Bodegas R'a.A. r. w. (p.) ⟦ ★★ ⟧ 75 76 78

Rioja bodega owned by Osborne (see Sherry), best known for its red and dry white Cumbrero, most reasonably priced and currently among the best of the 3° año wines.

Montecristo, Bodegas

Well-known brand of MONTILLA-MORILES wines, owned by RUMASA.

Monterrey Gal. r. ★

Demarcated region near the n. border of Portugal, making wines like those of VERIN.

Montilla-Moriles And. g. ⟦ ★★★ ⟧

Demarcated region near Cordoba. Its crisp, sherry-like FINO and AMONTILLADO contain 14% to 17.5% natural alcohol and remain unfortified and singularly toothsome.

RIOJA'S CHARACTERISTIC STYLE

To the Spanish palate the taste of luxury in wine is essentially the taste of oak. Oak contains vanillin, the taste of vanilla. Hence the characteristic vanilla flavour of all mature Spanish table wines of high quality — exemplified by the reservas of Rioja (both red and white).

Historically the reason for long oak-ageing was to stabilize the best wines while their simple fruity flavours developed into something more complex and characteristically winy. Today fashion has turned against such treatment for white wines. We tend to prefer them grapy. But the marriage of ripe fruit and oak in red Rioja is still highly appreciated.

Muga, Bodegas R'a.A. r. (w.) res. (sp.) ⟦ ★★★ ⟧ 70 73

Small family firm in HARO, making some of the best red Rioja now available by strictly traditional methods in oak. Its wines are fruity, intensely aromatic, with long complex finish.

Navarra Nav. r. (w.) ★→★★

Demarcated region, rather better than ordinary sturdy wine for everyday drinking.

Olarra, Bodegas R'a.A. r. (w. p.) ★★→★★★ 70 73 75 76

A new and vast bodega near LOGROÑO, one of the show-pieces of the RIOJA, making good red and white wines and excellent Cerro Añon reservas.

Paternina, S.A., Bodegas R'a.A. r. (p.) w. dr. or sw. res. ★→★★★★ 28 59 67 71 73 76 78

Bodega at Ollauri and a household name. Its best wines are the red Viña Vial and the magnificent older reservas.

Pazo Gal. r. p. w. dr. ★

Brand name of the co-operative at RIBEIRO, making "GREEN WINES". The rasping red is the local favourite. The pleasant fizzy white is safer.

Peñafiel O.Cas. r. and w. dr. ★★

Village on the R. Duero near Valladolid. Best wines are fruity reds from the cooperativa de Ribero del Duero, including the 5° año Protos.

Penedès Cat. r. w. dr. sp. ★→★★★

Demarcated region including Vilafranca del Penedès, SAN SADURNÍ DE NOYA and SITGES. See also Torres.

Perelada Cat. (r. p.) w. sp. ★★

In the demarcated region of Ampurdan on the Costa Brava. Best known for sparkling wines made both by the champagne and tank or *cuve close* system.

Priorato Cat. br. dr. r. ★★

Demarcated region, an enclave in that of TARRAGONA, known for its alcoholic "rancio" wines and also for strong dark full-bodied reds, often used for blending. Lighter blended Priorato is a good carafe wine in Barcelona restaurants.

Protos

See Peñafiel

Raimat Cat. r. w. p. ★→★★

Sound but unexciting wines from old v'yds. near Lérida recently replanted by CODORNÍU.

Reserva

Good-quality wine matured for long periods in cask. Gran Reserva, in Rioja, must have 8 years in the barrel.

Ribeiro Gal. r. (p.) w. dr. ★→★★

Demarcated region on the n. border of Portugal—the heart of the "GREEN WINE" country.

Rioja O.Cas. r. p. w. sp. esp. **64 66 68 70 73 75** 76 78

This upland region along the R. Ebro in the n. of Spain produces most of the country's best table wines in some 50 BODEGAS DE EXPORTACIÓN. It is sub-divided into:

Rioja Alavesa

North of the R. Ebro, the R'a.Al. produces fine red wines, mostly the lighter CLARETES.

Rioja Alta

South of the R. Ebro and w. of LOGROÑO, the R'a.A. grows fine red and white wines and also makes some rosé.

Rioja Baja

Stretching e. from LOGROÑO, the Rioja Baja makes coarser red wines, high in alcohol and often used for blending.

Riojanas, Bodegas R'a.A. r. (w. p.) res. ★★→★★★ **34 42 56 64 66 68 70 73** 78

One of the older bodegas, making a good traditional Viña Albina. Monte Real reservas are big, mellow, above average.

Rioja Santiago, S.A. R'a.A. r. (w. dr. or sw. p.) res. ★→★★★ 78

Bodega at HARO with well-known wines. The flavour sometimes suffers from pasteurization, and appropriately, as it now belongs to Pepsi-Cola, it makes the biggest-selling bottled SANGRÍA. Top red: Gran Enológica.

Rosado

Rosé.

Rueda O.Cas. br. w. dr. ★→★★

Small area w. of Valladolid. Traditional producer of golden flor-growing sherry-like wines up to 17° of alcohol, now making fresh young whites such as that of the MARQUES DE RISCAL.

Rumasa

The great Spanish conglomerate, which has absorbed many bodegas, incl. Williams and Humbert, Garvey, Paternina, Franco-Españolas and, in England, Augustus Barnett.

Salceda, S.A., Bodegas Viña R'a.Al. r. res. ★★→★★★

Makes fruity, well-balanced red wines.

Sangre de Toro

Brand name for a rich-flavoured red wine from TORRES S.A.

Sangría

Cold red wine cup, best made fresh by adding ice, citrus fruit, fizzy lemonade and brandy to red wine.

Sanlúcar de Barrameda

Centre of the Manzanilla district. (See Sherry p. 122.)

San Sadurní de Noya Cat. sp. ★★→★★★

Town s. of Barcelona, hollow with cellars where dozens of firms produce sparkling wine by the champagne method. Standards are high, even if the ultimate finesse is lacking.

Sarría, Senorio de Nav. r. (p. w. dr.) res. `★★→★★★` 70 73 75 78
The model winery of H. Beaumont y Cia. near Pamplona produces wines up to RIOJA standards.

Scholtz, Hermanos, S.A. And. br. ★★→ `★★★`
Makers of the best MALAGA, including a good, dry 10-year-old amontillado. Best is the dessert Solera Scholtz 1885.

Seco Dry.

Siglo Popular sack-wrapped RIOJA brand of Bodegas Age. Medium quality.

Sitges Cat. w. sw. ★★
Coastal resort s. of Barcelona noted for sweet dessert wine made from Moscatel and Malvasia grapes.

Solar de Samaniego
See Alavesas, Bodegas

Tarragona Cat. r. w. dr. or sw. br. ★→★★★
1. Table wines from the demarcated region; of little note. 2. Dessert wines from firms such as de Muller, comparable with good cream sherries. 3. The town makes vermouth and Chartreuse and exports cheap blended wine.

Tierra del Vino O.Cas. w. ★→★★
Area w. of Valladolid including the wine villages of La Nava and RUEDA.

Tinto Red.

Toro O.Cas. r. ★→★★
Town, 150 m. n.w. of Madrid, and its powerful (to 16°) wine. Leading producer Bodegas Mateos. His 3 año is good.

Torres, Bodegas Cat. r. w. dr. or semi-sw. p. res. `★★→★★★★` 70 71 73 74 75 76 78
Distinguished family firm making the best wines of Penedés, esp. the flowery white Viña Sol and Gran Viña Sol, the semi-dry Esmeralda, the red Tres Torres and Gran Sangredetoro, the beautiful Gran Coronas reservas, and the red Santa Digna (alias Viña Magdala) from the Pinot Noir grape.

Utiel-Requeña Lev. r. (w.) p.
Demarcated region w. of Valencia. Apart from sturdy reds and chewy vino de doble pasta for blending, it makes some deliciously light and fragrant rosé.

Valbuena O.Cas. r. ★★★ p.
Made with the same grapes as VEGA SICILIA but sold as 3° año or 5° año.

Valdeorras Gal. r. w. dr. `★→★★`
Demarcated region e. of Orense. Dry and refreshing wines.

Valdepeñas N.Cas. r. (w.) ★→★★
Demarcated region near the border of Andalucia. The supplier of most of the carafe wine to Madrid. Its wines, though high in alcohol, are sometimes surprisingly light in flavour.

Valencia Lev. r. w. ★
Demarcated region producing earthy high-strength wine.

Vega Sicilia O.Cas. r. res. ★★★★ 41 48 53 59 61 64 66 67
One of the very best Spanish wines, full-bodied, fruity and almost impossible to find. Containing up to 16% alcohol. Valbuena is (excellent) second quality.

Vendimia
Vintage.

Verín Gal. r. ★
Town near n. border of Portugal. Its wines are the strongest from Galicia, without a bubble, and up to 14% alcohol.

Vicente, Suso y Pérez, S.A. Ara. r. ★★
A bodega s. of Sarragossa producing superior Cariñena.

Viña Vineyard. Several of the best Rioja reservas are named for their Viña, e.g. Tondonia and Bosconia (LOPEZ), Zaco (BILBAINAS), etc.

Viuda Seguras, Cavas Cat. sp. ★★→ ★★★
> Cava making excellent sparkling wines by the champagne method. Part of the RUMASA group.

Vino Blanco
> White wine.

Vino commun/corriente Ordinary wine.
> **clarete** Light red wine.
> **dulce** Sweet wine.
> **espumoso** Sparkling wine.
> **generoso** Apéritif or dessert wine rich in alcohol.
> **rancio** Maderized (brown) white wine.
> **rosado** Rosé wine.
> **seco** Dry wine.
> **tinto** Red wine.
> **verde** See Green wine under Portugal.

Yecla Lev. r. w. ★
> Demarcated region n. of Murcia. Its co-operative-made wines, once heavy-weight champions, have been lightened and improved for export.

Ygay See Marqués de Murrieta

Portugal

For Port and Madeira see pages 122 to 127.

Adega
> A cellar or winery.

Aguardente
> The Portuguese word for brandy, made by a multiplicity of firms. Safest to ask for Adega Velha from Aveleda or one from a port concern.

Alentejo Alen. r. ★→★★
> Vast and long-neglected area s. of the R. Tagus, now being developed as a wine region, chiefly for red wine.

Algarve Alg. r. w. ★
> Lagoa is the wine centre of the holiday area. It is nothing to write home about.

Aliança Caves r. w. dr. sp. res. ★★→★★★
> Large Oporto-based firm, making sparkling wine by the champagne method and a variety of reds and whites, including mature DÃOS.

Amarante
> Sub-region in the VINHOS VERDES area. Rather heavier and stronger wines than those from farther n.

Aveleda Douro w. dr. ★★
> A first-class "GREEN WINE" made on the Aveleda estate of the Guedes family, proprietors of SOGRAPE. Sold dry in Portugal but sweetened for export.

Bagaceira
> A potent spirit made like the Spanish *aguardiente*. One of the best is CEPA VELHA from MONÇÃO.

Bairrada Bei. Lit. r. and sp. ★→★★
> Newly demarcated region supplying much of Oporto's (often good) carafe wine. Also makes good-quality sparkling wines by the champagne method.

Barca Velha (Ferreirinha) Trás-os-M. r. res. ★★★★ 57 64 66
> One of Portugal's best wines, made in very limited quantity by the port firm of Ferreira. Fruity and fine with deep bouquet.

Barrocão, Cavas do Bei. Lit. r. w. dr. res. ★→ ★★★
> Based in the BAIRRADA, the firm blends good red DÃOS and makes first-rate old Bairrada garrafeiras, such as 60 and 64.

Basto

A sub-region of the VINHOS VERDES area on the R. Tamego, producing more astringent red wine than white.

Borba Alen. r. ★

Small enclave near Evora, making some of the best wine from the ALENTEJO.

Braga

Sub-region of the VINHOS VERDES area, good for both red and white.

Buçaco B'a.Al. r. (w.) res. ★★★ 40 45 47 51 53 59 62 63 70

The speciality of the luxury Buçaco hotel near Coimbra, not seen elsewhere.

Bucelas Est'a. w. dr. ★★★

Tiny demarcated region just n. of Lisbon. João Camilo Alves Lda. and Caves Velhas make delicate, perfumed wines with 11% to 12% alcohol.

Camarate Est'a. r. ★★

Reliable CLARETE from FONSECA at Azeitão, s. of Lisbon.

Carcavelos Est'a. br. sw. ★★★

Minute demarcated region w. of Lisbon. Its excellent sweet wines average 19% alcohol and are drunk cold as an apéritif or with dessert.

Cartaxo Rib. r. w. ★

Brand name of adequate carafe wine from the Ribatejo n. of Lisbon, popular in the capital.

Casal García Douro w. dr. ★★

One of the biggest-selling "GREEN WINES" in Portugal, made by SOGRAPE.

Casal Mendes M'o. w. dr. ★★

The "GREEN WINE" from Caves Aliança.

Casaleiro

Trade mark of Caves Dom Teodosio—João T. Barbosa, who make a variety of reliable wines: DÃO, VINHOS VERDES, etc.

Cepa Velha M'o. (r.) w. dr. ★★★

Brand name of Vinhos de Monção, Lda. Their Alvarinho, from the grape of that name, is one of the best "GREEN WINES".

Clarete

Light red wine.

Colares Est'a. r. ★★★

Small demarcated region on the coast w. of Lisbon. Its classical dark red wines, rich in tannin, are from vines which survived the phylloxera epidemic. Drink the oldest available.

Conde de Santar B'a.A. r. (w. dr.) res. ★★→★★★

The only estate-grown DAO, later matured and sold by Carvalho, Ribeiro & Ferreira. The reservas are fruity, full-bodied and exceptionally smooth.

Dão B'a.Al. r. w. res. ★★★ ★★★

Demarcated region round Viseu on the R. Mondego. Produces some of Portugal's best table wines: solid reds of some subtlety with age: substantial dry whites. All are sold under brand names. 1970 was the best year of the decade.

Douro

The n. river whose valley produces port and more than adequate (though undemarcated) table wines.

Evel Trás-os-M. r. ★→★★

Reliable middle-weight red made near VILA REAL by Real Companhia Vinícola do Norte de Portugal. Ages well in bottle.

Faisca Est'a. p. ★

Big-selling sweet carbonated rosé from J. M. da Fonseca.

Fonseca, J. M. da

See Camarate and Moscatel de Setúbal.

Gaeiras Est'a. r. ★★
>Dry, full-bodied and well-balanced red made in the neighbourhood of Óbidos.

Gatão M'o. w. dr. ★★
>Reliable "GREEN WINE" from the firm of Borges & Irmão, fragrant but somewhat sweetened.

Grão Vasco B'a.A. r. w. res. ★★→★★★
>One of the best brands of DÃO, blended and matured at Viseu by SOGRAPE. Fine red reservas; fresh young white (D.Y.A.).

Green Wine (Vinho verde)
>Wine made from barely ripe grapes and undergoing a special secondary fermentation, which leaves it with a slight sparkle. Ready for drinking in the spring after the harvest. It may be white or red.

Lagoa See Algarve.

Lagosta M'o. w. dr. ★★
>Well-known "GREEN WINE" from the Real Companhia Vinícola do Norte de Portugal.

Lancers Est'a. p. ★
>Sweet carbonated rosé extensively shipped to the USA by J. M. da Fonseca.

Lima Sub-region in the n. of the VINHOS VERDES area making mainly harsh red wines.

Madeira Island br. dr./sw. ★★→★★★★
>Producer of the famous apéritif and dessert wines. See pages 122 to 127.

Magrico M'o. w. dr. ★★
>At a time when many VINHOS VERDES are being slightly sweetened for export, this is a genuinely dry "GREEN WINE".

Mateus Rosé Trás-os-M. p. ★
>World's biggest-selling medium-sweet carbonated rosé, made by SOGRAPE at VILA REAL.

Monção
>Sub-region of the VINHOS VERDES area on R. Minho, producing the best of "GREEN WINES" from the ALVARINHO grape.

Moscatel de Setúbal Est'a. br. ★★★
>Small demarcated region s. of the R. Tagus, where J. M. da Fonseca make an aromatic dessert muscat, 6 and 25 years old.

Palacio de Brejoeira M'o. (r.) w. dr. ★★★
>Outstanding estate-made "GREEN WINE" from Monção, with astonishing fragrant nose and full, fruity flavour.

Penafiel
>Sub-region in the s. of the VINHOS VERDES area.

Periquita Est'a. r. ★★
>One of Portugal's more robust reds, made by J. M. da Fonseca at Azeitão s. of Lisbon from a grape of that name.

Pinhel B'a.Al. r. ★
>Undemarcated region e. of the DÃO, making similar wine.

Ponte de Lima, cooperativa de M'o. r. ★★
>Maker of one of the best bone dry *red* VINHOS VERDES.

Quinta de S. Claudio M'o. w. dr. ★★★
>Estate at Esposende and maker of the best "GREEN WINE" outside MONÇÃO.

Quinta do Corval Trás-os-M. r. ★★
>Estate near Pinhão making good light CLARETES.

Raposeira B'a.Al. sp. ★★
>One of the best-known Portuguese sparkling wines, made by the champagne method at Lamego. Ask for the *bruto* (extra dry).

Santola B'a. Al. w. dr. ★★
>A refreshing and completely dry "GREEN WINE" from Vinhos Messias.

Serradayres Est'a. r. (w.) res. `** → ***`
> Blended table wines from Carvalho, Ribeiro & Ferreira, Lda.
> Sound and very drinkable.

Setúbal
> See Moscatel.

Sogrape
> Sociedad Comercial dos Vinhos de Mesa de Portugal. Largest
> wine concern in the country, making VINHOS VERDES, DÃO,
> MATEUS ROSÉ, VILA REAL red, etc.

Terras Altas B'a.Al. r. w. res. **
> Good DÃO wines made by J. M. da Fonseca.

Vila Real Trás-os-M. r. * → `**`
> Town in the upper DOURO now making some good undemar-
> cated red table wine.

Vinho branco White wine.
> **consumo** Ordinary wine.
> **doce** Sweet wine.
> **espumante** Sparkling wine.
> **garrafeira** A reserve with long bottle age.
> **generoso** Apéritif or dessert wine rich in alcohol.
> **maduro** A normal, mature table wine—as opposed to a
> VINHO VERDE.
> **rosado** Rosé wine.
> **seco** Dry wine.
> **tinto** Red wine.
> **verde** See under Green Wines.

Vinhos Verdes M'o. and D'o. r. * w. dr. * → ***
> Demarcated region between R. Douro and n. frontier with
> Spain, producing "GREEN WINES".

Sherry, Port & Madeira

The original, classical sherries of Spain, ports of Portugal
and madeiras of Madeira are listed in the A–Z below. Their
many imitators in South Africa, California, Australia,
Cyprus, Argentina are not. References to them will be
found under their respective countries.

The map on page 111 locates the port and sherry districts.
Madeira is an island 400 miles out in the Atlantic from the
coast of Morocco, a port of call for west-bound ships: hence its
traditional market in North America.

In this section most of the entries are shippers' names
followed by a brief account of their wines. The names of
wine-types are included in the alphabetical listing.

Amontillado
> In general use means medium sherry; technically means a
> wine which has been aged to become more powerful and
> pungent. A FINO can be amontillado.

Amoroso
> Type of sw. sherry, not much different from a sweet OLOROSO.

Barbeito
> Shippers of good-quality Madeira, including the driest and
> best apéritif Madeira, "Island Dry".

Bertola
> Sherry shippers, owned by the giant Rumasa group, best
> known for their Bertola Cream Sherry.

Blandy
> Old family firm of Madeira shippers at Funchal. Duke of
> Clarence Malmsey is their most famous wine.

Vazquez

Sherry bodega at JEREZ with outstanding FINO, "Carta Blanca", and "Carta Oro" amontillado "al natural" (unsweetened).

Brown sherry

British term for a style of dark sweet sherry, not normally of the best quality.

Bual

One of the grapes of Madeira, making a soft smoky sweet wine, not as sweet as Malmsey.

Caballero

Sherry shippers best known for Gran Señor Choice Old Cream. Their best FINO is Don Guisa.

Cockburn

British-owned port shippers with a range of good wines. Fine vintage port from very high v'yds. can look deceptively light when young, but has great lasting power. Vintages: **55 60** 63 67 70 75.

Cossart Gordon

Leading firm of Madeira shippers founded 1745, best known for their "Good Company" range of wines but also producing old vintages and soleras.

Cream sherry

A style of fairly pale sweet sherry made by sweetening a blend of well-aged OLOROSOS.

Crofts

One of the oldest firms shipping vintage port: 300 years old in 1978. Bought early this century by Gilbey's. Well-balanced vintage wines last as long as any. Vintages: **55 60** 63 66 70 75 77, and lighter vintage wines under the name of their Quinta da Roeda in several other years. Also now in the sherry business with Croft Original (pale cream), Delicado (fino).

Crusted

Term for a vintage-style port, but blended from several vintages not one, bottled young and aged in bottle, so forming a "crust" in the bottle. Needs decanting.

Cuvillo

Sherry bodega at Puerto de Santa Maria best known for their Cream, dry Oloroso Sangre y Trabajadero and Fino "C" and a fine Palo Cortado.

Delaforce

Port shippers particularly well known in Germany. "His Eminence" is an excellent tawny. "Vintage character" is also good. Vintage wines are very fine, among the lighter kind: **55 58 60** 63 **66** 70 75 77.

Domecq

Giant family-owned sherry bodegas at JEREZ. Double Century Original Oloroso is their biggest brand, La Ina their excellent FINO, Guitar a new pale cream. Other famous wines incl. Celebration Cream, Botaina (old amontillado) and Rio Viejo (dry oloroso). Now also in Rioja (p. 117).

Dow

Old name used on the British market by the port shippers Silva & Cosens, well known for their relatively dry vintage wines, said to have a faint "cedarwood" character. Vintages: **55 57 58 60** 63 66 70 75 77.

Dry Sack

See Williams & Humbert.

Duff Gordon

Sherry shippers best known for their El Cid AMONTILLADO. Owned by the big Spanish firm Bodegas Osborne.

Duke of Wellington

Luxury range of sherries from Bodegas Internacionales, owned by RUMASA.

Eira Velha, Quinta da

Small port estate with old-style vintage wines shipped b HARVEY's of Bristol. Vintages: 72 78.

Ferreira

Portuguese-owned port growers and shippers (since 1751 well-known for old tawnies and good, relatively light, vir tages: **60 63 66** 70 75 77. Also Special Reserve (vintag character) Donna Antonia.

Findlater's

Old established London wine merchant shipping his own ver successful brand of medium sherry: Dry Fly amontillado.

Fino Term for the lightest and finest of sherries, completely dry very pale and with great delicacy. Fino should always b drunk cool and fresh: it deteriorates rapidly once opened. TI PEPE is the classic example.

Flor The characteristic natural yeast which gives FINO sherry it unique flavour.

Fonseca

British-owned port shipper of high reputation. Vintag character "Bin 27" makes robust, deeply coloured vintag wine, sometimes said to have a slight "burnt" flavour. Vir tages: **55 60** 63 **66** 70 75 77.

Garvey's

Famous old sherry shippers at JEREZ owned by RUMASA. Thei finest wines are Fino San Patricio, Tio Guillermo Dry Amon tillado and Ochavico Dry Oloroso. San Angelo Mediur Amontillado is their most popular. Also Bicentenary Pal Cream.

Gonzalez Byass

Enormous concern shipping the world's most famous and on of the best sherries: Tio Pepe. Other brands incl. La Conch. Medium Amontillado, Elegante Dry Fino, San Domingo Pal Cream, Romano Cream.

Graham

Port shippers famous for one of the richest and sweetest o vintage ports, largely from their own Quinta Malvedos, als excellent brands, incl. Ruby, Late Bottled 10- and 20-year-ol Tawny. Vintages: **55 58 60 63** 66 70 75 77.

Harvey's

World-famous Bristol shippers of Bristol Cream and Bristo Milk sweet sherries, Club Amontillado and Bristol Dry which are medium. Luncheon Dry and Bristol Fino, which ar dry and excellent Palo Cortado.

Henriques & Henriques

Well-known Madeira shippers of Funchal. Their wide rang includes a good dry apéritif wine: Ribeiro Seco.

Jerez de la Frontera

Centre of the sherry industry, between Cadiz and Sevill in s. Spain. The word sherry is a corruption of the name pronounced in Spanish "Hereth". In French, Xérés.

Late-bottled vintage

Port of a single good vintage kept in wood for twice as long a vintage port (about 5 years). Therefore lighter when bottle and ageing quicker.

Leacock

One of the oldest firms of Madeira shippers. Most famou wine is "Penny Black" Malmsey.

Lustau

The largest independent family-owned sherry bodega i JEREZ, making many wines for other shippers, but with a ver good "Dry Lustau" range (particularly the oloroso) and "Jere Lustau" Palo Cortado.

acharnudo

One of the best parts of the sherry v'yds., n. of Jerez, famous for wines of the highest quality, both FINO and OLOROSO.

almsey

The sweetest form of Madeira; dark amber, rich and honeyed yet with Madeira's unique sharp tang.

anzanilla

Sherry, normally FINO, which has acquired a peculiar bracing salty character from being kept in bodegas at Sanlucar de Barrameda, on the Guadalquivir estuary near JEREZ.

isa, Marques de

Old sherry bodega now in the RUMASA group.

ffley Forester

Port shippers and owners of the famous Quinta Boa Vista. Their vintage wines tend to be round, "fat" and sweet, good for relatively early drinking. Vintages: 55 60 62 63 66 67 70 72 75 77 (an exception to the "early-drinking" rule).

loroso

Style of sherry, heavier and less brilliant than FINO when young, but maturing to greater richness and roundness. Naturally dry, but generally sweetened for sale, as CREAM.

alo Cortado

A style of sherry close to OLOROSO but with some of the character of a FINO. Dry but rich and soft. Not often seen.

alomino & Vergara

Sherry shippers of JEREZ, best known for Palomino Cream, Medium and Dry. Best FINO: Tio Mateo. Rumasa group.

ASTERS OF WINE

he British wine trade has its own advanced practitioners' amination with such high standards that it is internationally cognized as the highest formal qualification a wine merchant can hieve. Candidates must pass a statutory five years in the wine trade fore sitting the exam, which has papers on such mundane matters as cise and E.E.C. regulations as well as both the theory and practice of nderstanding and appreciating wine. The final tests are "blind" stings at which candidates must assess and comment on over 30 nidentified wines. The 100-odd men and women who have passed are embers of the Institute of Masters of Wine, or "M.W.s".

---

emartin

Jerez bodega in the RUMASA group.

uerto de Santa Maria

The port and second city of the sherry area with a number of important bodegas.

.X.

Short for Pedro Ximenez, the grape used in JEREZ for sweetening blends. P.X. wine alone is almost like treacle.

uinta

Portuguese for "estate".

uinta do Noval

Great Portuguese port house making splendidly dark, rich and full-bodied vintage port; a few pre-phylloxera vines still at the Quinta make a small quantity of "Nacional"—very dark, full and slow-maturing wine. Vintages: 55 58 60 63 66 67 70 75 78.

ainwater

A fairly light, not very sweet blend of Madeira—in fact of VERDELHO wine—popular in the USA and Canada.

Real Tesoro, Marques de

Sherry shippers of SANLUCAR and JEREZ, specializing in MA ZANILLA, esp. "La Capitala".

Rebello Valente

Name used for the vintage port of ROBERTSON. Their vinta wines are light but elegant and well-balanced, maturi rather early. Vintages: **55 60 63 66 67** 70 75 77.

La Riva

Distinguished firm of sherry shippers making one of the be FINOS, Tres Palmas, among many good wines.

Rivero

Considerable sherry concern best known for CZ range.

Robertson

Subsidiary of SANDEMAN'S, shipping REBELLO VALEN vintage port and Gamebird Tawny and Ruby.

Fino sherries – the palest, driest and most delicate – need handling with more care than the older, heavier and/or sweeter amontillados and olorosos. They lose their vital freshness quite rapidly after bottling, and very rapidly indeed once the bottle is opened. For this reason the Spanish often use half-bottles. Buy fino in small quantitie and use it straight away, keeping bottle in fridge if not finished at a sitting.

Rozes Port shippers controlled by Moët-Hennessy. Tawny ver popular in France; also Ruby and 77.

Ruby The youngest (and cheapest) style of port: very sweet and re The best are vigorous and full of flavour. Others can I merely strong and rather thin.

Ruiz Mateos

The sherry bodega which gave its name to the mammo Rumasa group of bodegas, banks, etc. Its Don Zoilo sherri are some of the most expensive and best. Ruiz Hermanos is cheaper range.

Rumasa

See Ruiz Mateos.

Rutherford & Miles

Madeira shippers with one of the best known of all Bu wines: Old Trinity House.

Saccone & Speed

British sherry shippers owned by Courage's the Brewer Popular Troubador and Cuesta ranges and a good Fino.

Sandeman

Giant of the port trade and a major figure in the sherry o owned by Seagrams. "Partners" is their best-known taw port; their vintage wines are robust—some of the old vintag were superlative [**55 58 60 63 66 67** 70 75 77]. Of the sherrie Medium Dry Amontillado is the best-seller, their Fi "Apitiv" is particularly good and Armada Cream and Dry D Amontillado are both well known.

Sanlucar

Seaside sherry-town (see Manzanilla) 15 miles from JEREZ.

Sercial

Grape (reputedly a RIESLING) grown in Madeira to make t driest of the island's wines—a good apéritif.

Solera

System used in making both sherry and Madeira, also so port. It consists of topping up progressively more matu barrels with slightly younger wine of the same sort: the obje to attain continuity in the final wine. Most commerci sherries are blends of several solera wines.

Tarquinio Lomelino

Madeira shippers famous for their collection of antique wines. Their standard range is called Dom Henriques.

Tawny

A style of port aged for many years in wood (in contrast to vintage port, which is aged in bottle) until tawny in colour.

Taylor

One of the best port shippers, particularly for their full, rich, long-lived vintage wine and tawnies of stated age (40-year-old, 20-year-old, etc.). Their Quinta de Vargellas is said to give Taylor's its distinctive scent of violets. Vintages: **55 60 63 66** 70 75 77. Vargellas is shipped unblended in certain (lesser) vintages.

De Terry, Carlos y Javier

Family-owned bodega at PUERTO DE SANTA MARIA with a good range of sherries.

Tio Pepe

The most famous of FINO sherries (see Gonzalez Byass).

Valdespino

Famous family-owned bodega at JEREZ, owner of the Inocente v'yd., making the excellent FINO of the same name. Tio Diego is their splendid dry AMONTILLADO, Solera 1842 a ditto oloroso, Matador the name of their popular range.

Varela

Sherry shippers, members of the RUMASA group, best-known for their Varela Medium and Cream.

Verdelho

Madeira grape making fairly dry wine without the distinction of SERCIAL. A pleasant apéritif.

Vintage Port

The best port of exceptional vintages is bottled after only 2 years in wood and matures very slowly, for up to 20 years or even more, in its bottle. It always leaves a heavy deposit and therefore needs decanting.

Vintage port is almost as much a ritual as a drink. It always needs to be decanted with great care (since the method of making it leaves a heavy deposit in the bottle). The simplest and surest way of doing this is by filtering it through clean muslin or a coffee filter-paper into either a decanter or a well-rinsed bottle. All except very old ports can safely be decanted the day before drinking. At table the decanter is traditionally passed from guest to guest clockwise. Vintage port can be immensely long-lived. Particularly good vintages older than those mentioned in the text include 1950, 48, 45, 35, 34, 27, 20, 11, 08, 04.

Vintage Character

Somewhat misleading term used for a good-quality full and meaty port like a first-class RUBY made by the solera system. Lacks the splendid "nose" of vintage port.

Warre

Probably the oldest of all port shippers (since 1670). Fine long-maturing vintage wines, a good TAWNY, Nimrod and Vintage Character Warrior. Vintages: **55 60** 63 **66** 70 75 77.

White Port

Port made of white grapes, golden in colour. Formerly made sweet, now more often dry: a good apéritif but a heavy one.

Williams & Humbert

Famous and first-class sherry bodega now owned by the giant Rumasa group. Dry Sack (medium AMONTILLADO) is their best-selling wine. Pando is an excellent FINO. Canasta Cream and Walnut Brown are good in their class.

Central & South-east Europe

Weinviertel
Langenlois
Wachau ● Vienna

AUSTRIA

Burgenland

Somló
Sopron

HUNGARY

Graz ●
Styria

Balaton

Mát...

●B...

Lutomer

Vilanyi-Pecs

Ljubljana ●

Slavonia

Slovenia

Trieste ●

Zagreb

Vojvo...

Croatia

Bosnia-Herzegovina

YUGOSLAVIA

Dalmatia

Split ●

Sarajevo

Monte...

Dubrovnik ●

The huge range of wines from the countries covered by this
map offers some of the best value for money in the world
today. Quality is moderate to high, tending to improve, and
reliability on the whole is excellent.

The references are arranged country by country, with all
geographical references back to the map on this page.

Labelling in all the countries involved except Greece is
based on the German, now international, pattern of place-
name plus grape-variety. The main grape-varieties are
therefore included alongside areas and other terms in the
alphabetical listings. Quality ratings in this section are
given where there is enough information to warrant it.

Tokay

Moldavia

Transylvania

Tîrnăve ●

ROMANIA   Focsani

nat   Dragaşani   Dealul Mare

rbia   Bucharest ●   Dobruja

R. Danube

Varna ●

Karlovo

● Sofia   **BULGARIA**

Plovdiv ●

Melnik   _R. Evros_

Macedonia   Istanbul ●

Thrace

● **Thessaloniki**

GREECE

● **Patras**   Attica   Samos

halonia   ● **Athens**

Peloponnese   Santorin

Rhodes

Crete

Austria

Austria has recently become recognized as one of Europe's most reliable sources of fresh, fruity, dry wines and succulent sweet ones at very fair prices. Most of her practices and terms are similar to the German; the basic difference is a higher alcoholic degree in almost all her wine. The Austrian Wine Quality Seal (Weingutesiegel or WGS), in the form of a red, white and gold disc on the bottle, means the wine has met fixed standards, been officially tested and approved.

Recent vintages:

1980	A difficult vintage, as in most of Europe.
1979	Reduced crop; excellent quality.
1978	Average quantity and quality.
1977	Average quantity; very good quality.
1976	Big; good average quality.

Apetlon Burgenland w. s./sw. or sw. ★→ ★★
> Village of the SEEWINKEL making tasty whites on sandy soil, incl. very good sweet wines.

Ausbruch
> Term used for very sweet wines between Beerenauslese and Trockenbeerenauslese (see Germany) in richness.

Baden Vienna (r.) w. dr. or sw. ★→★★★
> Town and area s. of VIENNA incl. GUMPOLDSKIRCHEN. Good lively high-flavoured wines, best from ROTGIPFLER and ZIERFÄNDLER grapes.

Blaufränkisch
> The GAMAY grape.

Blue Danube
> Popular GEWÜRZTRAMINER/WÄLSCHRIESLING blend from LENZ MOSER.

Bouvier
> Native Austrian grape giving soft but aromatic wine.

Burgenland Burgenland r. w. dr. w. ★→ ★★★★
> Region on the Hungarian border with ideal conditions for sweet wines. "Noble rot" occurs regularly and Ausleses are abundant. (See Rust, etc.)

Dürnstein w. dr. sw. ★★→★★★
> Wine centre of the WACHAU with a famous ruined castle and important WINZERGENOSSENSCHAFT. Some of Austria's best whites, esp. Rheinriesling and GRÜNER VELTLINER.

Eisenstadt Burgenland (r.) w. dr. or sw. ★★→★★★★
> Town in BURGENLAND and historic seat of the ESTERHAZYS.

Esterhazy
> Quasi-royal family whose AUSBRUCH and other BURGENLAND wines are of superlative quality.

Grinzing Vienna w. ★★ D.Y.A.
> Suburb of VIENNA with delicious lively HEURIGE wines.

Grüner Veltliner
> Austria's most characteristic white grape (31% of her white v'yds.) making short-lived but marvellously spicy and flowery, racy and vital wine.

Gumpoldskirchen Vienna (r.) w. dr. or sw. ★★→★★★
> Pretty resort s. of VIENNA with wines of great character.

Heiligenkreuz, Stift
> Cistercian Monastery at THALLERN making some of Austria's best wine, particularly from a fine steep v'yd.: Wiege.

Heurige
> Means both new wine and the tavern where it is drunk.

Kahlenberg Vienna w. ★★ D.Y.A.
> Village and v'yd. hill n. of VIENNA, famous for HEURIGEN.

Kamp Langenlois (r.) w. dr. or sw. *→**
  Tributary of the Danube (Donau) giving its name to wines from its valley, n. and e. of the WACHAU, incl. pleasant Veltliner (see Grüner Veltliner) and RIESLING.

Klöch Steiermark (r.) p. w. dr. ★
  The chief wine town of Styria, the s.e. province. No famous wines, but agreeable ones, esp. Traminer.

Klosterneuberg
  Famous monastery, now a wine college and research station with magnificent cellars, just n. of VIENNA.

Krems Danube w. *→***
  Town and district just e. of the WACHAU with good GRÜNER VELTLINER and Rheinriesling (see Riesling) esp. from Austria's biggest WINZERGENOSSENSCHAFT.

Langenlois Langenlois r. w. *→**
  Chief town of the KAMP valley with many modest and some good wines, esp. peppery GRÜNER VELTLINER and Rheinriesling (see Riesling). Reds less interesting.

Lenz Moser
  Austria's best known and most progressive grower, invented a high vine system and makes good to excellent wine at Röhrendorf near KREMS, APETLON, MAILBERG and elsewhere.

Mailberg Weinviertel w. ★★
  Town of the WEINVIERTEL known for lively light wine, esp. LENZ MOSER's Malteser.

Morandell, Alois
  Big-scale Viennese wine-merchant.

Mörbisch Burgenland r. w. dr. or sw. *→***
  Leading wine-village of BURGENLAND. Good sweet wines. Reds and dry whites not inspiring.

Müller-Thurgau
  9% of all Austria's white grapes are Müller-Thurgau.

Muskat-Ottonel
  The strain of muscat grape grown in e. Europe, incl. Austria.

Niederösterreich
  Lower Austria: i.e. all the n.e. corner of the country.

Neuberger
  Popular white grape: pleasant wine in KREMS/LANGENLOIS but soft and coarse in BURGENLAND.

Neusiedlersee
  Shallow lake in sandy country on the Hungarian border, creating autumn mists and giving character to the sweet wines of BURGENLAND.

Nussdorf Vienna w. ★★
  Suburb of VIENNA with well-known HEURIGEN.

Oggau Burgenland (r.) w. sw. ★★→***
  One of the wine-centres of BURGENLAND, famous for Beerenausleses (see Germany) and AUSBRUCH.

Portugieser
  With BLAUFRÄNKISCH, one of the two main red-wine grapes of Austria, giving dark but rather characterless wine.

Retz Weinviertel (r.) w. ★
  Leading wine-centre of the WEINVIERTEL, known for pleasant GRÜNER VELTLINER, etc.

Ried Vineyard: when named it is usually a good one.

Riesling
  German Riesling is always called Rheinriesling. "Riesling" is Wälschriesling.

Rotgipfler
  Good and high-flavoured grape peculiar to BADEN and GUMPOLDSKIRCHEN. Used with ZIERFÄNDLER to make lively whites. Very heavy/sweet on its own.

Ruländer

The PINOT GRIS grape.

Rust Burgenland (r.) w. dr. or sw. ✶→✶✶✶

Most famous wine centre of BURGENLAND, long and justly famous for its AUSBRUCH, often made of mixed grapes.

St. Laurent

Traditional Austrian red grape, faintly muscat-flavoured.

Schilcher

Pleasant sharp rosé, speciality of STYRIA.

Schloss Grafenegg

Famous property of the Metternich family near KREMS. Good standard white and excellent Ausleses.

Schluck

Name for the common white wine of the WACHAU, good when drunk very young.

Seewinkel

"Sea corner": the sandy district around the NEUSIEDLERSEE.

Sepp Hold

Well-known EISENSTADT grower and merchant.

Siegendorf, Klosterkeller

First-class private BURGENLAND wine estate.

Sievering Vienna w. ✶✶

Suburb of VIENNA with notable HEURIGEN.

Spätrot

Another name for ZIERFÄNDLER.

Spitzenwein

Top wines—as opposed to TISCHWEIN: ordinary table wines.

Steiermark (Styria)

Province in the s.e., not remarkable for wine but well-supplied with it.

Stift

The word for a monastery. Monasteries have been, and still are, very important in Austria's wine-making, combining tradition and high standards with modern resources.

Thallern Vienna (r.) w. dr. or sw. ✶✶ →✶✶✶

Village near GUMPOLDSKIRCHEN and trade-name of wines from Stift HEILIGENKREUZ.

Tischwein

Everyday wine, as opposed to SPITZENWEIN.

Traiskirchen Vienna (r.) w. ✶✶

Village near GUMPOLDSKIRCHEN with similar wine.

Veltliner

See Grüner Veltliner

Vöslau Baden r. (w.) ✶

Spa town s. of BADEN (and WIEN) known for its reds made of PORTUGIESER and BLAUFRÄNKISCH: refreshing but no more.

Wachau

District on the n. bank of the Danube round DÜRNSTEIN with cliff-like slopes giving some of Austria's best whites, esp. Rheinriesling (see Riesling) and GRÜNER VELTLINER.

Weinviertel

"The wine quarter": name given to the huge and productive district between VIENNA and the Czech border. Mainly light white wines.

Wien (Vienna)

The capital city, with 1,800 acres of v'yds. in its suburbs to supply its cafés and HEURIGEN.

Winzergenossenschaft

Growers' co-operative.

Zierfändler

White grape of high flavour peculiar to the BADEN area. Used with ROTGIPFLER.

Hungary

The traditional and characteristic firmness and strength of character which can make Hungarian wine the most exciting of Eastern Europe have been modified by modern ideas. Average quality is still high; whites are lively and reds made to last, but much of the drama has gone—at least from the standard exported lines. Visitors to the country will find plenty of excellent wine.

Aszu

Word meaning "syrupy" applied to very sweet wines, esp. Tokay (TOKAJI), where the "aszu" is late-picked and "nobly rotten" as in Sauternes. (See p. 47.)

Badacsony Balaton w. dr. sw. ⋆⋆→⋆⋆⋆

1,400 ft. hill on the n. shore of La. BALATON whose basalt soil can give rich high-flavoured wines, among Hungary's best.

Balatonfüred Balaton (r.) w. dr. sw. ⋆⋆

Town on the n. shore of La. BALATON e. of BADACSONY. Good but softer, less fiery wines.

Balaton Balaton r. w. dr. sw. ⋆ →⋆⋆⋆

Hungary's inland sea and Europe's largest lake. Many wines take its name and most are good. The ending "i" (e.g. Balatoni, Egri) is the equivalent of -er in German names, or in Londoner.

Bársonyos-Császár

Wine-district of n. Hungary. MÓR is its best-known centre.

Bikavér

"Bull's Blood"—or words to that effect. The historic name of the best-selling red wine of EGER: full-bodied and well-balanced, improving considerably with age.

Csopak

Village next to BALATONFÜRED, with similar wines.

Debrö Mátraalya w. sw. ⋆⋆⋆

Important centre of the MÁTRAALYA famous for its pale, aromatic and sweet HÁRSLEVELÜ.

Eger Mátraalya r. w. dr. sw. ⋆→ ⋆⋆

Best-known MÁTRAALYA wine-centre: fine baroque city of cellars full of BIKAVÉR. Also delicate white LEÁNYKA and dark sweetish MERLOT, known as MÉDOC NOIR.

Eszencia

The fabulous quintessence of Tokay (TOKAJI): intensely sweet grape-juice of very low, if any, alcoholic strength, reputed to have miraculous properties. Now almost unobtainable.

Ezerjó

The grape grown at MÓR to make one of Hungary's best dry white wines: potentially distinguished, fragrant and fine.

Furmint

The classic grape of Tokay (TOKAJI), with great flavour and fire, also grown for table wine on La. BALATON, sometimes with excellent results.

Hajós Mecsek r. ⋆

Town in s. Hungary becoming known as a centre for good CABERNET SAUVIGNON reds.

Hárslevelü

The "lime-leaved" grape used at DEBRÖ to make good gently sweet wine.

Kadarka

The commonest red grape of Hungary, grown in vast quantities for everyday wine on the plains in the s.; also used at EGER; capable of ample flavour and interesting maturity.

Kékfrankos

Hungarian for GAMAY, literally "blue French". Makes good light red at SOPRON on the Austrian border.

Kéknelyü

High-flavoured white grape making the best and "stiffest" wine of Mt. BADACSONY. It should be fiery and spicy stuff.

Leanyka

East-European white grape better known in Romania but making admirable pale soft wine at EGER.

Mátraalya

Wine-district in the foothills of the Matra range in n. Hungary, incl. DEBRÖ and EGER.

Mecsek

District in s. Hungary known for the good reds of VILÁNY and whites of PÉCS.

Médoc Noir

Hungarian name for MERLOT, used to make sweet red at EGER.

Monimpex

The Hungarian state export monopoly, with great cellars at Budafok, near Budapest.

Mór North Hungary w. dr. ★★★

Town in n. Hungary famous for its fresh dry EZERJÓ.

Muskotály

Hungarian muscat, used to add aroma to Tokay (TOKAJI) and occasionally alone at EGER, where its wine is long-lived and worth tasting.

Nágyburgundi

Literally "black burgundy"—the PINOT NOIR makes admirable wine in s. Hungary, esp. round VILÁNY.

Olasz Riesling

The Hungarian name for the Italian, or Wälschriesling.

Pécs Mecsek (r.) w. dr. ★ → ★★

Town in the Mecsek hills known in the West for its agreeable well-balanced (if rather sweet) Riesling.

Puttonyos

The measure of sweetness in Tokay (TOKAJI). A 7-gal. container from which ASZU is added to SZAMORODNI. One "putt" makes it sweetish; 6 (the maximum) very sweet indeed.

Siller

Pale red or rosé. Usually made from KADARKA grapes.

Somló North Hungary w. dr. ★★★

Isolated small v'yd. district n. of BALATON making intense white wines of high repute from FURMINT and RIESLING.

Sopron Burgenland r. ★★

Little Hungarian enclave in Burgenland s. of the Neusiedlersee (see Austria) specializing in KÉKFRANKOS (Gamay) red.

Szamorodni

Word meaning "as it comes": i.e. fully fermented (therefore dry) wine from all the grapes not specially selected. Used to describe the unsweetened form of Tokay (TOKAJI).

Szürkebarát

Literally means "grey friar": Hungarian for PINOT GRIS, which makes rich heavy wine in the BALATON v'yds.

Szekszárdi Vörös Mecsek r. ★★

The red (KADARKA) wine of Szekszárd in south-central Hungary. Dark strong wine which needs age.

Tokaji (Tokay) Tokaji w. dr. sw. ★★ → ★★★★

Hungary's famous strong sweet wine, comparable to an oxidized Sauternes, from hills on the Russian border in the n.e. See Aszu, Eszencia, Furmint, Puttonyos, Szamorodni.

Tramini

The TRAMINER grape; little grown in Hungary.

Vilány Mecsek r. p. (w.) [**★★**]

Southernmost city of Hungary and well-known centre of red wine production. Vilányi Burgundi is largely PINOT NOIR—and very good.

Wälschriesling

Austrian name sometimes used for Olasz (Italian) Riesling.

Zöldszilváni

"Green Sylvaner"—i.e. Sylvaner. Grown round La. BALATON.

Romania

The wine industry is orientated towards Russia as its biggest customer, and consequently specializes in the sweet wines that Russians like. The need for foreign currency makes. export to the West highly desirable, so the best qualities are available at subsidized prices. They include sound and good-value reds and whites, including dry ones, but at present nothing memorable.

Alba Iulia

Town in the TIRNAVE area in Transylvania, known for off-dry whites blended from Italian Riesling, FETEASCA and MUSKAT-OTTONEL.

AligotéThe junior white burgundy grape makes pleasantly fresh white wine in Romania.

Babeaşca

Traditional red grape of the FOCSANI area: agreeably sharp wine tasting slightly of cloves.

Banat The plain on the border with Serbia. Workaday Riesling and light red CADARCA.

Cabernet

Increasingly grown in Romania, particularly at DEALUL MARE, to make dark intense wines though sometimes too sweet for French-trained palates.

Cadarca

Romanian spelling of the Hungarian Kadarka.

Chardonnay

The great white burgundy grape is used at MURFATLAR to make honey-sweet dessert wine.

Cotesti

Part of the FOCSANI area making reds of PINOT NOIR, MERLOT, etc., and dry whites said to resemble Alsace wines.

Cotnari

Romania's most famous historical wine: light dessert wine from MOLDAVIA. Like very delicate Tokay.

Dealul Mare

Important up-to-date v'yd. area in the s.e. Carpathian foot-hills. Red wines from CABERNET, MERLOT, PINOT NOIR, etc.

Dobruja

Black Sea region round the port of Constanta. MURFATLAR is the main v'yd. area.

Dragaşani

Region on the R. Olt s. of the Carpathians, growing both traditional and "modern" grapes. Good MUSKAT-OTTONEL.

Feteasca

Romanian white grape of mild character, the same as Hungary's Leanyka (and some say Switzerland's Chasselas).

Focsani

Important eastern wine region including those of COTESTI, ODOBESTI and NICORESTI.

Grasa
> A form of the Hungarian Furmint grape grown in Romania and used in, among other wines, COTNARI.

Moldavia
> The n.e. province, now largely within the USSR.

Murfatlar
> Big modern v'yds. near the Black Sea specializing in sweet wines, incl. CHARDONNAY. Now also dry reds and whites.

Muskat-Ottonel
> The e. European muscat, at its best in Romania.

Nicoresti
> Eastern area of FOCSANI best known for its red BABEAȘCA.

Odobesti
> The central part of FOCSANI; mainly white wines of FETEASCA, RIESLING, etc.

Perla
> The speciality of TÎRNAVE: a pleasant blended semi-sweet white of RIESLING, FETEASCA and MUSKAT-OTTONEL.

Pitesti
> Principal town of the Arges region s. of the Carpathians. Traditionally whites from FETEASCA, TAMIIOASA, RIESLING.

Premiat
> Reliable range of mid-quality wines for export.

Riesling
> Italian Riesling. Very widely planted. No exceptional wines.

Sadova
> Town in the SEGARCEA area exporting a rosé.

Segarcea
> Southern wine area near the Danube. Exports rather sweet CABERNET.

Tamiioasa
> A traditional white-wine grape variety of no very distinct character.

Tîrnave
> Important Transylvanian wine region, known for its PERLA and MUSKAT-OTTONEL.

Valea Calugareasca
> "The Valley of the Monks", part of the DEALUL MARE v'yd. with a well-known research station. CABERNET, MERLOT and PINOT NOIR are generally made into heavy sweetish wines.

Yugoslavia

A well-established supplier of wines of international calibre at very reasonable prices. Yugoslav Riesling was the pioneer, now followed by Cabernet, Pinot Blanc and Traminer of equal quality as well as such worthwhile specialities as Zilavka and Prokupac. All parts of the country except the central highlands make wine, almost entirely in giant co-operatives. Tourists on the Dalmatian coast will find more original products—all well worth trying.

Amselfelder
> German marketing name for the Red Burgundac (Spätburgunder or PINOT NOIR) wine of KOSOVO.

Banat
> North-eastern area, partly in Romania, with up-to-date wineries making adequate RIESLING.

Beli Pinot
> The PINOT BLANC, a popular grape in SLOVENIA.

Bijelo White.

Blatina

The red grape and wine of MOSTAR. Not in the same class as the white ZILAVKA.

Bogdanuša

Local white grape of the Dalmatian islands, esp. Hvar and Brac. Pleasant fresh faintly fragrant wine.

Burgundac Bijeli

The CHARDONNAY, grown a little in SLAVONIA and VOJVODINA.

Cabernet

See Grapes for red wine. Now introduced in many places with increasingly pleasant, occasionally exciting, results.

Crno

Black—i.e. red wine.

Ćviček

Traditional pale red or dark rosé of SLOVENIA.

Dalmaciajavino

Important co-operative based at Split and selling a full range of coastal and island wines.

Dalmatia

The middle coast of Yugoslavia from Rijeka to Dubrovnik. Has a remarkable variety of wines of character.

Dingac

Heavy sweetish red from the local PLAVAC grape, speciality of the mid-Dalmatian coast.

Fruska Gora

Hills in VOJVODINA, on the Danube n.w. of Belgrade, with a growing modern v'yd. and a wide range of wines, incl. good Traminer and Sauvignon Blanc.

Graševina

Slovenian for Italian Riesling (also called Wälschriesling, LASKI RIZLING, etc.). The normal Riesling of Yugoslavia.

Grk

Strong almost sherry-like white from the Grk grape. Speciality of the island of Korcula.

Istria

Peninsula in the n. Adriatic, Porec its centre, with a variety of pleasant wines, the MERLOT as good as any.

Jerusalem

Yugoslavia's most famous v'yd., at LJUTOMER.

Kadarka

The major red grape of Hungary, widely grown in SERBIA.

Kosovo

Region in the s., between SERBIA and Macedonia, with modern v'yds. The source of AMSELFELDER and good light CABERNET.

Laski Rizling

Yet another name for Italian Riesling.

Ljutomer (or Lutomer)-Ormoz

Yugoslavia's best known and probably best wine district, in n.e. SLOVENIA, famous for its RIESLING: full-flavoured, full-strength and at its best rich and satisfying wine.

Malvasia

White grape giving luscious heavy wine, used in w. SLOVENIA.

Marastina

Strong dry white of the Dalmatian islands.

Maribor

Important wine-centre of n. SLOVENIA. White wines incl. SIPON, Ruländer, etc., as well as RIESLING and Austrian BOUVIER (see Austria).

Merlot

The Bordeaux red grape, grown in SLOVENIA and ISTRIA with reasonable results.

Mostar

Islamic-looking little city inland from DALMATIA, making admirable dry white from the ZILAVKA grape. Also BLATINA.

Muskat-Ottonel

The East European muscat, grown in VOJVODINA.

Navip

The big growers' co-operative of SERBIA, with its headquarters at Belgrade.

Opol

Pleasantly light pale red made of PLAVAĆ grapes round Split and Sibenik in DALMATIA.

Plavać Mali

Native red grape of SLOVENIA and DALMATIA: makes DINGAC, POSTUP, OPOL, etc.

Plavina

Light red of the DALMATIAN coast round Zadar.

Plovdina

Native red grape of Macedonia in the s., giving mild wine. Grown and generally blended with PROKUPAC.

Portugizac

Austria's Portugieser: plain red wine.

Posip

Pleasant, not-too-heavy white wine of the Dalmatian islands, notably Korcula.

Postup

Sweet and heavy DALMATIAN red from the Peljesac peninsula near Korcula. Highly esteemed locally.

Prokupac

Principal native red grape of s. SERBIA and Macedonia: 85% of the production. Makes good dark rosé (RUZICA) and full-bodied red of character. Some of the best comes from ZUPA. PLOVDINA is often added for smoothness.

Prosek

The dessert wine of DALMATIA, of stupefying natural strength and variable quality. The best is excellent, but hard to find.

Radgonska Ranina

Ranina is Austria's BOUVIER grape (see Austria). Radgona is near MARIBOR. The wine is sweet and carries the trade name TIGROVO MLJEKO (Tiger's Milk).

Rajnski Rizling

The Rhine Riesling, rare in Yugoslavia but grown a little in LJUTOMER-ORMOZ.

Refosco

Italian grape grown in e. SLOVENIA and ISTRIA under the name TERAN.

Renski Rizling

Alternative spelling for Rhine Riesling.

Riesling

Without qualification means Italian Riesling.

Ruzica

Rosé, usually from PROKUPAC. Darker than most; and better.

Serbia

The e. state of Yugoslavia, with nearly half the country's v'yds., stretching from VOJVODINA to Macedonia.

Sipon

Yugoslav name for the FURMINT grape of Hungary, also grown in SLOVENIA.

Slavonia

Northern Croatia, on the Hungarian border between SLOVENIA and SERBIA. A big producer of standard wines, mainly white.

Slovenia

The n.w. state, incl. Yugoslavia's most European-style v'yds. and wines: LJUTOMER, etc. Slovenija-vino, the sales organization, is Yugoslavia's biggest.

Teran

Stout dark red of ISTRIA. See REFOSCO.

Tigrovo Mljeko

See Radgonska Ranina

Tocai The PINOT GRIS, making rather heavy white wine in SLOVENIA.

Traminac

The TRAMINER. Grown in SLOVENIA and VOJVODINA. Particularly successful in the latter.

Vojvodina

An autonomous province of n. SERBIA with substantial, growing and improving v'yds. Wide range of grapes, both European and Balkan.

Zilavka

The white wine of MOSTAR in Hercegovina. One of Yugoslavia's best: dry, pungent and memorably fruity, with a faint flavour of apricots.

Zupa Central SERBIAN district giving its name to above-average red and rosé (or dark and light red) of PROKUPAC and PLOVDINA: respectively Zupsko Crno and Zupsko Ruzica.

Bulgaria

A dramatic new entry into the world's wine-diet. State-run and state-subsidized wineries seem to have learnt a great deal from the New World and offer Cabernet and Chardonnay at bargain prices—though there is more subtlety in some of the traditional local wines.

Cabernet

The Bordeaux grape is highly successful in n. Bulgaria. Dark, vigorous, fruity and well-balanced wine, needs aging.

Chardonnay

The white burgundy grape is scarcely less successful . Very dry but full-flavoured wine improves with a year in bottle.

Dimiat

The common native white grape, grown in the e. towards the coast. Agreeable dry white without memorable character.

Euxinograd

Brand of blended white wine produced for export.

Fetiaska

The same grape as Romania's Feteasca and Hungary's Leanyka. Rather neutral but pleasant pale wine, best a trifle sweet, sold as Donau Perle.

Gamza

The common red grape, Hungary's Kadarka: gives fairly light but "stiff" and worthwhile wine.

Hemus

A pale medium to sweet muscat from KARLOVO.

Iskra The national brand of sparkling wine, normally sweet but of fair quality.

Karlovo

Town in central Bulgaria famous for the "Valley of Roses" and its very pleasant white MISKET.

Mavrud

Darkly plummy red from s. Bulgaria. Improves with age. Generally considered the country's best.

Melnik
City of the extreme s.e. Such concentrated MAVRUD that the locals say it can be carried in a handkerchief.

Misket
Bulgaria's muscat: locally popular flavour in sweet whites.

Pamid
The light, quite soft, everyday red of s. and central Bulgaria.

Rcatzitelli
One of Russia's favourite white grapes for strong sweet wine. Grown in n.e. Bulgaria.

Riesling
Normally refers to Italian Riesling. Some Rhine Riesling is grown but at present is made over-dry.

Saperavi
Russian red grape, presumably used for export to Russia: the biggest export market.

Sonnenküste
Brand of medium-sweet white sold in Germany.

Sungurlare
Eastern town giving its name to a sweet MISKET, similar to that of KARLOVO.

Sylvaner
Some pleasant dry SYLVANER is exported as "Klosterkeller".

Tamianka
Sweet white; sweeter than HEMUS.

Tirnovo
Strong sweet red wine.

Trakia
"Thrace". Brand name of a good export range.

Vinimpex
The "State Commercial Enterprise for Export and Import of Wines and Spirits".

Greece

Entry into the E.E.C. gives Greece the challenge of modernizing and internationalizing a wine industry that has been up a backwater for two thousand years, concentrating on resin-flavoured white Retsina. (The resin is that of the Aleppo pine.) To those unenthusiastic about Greek food its strong flavour has at least one advantage. Recently there have been signs of experiment and investment, which promise well for the future.

Achaia-Clauss
The best-known Greek wine-merchant, with cellars a Patras, n. PELOPONNESE.

Attica
Region round Athens, the chief source of RETSINA.

Cambas, Andrew
Important Athenian wine-growers and merchants.

Carras, John
Hotelier at Chalkidiki, n. Greece, producing interesting new red and white wines under the name Porto Carra.

Castel Danielis
One of the best brands of dry red wine, from ACHAIA-CLAUSS.

Corfu Adriatic island with wines scarcely worthy of it. Ropa is the traditional red.

Crete Island with the name for some of Greece's better wine, esp MAVRO ROMEIKO.

Demestica

A well-established export of strong dry red and white from ACHAIA-CLAUSS.

Gortys

Adequate Cretan white.

Hymettus

Standard brand of red and dry white without resin.

Kokkineli

The rosé version of RETSINA: like the white. Drink very cold.

Lindos

Name for the higher quality of RHODES wine, whether from Lindos itself or not. Acceptable; no more.

Malvasia

The famous grape is said to originate from Monemvasia in the s. PELOPONNESE.

Mavro

"Black"—the word for dark red wine.

Mavrodaphne

Literally "black laurel": dark sweet concentrated red; a speciality of the Patras region, n. PELOPONNESE.

Mavro Romeiko

The best red wine of Crete, reputedly among the best of Greece: dry and full-bodied.

Mavroudi

The red wine of Delphi and the n. shore of the Gulf of Corinth: dark and plummy.

Minos

Popular Cretan brand; the Castello red is best.

Naoussa

Above-average strong dry red from Macedonia in the n.

Nemea

Town in the e. PELOPONNESE famous for its lion (a victim of Hercules) and its fittingly forceful MAVRO.

Peloponnese

The s. landmass of mainland Greece, with a third of the whole country's v'yds.

Pendeli

Reliable brand of dry red from ATTICA, grown and bottled by Andrew CAMBAS.

Retsina

White wine with pine resin added, tasting of turpentine and oddly appropriate with Greek food. The speciality of ATTICA. Drink it very cold.

Rhodes

Easternmost Greek island. Its sweet MALVASIAS are its best wines. LINDOS is the brand name for tolerable table wines.

Rombola

The dry white of Cephalonia; island off the Gulf of Corinth.

Ropa

See Corfu

Samos

Island off the Turkish coast with a reputation for its sweet pale-golden muscat. The normal commercial quality is nothing much.

Santorin

Island north of Crete, making sweet Vinsanto from sun-dried grapes, and dry white Thira.

Santalis

Merchants of Thessaloniki with a wide range of table wines.

Verdea

The dry white of Zakinthos, the island just w. of the PELOPONNESE.

Cyprus

A well-established exporter of strong wines of reasonable quality, best known for very passable Cyprus sherry, though old Commandaria, a treacly dessert wine, is the island's finest product. Until recently only traditional grape varieties of limited potential were available; now better kinds are beginning to improve standards.

Afames
> Village at the foot of Mt. Olympus, giving its name to one of the better red (MAVRON) wines.

Aphrodite
> Full-bodied medium-dry white from KEO, named after the Greek goddess of love.

Arsinöe
> Dry white wine from SODAP, named after an unfortunate female whom Aphrodite turned to stone.

Bellapais
> Rather fizzy medium-sweet white from KEO named after the famous abbey near Kyrenia.

Christoforou
> Family-directed wine firm at LIMASSOL.

Commandaria
> Good-quality brown dessert wine made since ancient times and named after a crusading order of knights. The best is superb, of incredible sweetness.

Emva Cream
> Best-selling sw. sherry from Etko, a HAGGIPAVLU subsidiary.

Haggipavlu
> Well-known wine-merchant at LIMASSOL.

Hirondelle
> The sweet white and some of the other wines of this popular brand are produced by Etko (see Emva).

Keo One of the biggest firms in the wine trade at LIMASSOL.

Kokkineli
> Rosé: the name is related to "cochineal".

Kolossi
> Red and white table wines from SODAP.

Limassol
> "The Bordeaux of Cyprus". The wine-port in the s.

Loel Major producer. Amathus and Kykko brands and Comman Cyprus sherry.

Mavron
> The black grape of Cyprus (and Greece) and its dark wine.

Mosaic
> The brand-name of KEO's Cyprus sherries.

Othello
> Perhaps the best dry red: solid, satisfying wine from KEO.

Pitsilia
> Region s. of Mt. Olympus producing the best white an COMMANDARIA wines.

Rosella
> Brand of strong medium-sweet rosé.

St Panteleimon
> Brand of strong sweet white.

Sherry
> Cyprus makes a full range of sherry-style wines, the be (particularly the dry) of very good quality.

SODAP
> Major wine firm at LIMASSOL.

Xynisteri
> The native white grape of Cyprus.

North Africa & Asia

Algeria

The massive v'yds. of Algeria have dwindled in the last ten years from 860,000 acres to under 500,000. Red wines of some quality are made in the coastal hills of Tlemcen, Mascara, Haut-Dahra, Zaccar and Ain-Bessem. Most goes for blending today. The Soviet Union is the biggest buyer.

Israel

Israeli wine, since the industry was re-established by a Rothschild in the 1880s, has been primarily of Kosher interest until recently, when CABERNET, SAUVIGNON BLANC, SEMILLON and GRENACHE of fair quality have been introduced. Carmel is the principal brand.

Lebanon

The small Lebanese wine industry, based on Ksara, has made red wine of real vigour and quality. Château Musar has recently made a great stir with splendid matured reds, largely of CABERNET SAUVIGNON.

Morocco

Morocco today makes North Africa's best wine from v'yds. along the Atlantic coast and round Meknes. In ten years the v'yds. have declined from 190,000 to 115,000 acres. Chante Bled and Tarik are the best reds, Gris de Guerrouane a very pale dry rosé.

Tunisia

Tunisia now has 90,000 acres compared with 120,000 ten years ago. Her speciality is sweet muscat, but reasonable reds come from Carthage, Grombalia and Cap Bon.

Turkey

Most of Turkey's huge v'yds. produce table grapes. But her wines, from Thrace, Anatolia and the Aegean, are remarkably good. Trakya (Thrace) white and Buzbag red are the well-known standards of the State wineries. Doluca and Kavaklidere are private firms of good quality. Villa Doluca red is remarkable: dry, full-bodied, deep-flavoured and vigorous.

USSR

With over 3 million acres of v'yds. the USSR is the world's fourth-biggest wine-producer—but almost entirely for home consumption. Ukraine (incl. the Crimea) is the biggest v'yd. republic, followed by Moldavia, the Russian Republic and Georgia. The Soviet consumer has a sweet tooth, for both table and dessert wines. Of the latter the best come from the Crimea (esp. Massandra). Moldavia and Ukraine use the same grapes as Romania, plus Cabernet, Riesling, Pinot Gris, etc. The Russian Republic makes the best Rieslings (esp. Arbau, Beshtau, Anapa) and sweet sparkling Tsimlanskoye "Champanski". Georgia uses mainly traditional grapes (esp. white Tsinandali and red Mukuzani) for good table wines.

Soviet wines are classified as ordinary (unmatured), "named" (matured in cask or vat) or "kollektsionye" (which are matured both in cask and bottle).

Japan

Japan has a small wine industry in Yamanashi Prefecture, w. of Tokyo. Standard wines are mainly blended with imports from Argentina, E. Europe, etc. Premium wines of Semillon, Cabernet and the local white grape, Koshu, are light but can be good, though expensive. Remarkable sweet wines with noble rot have been made in an area with high humidity. The main producers are Suntory, Mercian, Mann's.

California

California has been making wine for 150 years, but he
modern wine industry has grown from scratch in scarcel
more than 25. Today it leads the world in good-quality chea
wines and startles it with a handful of luxury wines o
brilliant quality. In the last seven years the industry ha
expanded and altered at a frenzied pace. The majority of th
wineries listed here have a history shorter than ten years
Quality-ratings must therefore be tentative.

Grape-varieties (combined with brand-names) are the key
to California wine. Since grapes in California play man
new roles they are separately listed on pages 146-147.

Vineyard areas

Amador
> County in the Sierra foothills e. of Sacramento. Grows fin
> Zinfandel, esp. in Shenandoah Valley.

Central Coast
> A long sweep of coast with scattered wine activity, from Sa
> Francisco Bay s. to Santa Barbara.

Central Coast/Santa Barbara
> Some of the most promising recent planting in the state is i
> the Santa Ynez Valley n. of Santa Barbara, where coastal fo
> gives particularly cool conditions.

Central Coast/Santa Cruz Mts.
> Wineries are scattered round the Santa Cruz Mts. s. of Sa
> Francisco Bay, from Saratoga down to the HECKER PASS.

Central Coast/Hecker Pass
> Pass through the Santa Cruz Mts. s. of San Francisco Ba
> with a cluster of small old-style wineries.

Central Coast/Salinas Valley
> The main concentration of new planting in the Central Coast
> the Salinas Valley runs inland s.e. from Monterey.

Central Coast/San Luis Obispo
> Edna Valley just s. of San Luis Obispo and new more scat
> tered v'yds. nr. Paso Robles.

Livermore
> Valley e. of San Francisco Bay long famous for white wine
> but now largely built over.

Lodi
> Town and district at the n. end of the San Joaquin Valley, it
> hot climate modified by a westerly air-stream.

Mendocino
> Northernmost coastal wine country; a varied climate coole
> in Anderson Valley nr. the coast, warm around Ukiah inland.

Napa
> The Napa Valley, n. of San Francisco Bay, well established a
> the top-quality wine area. Coolest at southern end (Carneros)

San Joaquin Valley
> The great central valley of California, fertile and hot, the
> source of most of the jug wines and dessert wines in the State.

Sonoma
> County n. of San Francisco Bay, between Napa and the sea
> Most v'yds. are in the north (see below). A few, historicall
> important, are in the Valley of the Moon in the south. Ken
> wood lies between the two.

Sonoma/Alexander Valley/Russian River
> High-quality area from Alexander Valley (n. of Napa Valley
> towards the sea (Russian River). Incl. Dry Creek Valley.

Temecula (Rancho California)
> Very new small area in s. California, 25 miles inland halfway
> between San Diego and Riverside.

Mendocino

Russian River

Sonoma

Russian R.

Napa

San Francisco

Santa Cruz

Salinas

CENTRAL COAST

Monterey

Sacramento

Lodi

Modesto

San Joaquin

San Luis Obispo

Santa Barbara

Los Angeles

Southern California

San Diego

Recent Vintages

The Californian climate is far from being as consistent as its reputation. Although on the whole the grapes ripen regularly, they are subject to severe spring frosts in many areas, sometimes a wet harvest-time, and such occasional calamities as the two-year drought of 1975–7.

Wines from the San Joaquin Valley tend to be most consistent year by year. The vintage date on these, where there is one, is more important for telling the age of the wine than from its character.

Vineyards in the Central Coast are mainly so new that no pattern of vintage qualities has yet emerged.

The Napa Valley is the one area where comment can be made on the last dozen vintages of the top varietal wines: Cabernet Sauvignon and Chardonnay.

	Chardonnay	Cabernet Sauvignon
1980	High alcohol. The best well-balanced.	Outstanding
1979	Excellent.	Generally disappointing.
1978	Very good if not too heady.	Promising.
1977	Generally excellent.	Attractive: ageing well.
1976	Difficult: variable.	Small crop but splendid.
1975	Very good.	Delicate; charming.
1974	Good.	Difficult: but many superb.
1973	Very good.	Big and good.
1972	The best wines of a cool year.	Uneven: rain: many poor wines.
1971	Good balance: long lived.	Average.
1970	Good all round: not great: mature.	Best ever.
1969	Weak.	Good, not great.
1968	Well-balanced: now ageing.	Fine, well-balanced, now ageing.

California: grape varieties

Barbera

Darkly plummy variety from Piemonte (see Italy). Gives full-blooded and astringent wine in cool areas, good but softer wine in hot ones.

Cabernet Sauvignon

The best red-wine grape in California with a wide range of styles from delicately woody to overpoweringly fruity. The classic Napa grape.

Carignane

Common bulk-producing red grape rarely used as a "varietal", but occasionally with some success.

Charbono

Rare red grape of Italian origin and no distinction.

Chardonnay

The best white-wine grape—indeed the best wine-grape—in California. Styles of making vary from merely clean and grapy to rich and complex like the best white burgundies.

Chenin Blanc

A work-horse white grape with a surprising turn of speed when made dry and in limited, concentrated quantities. But usually made soft and sweet.

Emerald Riesling

A Californian original in the German manner. Clean, flowery/fruity and a touch tart.

Flora   California-bred white. Mildly flowery; best made sweet.

French Colombard

High-acid white coming into favour for clean semi-dry wines made more German-style than French.

Fumé Blanc

See Sauvignon Blanc.

Gamay (or Napa Gamay)

The red grape of Beaujolais. Never remarkable in California.

CALIFORNIAN VINTAGES TO NOTE
For Cabernets: **70, 73,** 74 **75,** 76, 77, 78, 80.
For Pinot Noir: **70, 74, 75, 76,** 78, 79, 80.
For Zinfandel: **70, 74, 76, 77,** 78, 80.
For Chardonnay: **71, 73, 75, 76, 77,** 78, 79, 80.
For Riesling: **73, 76, 77,** 78, 79, 80.
For Sauvignon Blanc: **77,** 78, 80.
For Gewürztraminer: **75, 77,** 78, 79, 80.

Gamay Beaujolais

Not the red grape of Beaujolais, but a selection of Pinot Noir capable of good Beaujolais-style reds in California.

Gewürztraminer

Generally softer and less aromatically thrilling in California than in France, but at best one of the real successes.

Green Hungarian

A minority interest: rather tasteless white. Can be lively.

Grenache

The most successful grape for rosé in California; generally, alas, made sweet.

Grey Riesling

Not a Riesling. Full-bodied but scarcely notable white.

Grignolino

Highly seasoned grape good for young reds and rosés.

Johannisberg Riesling

Real Rhine Riesling (also known as White Riesling). Often rather strong and bland in California, but at its best (esp. in Auslese-style wines) gloriously complex and satisfying

Merlot

> The St-Emilion grape has a growing acreage in California. Very good heavy reds have been made.

Muscat Light sweet pale gold muscat is one of California's treats.

Petite Syrah or **Syrah**

> The name of the Rhône's and Australia's great red grape has been wrongly applied to a poor one. Generally used in Burgundy blends. But the real one (Syrah) is present in small quantities, and has great promise. See Phelps, Estrella River.

Pinot Blanc

> Much in the shade of the better Chardonnay.

Pinot Noir

> Has yet to reach consummation in California. Most wine with the name is disappointing; a minute proportion thrilling.

Pinot St George

> Used by two or three wineries to make a thoroughly agreeable sturdy red.

Riesling

> See Johannisberg Riesling. Also Sylvaner.

Ruby Cabernet

> A California-bred cross between Carignan and Cabernet Sauvignon with enough of the character of the latter to be interesting. Good in hot conditions.

Sauvignon Blanc

> Excellent white grape used either Sancerre style (fresh, aromatic, effervescent) or Graves style (fat, chewable). The former usually called Fumé Blanc.

Semillon

> High-flavoured whites from the cooler areas; bland ones from hotter places. The most memorable are sweet.

Zinfandel

> California's own red grape, open to many interpretations from light-weight fruity to galumphing. Capable of ageing to great quality.

California wineries

Acacia Napa. Table

> New Carneros winery (first wine 1980) specializing in CHARDONNAY and PINOT NOIR. To watch.

Alexander Valley Vineyards Alexander Valley. Table `**→***`

> New small winery. CHARDONNAY, JOH. RIESLING esp. good.

Almaden Central Coast. Full range `*→` `**` (rising)

> Big winery famous for pioneer varietal labelling and planting in Central Coast. Now owned by National Distillers. Best regular wines incl. SAUV BL., CHARDONNAY, CABERNET. New Charles le Franc label for top vintage wines.

Ambassador

> Brand name of PERELLI-MINETTI.

Assumption Abbey

> Brand name of BROOKSIDE.

Barengo Lodi. Table and dessert `*→**`

> Small firm making wines of character, especially ZINFANDEL and RUBY CABERNET.

Beaulieu Napa. Table and sp. `**→****`

> Rightly famous medium-size growers and makers of esp. CABERNET. CHARDONNAY now less good. Top wine: De Latour Private Reserve Cabernet. Now owned by Heublein Corp.

Beringer Napa. Table and dessert `**` `→***`

> Century-old winery recently modernized by Nestlé Co. Increasingly interesting wines incl. Auslese types.

Boeger   Amador. Table ★→★★
  Small winery in Sierra foothills. Good ZIN.

Brookside   S. California. Table and dessert ★→★★
  Traditional dessert wine firm also making table varietals from TEMECULA under the Assumption Abbey label.

Bruce, David   Central Coast. Table ★★★
  Small luxury winery with heavy-weight old-style wines.

Buena Vista   Sonoma. Table ★★
  Historic pioneer winery with improving recent record esp. in whites (RIESLING, FUMÉ BLANC). Reds include old-style ZINFANDEL from its reputed original v'yd.

Burgess Cellars   Napa. Table ★★★
  Small hillside winery, originally called Souverain, making good CHARDONNAY, late harvest RIESLING, CABERNET.

B.V.   Abbreviation of BEAULIEU VINEYARDS used on their labels.

Cakebread   Napa. Table ★★★
  Started 1974. Increasing reputation, esp. for SAUVIGNON BLANC; also CHARDONNAY, CABERNET, ZIN.

Calera   Monterey-San Benito. Table ★★
  1975 winery growing good ZIN and ambitious with PINOT NOIR.

California Growers   San Joaquin. Table and dessert ★
  Known for sherry and brandy, now also varietal table wines.

Callaway   S. California. Table ★★
  Small new winery in new territory at TEMECULA. Early reds are strong, dark, conservative.

Cassayre-Forni   Napa. Table
  Small new Rutherford winery. Good CABERNET, ZIN and dry CHENIN BLANC.

Carneros Creek   Napa. Table ★★★
  The first winery in the cool Carneros area between Napa and San Francisco Bay. First PINOT NOIR ('77) was sensational. Fine CHARDONNAY (Giles v'yd.) and CABERNET.

Caymus   Napa. Table ★★★
  Small winery at Rutherford with Spätlese-style RIESLING and notable CABERNET. Second label: Liberty School.

Chalone   Central Coast/Salinas. Table ★★★★
  Unique small hilltop v'yd/winery at the Pinnacles. French-style CHARDONNAY and PINOT NOIR of superb quality, good FRENCH COLOMBARD.

Chappellet   Napa. Table ★★★
  Small modern luxury winery and hillside v'yd. Good CABERNET SAUVIGNON and RIESLING, very good dry CHENIN BLANC.

Château Montelena   Napa. Table ★★★→★★★★
  Small 1969 winery making very good distinctive CHARDONNAY and CABERNET SAUVIGNON.

Château St Jean   Sonoma. Table and sp. ★★★★
  Impressive winery specializing in richly flavoured whites from individual v'yds., incl. CHARDONNAY, PINOT BLANC and esp. late harvest RIESLING.

Château Chevalier   Napa. Table ★★
  Small estate in hills above St. Helena known for darkly concentrated CABERNET.

Christian Brothers   Napa and San Joaquin. Full range ★★→★★★
  The biggest Napa winery, run by a religious order, specializing in consistent blends, incl. excellent CABERNET, useful PINOT ST GEORGE, sweet white Ch. La Salle and very good brandy. Also vintage-dated special lots.

Clos du Bois   Sonoma. Table ★★→★★★
  Healdsburg winery of considerable grower in Dry Creek Valley. Good GEWÜRZ and CABERNET.

Clos du Val   Napa. Table ★★★
  French-owned. Strong, rustic ZIN, fine delicate CABERNET.

Concannon Livermore. Table ★★
  Substantial winery famous for SAUVIGNON BLANC and SEMIL-LON, but with reds of similar quality. In new ownership.

Congress Springs Santa Clara/Santa Cruz. Table ★★
  Tiny winery above Saratoga. Well-made whites, esp. SAUVIG-NON BLANC, SEMILLON.

Conn Creek Napa. Table ★★→★★★
  Still formative. New winery building on Silverado Trail in 1979. Best known for CABERNET.

Cresta Blanca Mendocino and San Joaquin. Table and dessert ★★
  Old name from Livermore revived on the n. coast by new owners, GUILD. Husky ZIN and PETITE SYRAH. Mild whites.

Cuvaison Napa. Table ★★→★★★
  Small winery with expert new direction. Shows promise. Austere CABERNET and CHARDONNAY for long ageing.

Davis Bynum Sonoma. Table ★→★★
  Established maker of standard varieties, w. of Healdsburg.

Dehlinger Sonoma. Table ★★→★★★
  Small winery and v'yd. w. of Santa Rosa. Promising CHARDON-NAY, CABERNET and ZIN since 1976.

Diamond Creek Napa. Table ★★★
  Small winery since the 60s with austere, long-ageing CABER-NET from hills w. of Calistoga. Growing in reputation.

Domaine Chandon Napa. sp. ★★★
  Californian outpost of Moët & Chandon Champagne. Launched 1976. Early promise is being fulfilled.

Dry Creek Sonoma. Table ★★★
  Small winery with high ideals, making old-fashioned dry wines, esp. whites, incl. CHARDONNAY, CHENIN BLANC and FUMÉ BLANC.

Durney Vineyard Central Coast/Monterey. Table
  Good CABERNET from Carmel Valley, riper than most in Monterey. Also CHENIN BLANC. Since '76.

East-Side San Joaquin. Table and dessert ★
  Progressive growers' co-operative best known for its Royal Host label. Good RUBY CABERNET, EMERALD RIESLING, ZIN.

Edmeades Mendocino. Table ★★
  Tiny winery in Anderson Valley near Pacific. Known for CABERNET and a French Colombard Ice Wine.

Eleven Cellars
  Brand name of PERELLI-MINETTI.

Estrella River San Luis Obispo/Santa Barbara. Table ★★
  Impressive new winery with 600 acres. CHARDONNAY, RIES-LING, MUSCAT, SYRAH are promising.

Felton-Empire Vineyards Cent. Coast/Santa Cruz Mts. Table ★★
  The old Hallcrest property recently revived by new owners. Excellent 1978 RIESLING. A label to watch.

Fetzer Mendocino. Table ★★
  Rapidly expanding 13-year-old winery with interesting but inconsistent wines, incl. CABERNET, SAUVIGNON BLANC, ZIN, RIESLING. Good-value jug wine.

Ficklin San Joaquin. Dessert (and table) ★★★
  Family firm making California's best "port" and minute quantities of table wine.

Field Stone Sonoma (Alexander Valley). Table ★★
  Small winery founded by mechanical harvester manufac-turer, pressing grapes in the v'yd. for whites and CABERNET rosé.

Firestone Central Coast/Santa Barbara. Table ★★★
  Ambitious 1975 winery in a new area n. of Santa Barbara. Cool conditions are producing very attractive wines, incl. PINOT NOIR, RIESLING, CHARDONNAY, GEWÜRZ.

Foppiano   Sonoma. Table ⟨**∗∗**⟩
> Old winery at Healdsburg refurbished with vintage varieties incl. CHENIN BLANC, FUMÉ BLANC, CAB, ZIN, PETITE SYRAH.

Franciscan Vineyard   Napa. Table ∗∗
> Small-to-medium winery run by an ex-Christian Brother. Good ZINFANDEL, CABERNET, CHARDONNAY and RIESLING.

Franzia   San Joaquin. Full range ∗
> Large old family winery now owned by Coca Cola Bottling Co. of N.Y. Various labels, but all say "made and bottled in Ripon". Noteworthy Burgundy and ZINFANDEL.

Freemark Abbey   Napa. Table ∗∗∗∗
> Small connoisseur's winery with high reputation for CABERNET, CHARDONNAY, PINOT NOIR and RIESLING.

Gallo, E. & J.   San Joaquin. Full range ⟨∗→∗∗⟩
> The world's biggest winery, pioneer in both quantity and quality. Family owned. Hearty Burgundy and Chablis Blanc set national standards. Varietals incl. GEWÜRZ, RIESLING, CHARDONNAY, CABERNET.

Gemello   Santa Clara/Santa Cruz. Full range ∗∗
> Old winery with reputation for reds, esp. PETITE SYRAH, ZIN.

Geyser Peak   Sonoma. Table ∗∗
> Old winery recently revived and expanded by Schlitz Brewery. More steady than inspired.

Giumarra   San Joaquin. Table ⟨**∗∗**⟩
> Recent installation expanding rapidly. Attractive RUBY CAB., CHENIN BLANC from family v'yds. in hottest part of valley.

Grand Cru   Sonoma. Table ∗∗→∗∗∗
> Small 1971 winery making good GEWÜRZ and increasingly CABERNET and SAUVIGNON BLANC.

Grgich-Hills Cellars   Napa. Table ∗∗∗
> Grgich (formerly of CH. MONTELENA) is wine-maker, Hills grows the grapes—esp. CHARDONNAY and RIESLING. Delicate, lively wines.

Guild   San Joaquin. Table and dessert ∗
> Big growers' co-operative famous for Vino da Tavola semi-sweet red and B. Cribari label. New line of varietals with Winemasters label incl. good ZINFANDEL.

Gundlach-Bundschu   Sonoma. Table ⟨**∗∗∗**⟩
> Very old small family winery revived by the new generation. Excellent CABERNET, MERLOT, ZIN and good whites: CHARDONNAY, GEWÜRZ, RIESLING.

Hacienda   Sonoma. Table ∗∗→∗∗∗
> Small winery at Sonoma specializing in high-quality CHARDONNAY and GEWÜRZ. Recently good CABERNET.

Hanzell   Sonoma. Table ∗∗∗
> Small winery which revolutionized Californian CHARDONNAYS in the '50s under its founder, now in new hands. PINOT NOIR now also good.

Harbor Winery   San Joaquin. Table ∗∗∗
> Tiny winery using AMADOR and NAPA grapes to make first-rate ZINFANDEL and CHARDONNAY.

Heitz   Napa. Table (and dessert) ∗∗∗∗
> In many eyes the first name in California. An inspired individual wine-maker who has set standards for the whole industry. His CABERNETS (esp. "Martha's Vineyard") are dark, deep and emphatic, his best CHARDONNAYS peers of Montrachet.

Hoffmann Mtn. Ranch   Cen. Coast/San Luis Obispo. Table ⟨**∗∗**⟩
> Small winery in new area near Paso Robles. CHARDONNAY and PINOT NOIR are promising.

Hop Kiln   Sonoma/Russian River. Table ∗∗
> Small winery. Individual, flavoury PETIT SIRAH, ZIN, GEWÜRZ.

Inglenook   Napa and San Joaquin. Table and dessert ⭐ →★★★
One of the great old Napa wineries recently much changed by new owners: Heublein Corp. Special Cask CABERNET SAUVIGNON remains best wine. Other varieties sound. Inglenook Vintage is a second label, Inglenook Navalle a third and the best value: good cheap RUBY, ZINFANDEL and FRENCH COLOMBARD.

(Italian Swiss) Colony   San Joaquin and Sonoma. Full range ★→★★
Honourable old name from Sonoma transferred to San Joaquin by new owners: Heublein Corp. Adequate standards. Lejon is a second label.

Jekel Vineyards   Central Coast/Monterey. Table ★★→★★★
Outstandingly well-made RIESLING and CHARDONNAY. Reds good but less exciting.

Johnsons of Alexander Valley   Sonoma. Table ★★
New small winery with good v'yd. land. CABERNET best.

Jordan   Sonoma. Table ★★★
Extravagant winery specializing in CABERNET. First vintage, '76, released in 1980, exceptionally elegant at a fair price. First CHARDONNAY in 1979.

Keenan, Robert   Napa. Table ★★★
Newcomer with very good first CHARDONNAY and CABERNET. V'yds. on Spring Mountain; wine-maker ex-CHAPPELLET.

Kenwood Vineyards   Sonoma. Table ★★→★★★
Steady small producer of increasingly stylish reds, esp. CABERNET and ZIN. Also good CHARDONNAY and CHENIN BLANC.

Kistler Vineyards   Sonoma. Table ★★
New small winery in hills. First CHARDONNAY (79) was overwhelming. CABERNET and PINOT NOIR to come.

Konocti Cellars   North Coast. Table
New winery in new area: Lake County, east of Sonoma/Mendocino. A growers' co-op. to specialize in reds.

Korbel   Sonoma. Sp. and table ★★★
Long-established sparkling wine specialists. "Natural" and "Brut" are among California's best standard "champagnes".

Kornell, Hanns   Napa. Sp. ★★★
Fine sparkling wine house making excellent full-flavoured dry wines: Brut and Sehr Trocken.

Krug, Charles   Napa. Table and dessert ★★→★★★
Important old winery with reliable range, incl. good CABERNET SAUVIGNON, sweet CHENIN BLANC and very sweet Moscato di Canelli. C.K. is the jug-wine brand.

Kruse, Thomas   Central Coast/Hecker Pass. Table ★★
Well-established maker of sound rustic varietals at Gilroy.

Lambert Bridge   Sonoma. Table ★★
Small 1975 winery nr. Healdsburg has made promising CHARDONNAY; also CABERNET.

Lamont, M.   San Joaquin. Table and dessert ⭐
New name for old Bear Mountain co-op, now owned by Labatt brewery. Well-made varietals, incl. FRENCH COLOMBARD.

Landmark   Sonoma. Table ★★
New winery nr. Windsor with sound CHARDONNAY and CABERNET tending to improve.

Lawrence Winery   Central Coast/San Luis Obispo. Table
Ambitious new mid-size winery.

Lejon   Brand name of ITALIAN SWISS COLONY.

Llords & Elwood   Central Coast. Table and dessert ★→★★
Specialist in sherry-type wines.

Long Vineyards   Napa. Table
New small winery in eastern hills nr. CHAPPELLET. Long is husband of SIMI wine-maker Zelma. So far good CHARDONNAY and late-harvest RIESLING.

Los Hermanos
>Second label of BERINGER.

Lytton Springs   Sonoma. Table ★★
>Small specialist in Russian River ZIN; thick, heady, tannic.

Mark West   Sonoma Table ★★
>New winery in cool sub-region starting well with whites GEWÜRZ, RIESLING, CHARDONNAY.

Markham   Napa. Table ★★?
>New winery with 200 acres. Early releases show promise.

Martin Ray   Central Coast/S. Cruz Mts. Table ★★
>Eccentric small winery famous for high prices.

Martini, Louis   Napa. Table and dessert ★★→ ⌈★★★⌉
>Large but individual winery with very high standards, from jug wines (called "Mountain") up. CABERNET SAUVIGNON one of California's best. BARBERA, PINOT NOIR, ZINFANDEL, GEWÜRZ FOLLE BLANCHE and Moscato Amabile are all fine.

Martini & Prati   Sonoma. Table ★★
>Important winery selling mainly in bulk to others. Uses the name Fountaingrove for a small quantity of good CABERNET.

Masson, Paul   Central Coast. Full range ★→ ⌈★★⌉
>Big, lively and reliable middle-quality winery with good-value varietals, incl. CHARDONNAY, ZINFANDEL. Also Emerald Dry (EM. RIES.) Rubion (RUBY), good cheap sparkling and very good Souzão port-type.

Matanzas Creek   Sonoma. Table ★★
>First wines ('79) were GEWÜRZ and very good PINOT BLANC CHARDONNAY even better. CABERNET to come.

Mayacamas   Napa. Table ★★★★
>First-rate very small v'yd. and winery offering CABERNET SAUVIGNON, CHARDONNAY, ZINFANDEL (sometimes).

McDowell Valley Vineyards   Mendocino. Table
>Big new development using old-established v'yd. to make wide range. To watch.

Mill Creek   Sonoma. Table ★★
>New winery near Healdsburg with ex-SIMI winemaker Mary Ann Graf. First wines are CHARDONNAY, MERLOT, CABERNET.

Mirassou   Central Coast. Full range ★★
>Dynamic mid-sized growers and makers, the fifth generation of the family. Pioneers in SALINAS v'yds. Notable ZINFANDEL, GAMAY BEAUJOLAIS, GEWÜRZ and sparkling.

Mondavi, Robert   Napa. Table ★★★→★★★★
>Twelve-year-old winery with a brilliant record of innovation in styles, equipment and technique. Wines of grace and character incl. CABERNET SAUVIGNON, SAUVIGNON BLANC (sold as Fumé Blanc), CHARDONNAY, PINOT NOIR.

Monterey Peninsula   Central Coast/Salinas. Table ★★
>Very small winery near Carmel making chunky chewable ZINFANDEL and CABERNET from SALINAS and other grapes.

Monterey Vineyard   Central Coast/Salinas. Table ★★
>The first big modern winery of SALINAS, opened 1974. Now owned by Coca Cola. Good ZINFANDEL, GEWÜRZ and SYLVANER and fruity feather-weight GAMAY BEAUJOLAIS.

Monteviña   Amador. Table ★★
>Pioneer small winery in revitalized area: the Shenandoah Valley, Amador County, in the Sierra foothills. ZINFANDEL BARBERA and SAUVIGNON BLANC.

J. W. Morris   North Coast (Oakland). Table and dessert ★★★
>Small specialist in high-quality port-types, both vintage and wood-aged. Mainly SONOMA grapes. Good CHARD., CAB. S., ZIN.

Mount Eden   Central Coast. Table ★★★
>Company owning a major share of what were MARTIN RAY Vineyards. Excellent (and expensive) early wines.

Mount Veeder   Napa. Table ✶✶
    Ambitious little 1973 winery. High prices but signs of quality in CABERNET.

Napa Wine Cellars   Napa. Table ✶✶
    Small Yountville winery with steady record, esp. for CABERNET and ZIN.

Navarro Vineyards   Mendocino. Table
    Small specialist in GEWÜRZ in cool Anderson Valley.

Nichelini   Napa. Table ✶✶
    Small old-style family winery selling sound varietals at the cellar door.

Novitiate of Los Gatos   Central Coast. Dessert and Table ✶✶
    Jesuit-run altar-wine-orientated unrevolutionary winery with some adequate varietals, inadequately distributed.

Orso Fumoso   Sonoma. Table ✶
    Small winery with brown fur specializing in FUMÉ BLANC.

Papagni, Angelo   San Joaquin. Table and sp.   ✶✶
    Grower of an old family with a technically outstanding modern winery at Madera. Dry coastal-style varietals incl. ex. ZIN, good Alicante Bouschet, light "Moscato d'Angelo".

Parducci   Mendocino. Table   ✶✶
    Well-established mid-sized winery with v'yds. in several locations. Good sturdy reds: CABERNET SAUVIGNON, PETITE SYRAH, ZINFANDEL, Burgundy. Also pleasant slightly sweet CHENIN BLANC and FRENCH COLOMBARD.

Pecota, Robert   Napa. Table   ✶✶
    New small cellar of ex-Beringer man with high standards. Wines are FLORA, CABERNET, SAUVIGNON BLANC, excellent Beaujolais-style GAMAY.

Pedroncelli   Sonoma R-R. Table   ✶✶
    Second-generation family business with recent reputation for well-above-average ZINFANDEL, PINOT NOIR and CHARDONNAY in a ripe rural style.

Perelli-Minetti   San Joaquin. Table and dessert ✶
    Big firm with chequered history as California Wine Association. Two principal labels: Ambassador and Guasti. Also "Greystone".

Phelps, Joseph   Napa. Table ✶✶✶→✶✶✶✶
    De-luxe mid-size winery and v'yd. Late harvest RIESLING exceptional. Very good CHARDONNAY, CABERNET, SYRAH and ZIN. Second label Le Fleuron.

Preston   Sonoma. Table (Possible ✶✶✶)
    Tiny winery with very high standards in Dry Creek Valley, Healdsburg. So far SAUVIGNON BLANC and CABERNET.

Rafanelli, J.   Sonoma. Table   ✶✶
    Tiny local cellar specializing in outstanding ZIN; also GAMAY BEAUJOLAIS.

Raymond Vineyards   Napa. Table   ✶✶✶
    Small 1974 winery near St. Helena with experienced owners. Early ZIN, CHARDONNAY, CHENIN BLANC and CABERNET all excellent.

Ridge   Central Coast S. CRUZ. Table ✶✶✶✶
    Small winery of high repute among connoisseurs for powerful concentrated reds needing long maturing in bottle. Notable CABERNET and very strong ZINFANDEL.

River Oaks   Sonoma. Table ✶→✶✶
    Sound commercial wines from same winery as CLOS DU BOIS.

Round Hill   Napa. Table   ✶✶
    Consistent good value, esp. GEWÜRZ and CABERNET, from St. Helena.

Roudon-Smith   Santa Clara/Santa Cruz. ✶✶→   ✶✶✶
    New small winery. Really stylish CHARDONNAY.

Royal Host

Brand name for EAST-SIDE winery.

Rutherford Hill Napa. Table **★★**

Recent larger stable-mate of FREEMARK ABBEY. Good early GEWÜRZ, MERLOT, ZIN. Promising CHARDONNAY and CABERNET.

Rutherford Vintners Napa. Table **★★★**

New small winery started in 1977 by Bernard Skoda, former LOUIS MARTINI manager. CABERNET and RIESLING will be specialities; also PINOT NOIR, MERLOT, CHARDONNAY.

St. Clement Napa. Table **★★★**

Small production of very good CABERNET and CHARDONNAY. Both need age.

St. Francis Sonoma. Table

New small winery to use excellent CABERNET, GEWÜRZ from older v'yd.

Sanford and Benedict Santa Barbara Table **★★★**

New winery whose first CHARDONNAY and PINOT NOIR (1976) caused a stir. Uneven quality.

San Martin Central Coast. Table and dessert **★★→ ★★★**

Newly restructured old company using SALINAS and SAN LUIS OBISPO grapes to make clean, correct varietals of increasing quality. "Select Vintage" is top-line label. Also pioneers in "soft" (low-alcohol) wines, esp. RIESLING.

San Pascual S. California. Table **★→★★**

New winery near San Diego with pleasant whites, esp. CHENIN BLANC, SAUVIGNON BLANC.

Santa Ynez Valley Winery Santa Barbara. Table **★★**

Promising whites, esp. SAUVIGNON BLANC, from new winery.

Sausal Sonoma. Table

Small specialist in stylish ZIN, etc.

Schramsberg Napa. Sp. **★★★★**

A dedicated specialist using historic old cellars to make California's best "champagne".

Sebastiani Sonoma. Table and dessert **★★**

Substantial and distinguished old family firm with robust appetizing wines, esp. BARBERA, GAMAY BEAUJOLAIS, PINOT NOIR. Top wines have SONOMA appellation.

Setrakian

See California Growers.

Shaw, Charles F., Vineyards and Winery Napa. Table

Off-beat St. Helena specialist in GAMAY light red.

Silver Oak Napa. Table **★★→★★★**

Small 1972 winery succeeding with oaky CABERNET.

Simi Alexander Valley. Table **★★★**

Restored old winery with expert direction. Several notable wines, incl. racy GEWÜRZ, gentle ZINFANDEL, delicate CABERNET.

Smith-Madrone Napa. Table **★★→★★★**

New v'yd. high on Spring Mountain made good RIESLING in '77, '78 CHARDONNAY excellent.

Smothers Santa Clara/Santa Cruz. Table

Tiny winery owned by T.V. comic made remarkable first wines, esp. late-harvest GEWÜRZ.

Sonoma Vineyards Sonoma R-R. Table and sp. **★★** **→★★★**

Quick-growing business, well-regarded for varietals, esp. RIESLING and CHARDONNAY. Range includes single-v'yd. wines, esp. Alexander's Crown CABERNET.

Souverain Alexander Valley. Table **★★**

Luxurious new mid-sized winery with highly competent wines, both red and white, if no great ones.

Spring Mountain Napa. Table ★★★
Recently renovated small 19th-century property with new winery already noted for good CHARDONNAY, SAUVIGNON BLANC and CABERNET.

Stag's Leap Wine Cellars Napa. Table ★★★→★★★★
New small v'yd. and cellar with high standards. Excellent CABERNET and MERLOT, fresh GAMAY, soft RIESLING, fine CHARDONNAY.

Sterling Napa. Table ★★★
Spectacular new mid-sized winery, now owned by Coca-Cola, with already startling achievements. Strong, tart SAUVIGNON BLANC and CHARDONNAY; fruity CABERNET and MERLOT.

Stonegate Napa. Table ★★→★★★
Small privately-owned winery and v'yd. making CABERNET, SAUVIGNON BLANC, CHARDONNAY.

Stony Hill Napa. Table ★★★★
Many of California's very best whites have come from this minute winery over 25 years. Alas owner Fred McCrea died in 1977, but his wife Eleanor carries on. Stony Hill CHARDONNAY, GEWÜRZ and RIESLING are all delicate and fine.

Sutter Home Napa. Table ★★
Small winery revived, specializing in ZINFANDEL from Amador County grapes: excellent heavy-weight.

Swan, J. Sonoma. Table ★★
New one-man winery with a name for rich ZINFANDEL.

Trefethen Napa. Table ★★★→★★★★
Small family-owned winery in Napa's finest old wooden building. Good RIESLING, CABERNET. Brilliant CHARDONNAY.

Trentadue Sonoma R-R. Table ★★
Small v'yd. and smaller winery making sound big-flavoured wines, incl. some from unorthodox varieties.

Tulocay Napa. Table
Tiny new winery at Napa City. First wines are good PINOT NOIR and CABERNET.

Turgeon & Lohr Central Coast. Table ★★
Small winery in San Jose with its own v'yds. in SALINAS. Reliable RIESLING and CABERNET.

Veedercrest Napa. Table ★★
Small winery with mixed performance; CABERNET best.

Ventana Central Coast/Monterey. Table
New in '78 with flavoury PINOT BLANC and CHARDONNAY.

Villa Armando Livermore/San Joaquin. Table ★
Specialist in the American-Italian market for coarse sweet table wines.

Villa Mount Eden Napa. ★★★
Small Oakville estate with excellent dry CHENIN BLANC, good CHARDONNAY, and CABERNET outstanding.

Weibel Central Coast. Table and sp. ★
Veteran mid-sized winery without high ambitions.

Wente Livermore and Central Coast. Table ★★→★★★
Important and historic specialists in Bordeaux-style whites. Fourth-generation Wentes are as dynamic as ever. CHARDONNAY, SAUVIGNON BLANC and RIESLING are all successful commercial wines.

Winemasters
Brand name of GUILD.

Zaca Mesa Central Coast/Santa Barbara. Table ★★
Santa Ynez Valley pioneer most successful with CHARDONNAY and RIESLING.

Z-D Wines Napa. Table ★★★
Very small winery (moved from Sonoma to Rutherford) with a name for powerful PINOT NOIR and CHARDONNAY.

The Pacific North-West

Vineyards have now been planted in at least half of the States in the Union — Texas included. So far the only ones that present a palpable challenge to California (for quality not quantity) are Oregon and Washington in the north-west and their inland neighbour, Idaho.

Oregon's vineyards lie in the cool-temperate Willamette and slightly warmer Umpqua valleys between the Coast and Cascades ranges. Those of Washington and Idaho are mainly east of the Cascades in the semi-arid Yakima Valley and Columbia basin areas, with very hot days and cold nights. Oregon-grown wines are consequently more delicate, Washington's more intensive in flavour. Several wineries use both. Whites are in the majority, though Oregon has high hopes for Pinot Noir.

The principal current producers are:

Amity Vineyards   Oregon
> Very small Willamette winery; uneven results but PINOT NOIR promising.

Associated Vintners   Washington
> A Washington pioneer at Redmond, nr. Seattle. CABERNET, SEMILLON, RIESLING and GEWÜRZTRAMINER have all been successful. Good value.

Château Ste. Chapelle   Idaho
> The only Idaho winery, near Boise. CHARDONNAY or RIESLING with exceptionally intense flavours are very promising.

Château Ste. Michelle   Washington
> The largest north-west winery, with very modern equipment and a wide range of labels. Best wines are CABERNET, SEMILLON, RIESLING and a dry MUSCAT. Sparkling wines to come.

Elk Cove Vineyards   Oregon
> Very small new winery. Good CHARDONNAY and RIESLING. Also PINOT NOIR.

The Eyrie Vineyards   Oregon
> Early (1965) Willamette Valley winery with Burgundian ideas; remarkable oak-aged PINOT NOIR and CHARDONNAY.

Hill Crest Vineyard   Oregon
> Early (1961) Umpqua Valley winery. Inconsistent, but RIESLING, GEWÜRZTRAMINER and PINOT NOIR can score well.

Knudsen-Erath   Oregon
> Willamette Valley vineyards with reliable good-value PINOT NOIR, RIESLING. CHARDONNAY and GEWÜRZTRAMINER can also be good.

Ponzi Vineyards   Oregon
> Tiny family winery near Portland. RIESLING and CHARDONNAY are best wines. "Oregon Harvest" is a CHARDONNAY/PINOT BLANC blend.

Preston Wine Cellars   Washington
> Rapidly growing new Yakima Valley winery already acclaimed, especially for SAUVIGNON BLANC and MERLOT. Also CHARDONNAY, RIESLING, GEWÜRZTRAMINER.

Sokol Blosser Vineyards   Oregon
> New Willamette Valley winery with wide range, including CHARDONNAY, SAUVIGNON BLANC, Müller-Thurgau, highly rated PINOT NOIR, MERLOT and (slightly sweet) RIESLING.

Tualatin Vineyards   Oregon
> Consistently good specialist (hitherto) in whites, west of Portland. Known for RIESLING, GEWÜRZTRAMINER and dry MUSCAT. Recently promising PINOT NOIR.

New York

New York State and its neighbours Ohio and Ontario make their own style of wine from grapes of native American ancestry, rather than the European vines of California. American grapes have a flavour known as "foxy"; a taste acquired by many easterners. Fashion is slowly moving in favour of hybrids between these and European grapes with less, or no, foxiness. The entries below include both wineries and grape varieties.

Aurora
One of the best white French-American hybrid grapes, the most widely planted in New York. Formerly known as Seibel 5279. Good for sparkling wine.

Baco Noir
One of the better red French-American hybrid grapes. High acidity but good clean dark wine.

Benmarl
Highly regarded and expanding v'yd. and winery at Marlboro on the Hudson River. Wines are mainly from French-American hybrids, but European vines also make good wine.

Boordy Vineyards
The winery which pioneered French-American hybrid grapes in the USA. Started by Philip Wagner in Maryland in the '50s.

Brights
Canada's biggest winery, in Ontario, now tending towards French-American hybrids and experiments with European vines. Their CHELOIS and BACO NOIR are pleasant reds, respectively lighter and more full-bodied.

Bully Hill
New (since 1970) FINGER LAKES winery using both American and hybrid grapes to make varietal wines.

Château Gai
Canadian (Ontario) winery making European and hybrid wines, incl. successful GAMAY and PINOT NOIR.

Catawba
One of the first American wine-grapes, still the second most widely grown. Pale red and foxy flavoured.

Chautauqua
The biggest grape-growing district in the e., along the s. shore of La. Erie from New York to Ohio.

Chelois
Popular red French-American hybrid grape, formerly called Seibel 10878. Makes dry red wine with some richness, slightly foxy.

Concord
The archetypal American grape, dark red, strongly foxy, making good grape jelly but dreadful wine. By far the most widely planted in New York (23,000 acres).

Delaware
Old American white-wine grape making pleasant, slightly foxy dry wines. Used in "Champagne" and for still wine.

De Chaunac
A good red French-American hybrid grape, popular in Canada as well as New York. Full-bodied dark wine.

Finger Lakes
Century-old wine district in upper New York State, best-known for its "Champagne". The centre is Hammondsport.

Fournier, Charles
The top quality of "Champagne" made by the GOLD SEAL company, named for a former pioneering wine-maker.

Frank, Dr. Konstantin
>A controversial figure in the FINGER LAKES: the protagonist of European vinifera vines. See Vinifera Wines.

Gold Seal
>One of New York's biggest wineries, makers of Charles FOURNIER "Champagne" and the HENRI MARCHANT range. Known for high quality and readiness to experiment.

Great Western
>The brand name of the PLEASANT VALLEY WINE CO's "Champagne", one of New York's best wines.

Hargrave Vineyard
>Trend-setting winery with 50 acres on North Fork of Long Island. Very promising CHARDONNAY, PINOT NOIR.

Henri Marchant
>Brand name of GOLD SEAL's standard range of mainly traditional American-grape wines.

Inniskillin
>Small new Canadian winery at Niagara making European and hybrid wines, incl. good MARÉCHAL FOCH.

Isabella
>Old CONCORD-style red grape making strongly foxy wine.

Phylloxera is an insect that lives on the roots of the vine. Its arrival in Europe from North America in the 1860s was an international catastrophe. It destroyed almost every vineyard on the continent before it was discovered that the native American vine is immune to its attacks. The remedy was (and still is) to graft European vines on to American rootstocks. Virtually all Europe's vineyards are so grafted today. Whether their produce is just as good as the wine of pre-phylloxera days is a favourite debate among old-school wine-lovers.

Maréchal Foch
>Promising red French hybrid between PINOT NOIR and GAMAY Makes good burgundy-style wine in Ontario.

Moore's Diamond
>Old American white grape still grown in New York.

Niagara
>Old American white grape used for sweet wine. Very foxy.

Pleasant Valley Wine Co.
>Winery at Hammondsport, FINGER LAKES, owned by TAYLOR'S, producing GREAT WESTERN wines.

Seibel
>One of the most famous French grape hybridists, responsible for many successful French-American crosses originally known by numbers, since christened with such names as AURORA, DE CHAUNAC, CHELOIS.

Seyve-Villard
>Another well-known French hybridist. His best-known cross no. 5276, is known as Seyval Blanc.

Taylor's
>The biggest wine-company of the Eastern States, based at Hammondsport in the FINGER LAKES. Brands incl. GREAT WESTERN and LAKE COUNTRY. Most vines are American.

Vinifera Wines
>Small but influential winery of Dr Frank, pioneer in growing European vines, incl. RIESLING, CHARDONNAY and PINOT NOIR in the FINGER LAKES area. Some excellent wines.

Widmers
>Major FINGER LAKES winery selling native American varietal wines: DELAWARE, NIAGARA, etc.

South America

The flourishing vineyards of Argentina (the world's fifth largest) and Chile are known to the world chiefly as a source of cheap wine of sometimes remarkable quality. Most of it is drunk within South America. Brazil also has an expanding wine industry in the Rio Grande do Sul area, but as yet no exports.

ARGENTINA

The quality vineyards are concentrated in Mendoza province in the Andean foothills at about 2,000 feet. They are all irrigated. San Raphael, 140 miles s. of Mendoza city, is centre of a slightly cooler area. San Juan, to the north, is hotter and specializes in sherry and brandy.

Andean Vineyards

Widely distributed brand of adequate quality from PEÑAFLOR.

Bianchi, Bodegas

Well-known premium wine producer at San Raphael owned by Seagrams. "Don Valentin" CABERNET is a best-seller. "1887" and "Particular" are top CABERNETS.

Castell Chandon

Excellent fresh "tipo Rhin" from a Moët offshoot.

Cooperation San Raphael

Enormous co-operative for bulk wines and concentrated grape juice.

Crillon, Bodegas

Brand-new (1972) winery owned by Seagram's, principally for tank-method sparkling wines.

Furlotti, Angel

Big bodega at Maipu, Mendoza. 2,500 acres making its best red wine from a blend of CABERNET, MERLOT and Lambrusco, white from PINOT BLANC and RIESLING. Owned by GRECO HERMANOS.

Giol

The enormous State winery of Maipu province. Mainly bulk wines. Premium range is called "Canciller".

Gonzales Videla, Bodegas

Old-established family firm re-equipped for modern methods. Brands include "Tromel" and "Panquehua".

Goyenechea, Bodegas

Basque family firm making old-style wines.

Greco Hermanos

1,750-acre v'yds. at St. Martin, Mendoza, with Malbec, Lambrusco, BARBERA, SEMILLON, PALOMINO, etc. Range incl. El Greco "selection" and Oro del Rhin (PINOT BLANC). The giant company has serious financial problems.

La Rural, Bodegas

Family-run winery at Coquimbito making some of Argentina's best Riesling and Traminer whites and some good reds.

Lopez, Bodegas

Family firm best known for their "Château Montchenot" red and white and "Château Vieux" CABERNET.

Norton, Bodegas

Old firm, originally English now owned by Seagrams, at Perdriol. "Perdriel" is brand-name of 10-year-old premium Cabernet in flask-bottles.

Orfila, José

Long-established bodega at St. Martin, Mendoza. Top export wines are CABERNET and white Extra Dry (PINOT BLANC).

Peñaflor

Four v. modern bodegas and 3,000 acres in San Juan and Mendoza. Range includes Andean and Trapiche brands of CABERNET, CHARDONNAY and PINOT BLANC; also good-value red in cans. Tio Quinto is their popular medium sherry.

Proviar, Bodega
Producers of "champaña" (sparkling wine) under contract with MOËT ET CHANDON. Premium brand is "Baron B".

Santa Ana, Bodegas
Old-established family firm at Guaymallen. Wide range of wines.

Suter, Bodegas
Swiss-founded firm best-known for "Etiquetta Marron" white and "Juan Suter" reds.

Toso, Pascual
Old Mendoza winery at San José, making one of Argentina's best reds, Cabernet Toso. Also RIESLING and sparkling wines.

Trapiche
Popular range of wines from PEÑAFLOR.

Weinert, Bodegas
New winery producing crisp, fruity, modern-style white.

CHILE

Natural conditions are ideal for wine-growing in central Chile, just south of Santiago. But political conditions have been very difficult, and the country's full potential still has to be explored. The Cabernets are best. The principal bodegas exporting wine from Chile are:

Canepa, José
A modern establishment at Valparaiso handling wine from several areas. Very good French-style CABERNET from Lontüé, Talca, 100 miles south; dry SEMILLON, sweet Moscatel.

Concha y Toro
The biggest and most outward-looking wine firm, with several bodegas and 2,500 acres in the Maipo valley. Remarkable dark and deep CABERNET, MERLOT, Verdot. Brands are St. Emiliana, Marques de Casa Concha, Cassillero del Diablo.

Cousiño Macul
Distinguished estate near Santiago. Very dry "green" SEMILLON and CHARDONNAY. Don Luis light red, Don Matias dark and tannic, are good CABERNETS.

Santa Carolina
A bodega with pleasant widely available dry wines mainly consumed in S. America.

Santa Helena/San Pedro
Brands now controlled by RUMASA (see Spain), long established at Lontüé, Talca. Range of good wines sold all over S. America, esp. Bordeaux-like CABERNET.

Santa Rita
Bodega in the Maipo valley s. of Santiago. Pleasant soft wines including the "120" brand.

Tocornal, José
Considerable exporter to Venezuela and Canada.

Torres, Miguel
New enterprise of Catalonian family firm (see Spain). Viña Santa Digna CABERNET and light gassy SAUVIGNON white.

Undurraga
Famous family business; one of the first to export to the U.S.A. Wines in both old and modern styles: good clean SAUVIGNON BLANC and oaky yellow "Viejo Roble". "Gran Vino Tinto" is one of the best buys in Chile.

Viña Linderos
Small family winery in the Maipo valley exports good full-bodied CABERNET.

England

The English wine industry started again in earnest in the late 1960s after a pause of some 400 years. More than a million bottles a year are now being made; almost all white and generally Germanic in style, many from new German and French grape varieties designed to ripen well in cool weather. In such a young industry results of prize competitions are studied with interest. The annual Gore-Brown Trophy is awarded for the best English wine.

Adgestone nr. Sandown, Isle of Wight. K. C. Barlow
Prize-winning 9-acre v'yd. on chalky hill site. Vines are MÜLLER-THURGAU, Reichensteiner, SEYVAL BLANC. First vintage was 1970. Light, fragrant, dryish wines.

Beaulieu nr. Lymington, Hampshire. The Hon. Ralph Douglas Scott-Montagu
6-acre v'yd, principally of MÜLLER-THURGAU, established in 1960 by the Gore-Brown family on an old monastic site.

Biddenden nr. Tenterden, Kent. R. A. Barnes
18-acre mixed v'yd. planted in 1970, making crisp medium-dry white of MÜLLER-THURGAU and Ortega; also a rosé with PINOT NOIR. First vintage 1973. Also makes wine for other growers.

Bosmere nr. Chippenham, Wiltshire. G. H. Walton
16 acres of MÜLLER-THURGAU and SEYVAL BLANC; some GAMAY and PINOT NOIR.

Bruisyard nr. Saxmundham, Suffolk. I. H. Berwick
10 acres of MÜLLER-THURGAU making medium-dry wines since 1976. Well distributed..

Carr Taylor Vineyards nr. Hastings, Sussex. D. Carr-Taylor
21 acres, planted 1974. Gutenborner, Huxelrebe, KERNER and Reichensteiner.

Cavendish Manor nr. Sudbury, Suffolk. B. T. Ambrose
10-acre v'yd. of MÜLLER-THURGAU planted on a farm. Fruity dry wine has won several awards at home and abroad since 1974.

Chilford Hundred Linton, nr. Cambridge. S. Alper
16 acres of MÜLLER-THURGAU, Schönburger, Huxelrebe, Siegerrebe and Ortega making fairly dry wines since 1974.

Chilsdown nr. Chichester, Sussex. I. R. Paget
10½ acres of MÜLLER-THURGAU, Reichensteiner and SEYVAL BLANC making full dry French-style white since 1974.

Elmham Park nr. East Dereham, Norfolk. R. Don
7½-acre v'yd. of a wine-merchant/fruit farmer, planted with MÜLLER-THURGAU, Madeleine-Angevine, etc. "Mosel-style" light dry flowery wines. First vintage 1974. Also a fine dry cider.

Felstar Felsted, nr. Dunmow, Essex J. G. Barrett
Well-established 10½-acre v'yd. of many varieties, selling Madeleine Sylvaner, MÜLLER-THURGAU, SEYVAL BLANC/ CHARDONNAY, MUSCAT and a PINOT NOIR red.

Gamlingay nr. Sandy, Bedfordshire. G. P. and N. Reece
10 acres of MÜLLER-THURGAU, Reichensteiner and SCHEUREBE making wine since 1970.

Hambledon nr. Petersfield, Hampshire. Maj. Gen. Sir Guy Salisbury Jones
The first modern English v'yd., planted in 1951 on a chalk slope with advice from Champagne. Grapes are CHARDONNAY, PINOT NOIR and Pinot Meunier. Now 5½ acres. Fairly dry wines.

Hascombe Godalming, Surrey. Lt. Cdr. T. P. Baillie-Grohman
5¾-acre v'yd., principally MÜLLER-THURGAU, making dry delicate wines since 1971.

Highwayman's nr. Bury St. Edmunds, Suffolk. Macrae Farms
25 acres, planted 1974. MÜLLER-THURGAU and PINOT NOIR.

Kelsale nr. Saxmundham, Suffolk. S. T. Edgerley
2¼-acre v'yd. owned by a retired barrister, making stylish
wines. Winner of 1977 Gore-Brown Trophy with a MÜLLER-
THURGAU/Seyve-Villard blend.

Lamberhurst Priory nr. Tunbridge Wells, Kent. K. McAlpine
England's biggest v'yd. with 35 acres, planted 1972. Largely
MÜLLER-THURGAU, SEYVAL BLANC, also Reichensteiner, Schönburger. Production capacity approx. half a million bottles a
year including wine-making for other small v'yds.

Lexham Hall nr. Kings Lynn, Norfolk. N. W. D. Foster
8 acres, planted 1975. MÜLLER-THURGAU, SCHEUREBE,
Reichensteiner and Madeleine-Angevine.

Merrydown Wine Co. Heathfield, E. Sussex. J. L. Ward
A major influence on English wine-making, having started in
1946 with cider and since 1969 acted as a co-operative for the
young wine industry. Now making an estate MÜLLER-
THURGAU, "Horam Manor" (2 acres).

New Hall nr. Maldon, Essex. S. W. Greenwood
22 acres of a mixed farm planted with Huxelrebe, MÜLLER-
THURGAU and PINOT NOIR. Makes award-winning whites.
Experimental reds.

Pilton Manor nr. Shepton Mallet, Somerset. N. de M. Godden
13-acre hillside v'yd., chiefly of MÜLLER-THURGAU and SEYVAL
BLANC, planted 1966. Twice winner of Gore-Brown Trophy.
Also a méthode champenoise sparkling wine.

Pulham nr. Norwich, Norfolk. P. W. Cook
6-acre v'yd. planted 1973; principally MÜLLER-THURGAU,
Auxerrois and experimental Bacchus.

Rock Lodge nr. Haywards Heath, Sussex. N. D. Cowderoy
3½-acre v'yd. of MÜLLER-THURGAU and Reichensteiner making
dry white since 1970.

St. Etheldreda nr. Ely, Cambridgeshire. N. Sneesby
2½-acre mixed v'yd. making a MÜLLER-THURGAU and a CHAR-
DONNAY since 1974.

Staple nr. Canterbury, Kent. W. T. Ash
7 acres, mainly MÜLLER-THURGAU. Some Huxelrebe and
Reichensteiner. First sales 1977. Dry and fruity wines.

Stocks nr. Suckley, Worcestershire. R. M. O. Capper
Successful 11-acre v'yd. All MÜLLER-THURGAU.

Tenterden nr. Tenterden, Kent. S. P. Skelton
6 acres of a 100-acre fruit farm. Planted 1977. Six wines from
very dry to sweet, incl. MÜLLER-THURGAU, Gutenborner,
SEYVAL BLANC.

Three Choirs nr. Newent, Gloucestershire. A. A. McKechnie
18 acres of MÜLLER-THURGAU and Reichensteiner.

Westbury nr. Reading, Berkshire. B. H. Theobald
16 acres of a mixed farm. 11 varieties in commercial quantities since 1975, incl. PINOT NOIR red.

Wootton nr. Wells, Somerset. Major C. L. B. Gillespie
6-acre v'yd. of Schönburger, MÜLLER-THURGAU, SEYVAL BLANC,
etc., making award-winning fresh and fruity wines since
1973.

Wraxall nr. Shepton Mallet, Somerset. A. S. Holmes
5 acres of MÜLLER-THURGAU and SEYVAL BLANC. Planted 1974.

Australia

S.A.

Clare/
Watervale
Barossa
Murray Valley
Adelaide
uthern Langhorne
ales Creek
Coonawarra

Hunter
Valley

Riverina   N.S.W.

Canberra ●
Rutherglen

N.E. VIC.

CENTRAL VIC.
Great
Western
● Melbourne

It is only 20 years since modern wine technology revolutionized Australia's 150-year-old wine industry, ending the
dominance of fortified wines and making table wines of top
quality possible. Already the results are as impressive as
California's. The Australians know it: little is left for export.

Traditional-style Australian wines were thick-set and
burly Shiraz reds or Semillon or Riesling whites. The modern taste is for lighter wines, especially Rhine Rieslings, and
for Cabernet reds, but the best still have great character and
the ability to age splendidly.

Australia's wine labels are among the world's most com-
municative. Since Australians started to take their own
wine seriously they have become longer and longer winded,
with information about grapes, soil, sunshine, fermenting
periods and temperatures, wine-makers' biographies and
serving hints. Little of this is pure salesmanship. It is
intended to be, and really is, helpful. Bin-numbers mean
something. They need to be noted and remembered. Prizes in
shows (which are highly competitive) mean a great deal. In a
country without any sort of established grades of quality the
buyer needs all the help he can get.

Wine areas

The vintages mentioned here are those rated as good or excellent for
the reds of the areas in question. Excellent recent vintages are
marked with an accent, e.g. 80'.

Adelaide   66 67 70 71 72 73 75 76 77 79 80' 81
    The capital of South Australia had the state's first v'yds. A
    few are still making wine.
Barossa   66 68 72 73 75 76 77 79 80' 81'
    Australia's biggest quality area, of German origin, specializ-
    ing in white (esp. Riesling; best from the Eden Valley at 1,500
    feet), good-quality reds and good dessert wines.
Clare-Watervale   66 68 70 71 72 75 76 77 78 79 81
    Small cool-climate area 90 miles n. of Adelaide best known
    for Riesling; also planted with Shiraz and Cabernet.

Central Victoria   66 68 71 73 74 76 79 80
>   Scattered v'yds. remaining from vast pre-phylloxera plantings include GT. WESTERN, CH. TAHBILK, AVOCA and BENDIGO.

Coonawarra   66 68 70 71 72 73 74 75 76 77 79 80 81
>   Southernmost v'yd. of South Australia, long famous for well-balanced reds, recently successful with Riesling.

Hunter Valley   66 67 70 72 73 74 75 76 77 79 80′ 81
>   The great name in N.S.W. Broad deep Shiraz reds and Semillon whites with a style of their own. Now also Cabernet and Chardonnay. Recent expansion at Wybong, etc., to the w.

Keppoch/Padthaway   75 76 77 78 79 80′ 81′
>   Large new area in southern S. Australia being developed by big companies as an overspill of Coonawarra. Cool climate and good potential for commercial reds and whites.

Langhorne Creek
>   See Southern Vales

Lilydale/Yarra Valley   77 78 80′ 81
>   Historic wine area near Melbourne destroyed by phylloxera, now being redeveloped by enthusiasts with small wineries. A bewildering range of varieties and styles.

N.E. Victoria   66 70 71 72 73 75 76 80′
>   Historic area incl. Rutherglen, Corowa, Wangaratta. Heavy reds and magnificent sweet dessert wines.

Margaret River/Busselton
>   New area of great promise for fine wines, s. of Perth in W. Australia.

McLaren Vale and S. Adelaide
>   See Southern Vales

Mudgee   73 74 75 77 78 79′
>   Small traditional wine area in a N.S.W. fruit-growing district. Big reds of considerable colour and flavour and full coarse whites recently being refined.

Murray Valley   N.V.
>   Important scattered v'yds. irrigated from the Murray river, incl. Swan Hill, Mildura, Renmark, Berri, Loxton, Waikerie. Largely sherry, brandy, "jug" and dessert wines.

Riverina   N.V.
>   Fruit- and vine-growing district irrigated from the Murrumbidgee river. Mainly jug wines, but good light "varietals".

Southern Vales   66 67 70 71 72 73 75 76 77 79 80′ 81
>   General name for several small pockets of wine-growing s. of Adelaide of which McLaren Vale is the most important. Big full-blooded reds and rather coarse whites.

Swan Valley
>   The main v'yd. of Western Australia, on the n. outskirts of Perth. Hot climate makes strong low-acid wines.

Upper Hunter   69 73 75 76 79 80 81′
>   New region 60 miles N.W. of Hunter Valley, N.S.W. with more extreme climate, specializing in white wines, lighter and quicker-developing than Hunter whites.

Wineries

All Saints   N.E. Vic. Full range ★→★★
>   Big old family-run winery in dessert-wine country. Sturdy reds. Sweet brown MUSCAT is sometimes exceptional.

Angove's   S.A. Table and dessert ★→★★
>   Family business in Adelaide and Renmark in the Murray Valley. Sound traditional wines.

Arrowfield   N.S.W. Table ★
>   The largest Upper Hunter vineyard, on irrigated land. Some pleasant dry whites, including RH. RIESLING.

Bailey's   N.E. Vic. Table and dessert ★★→★★★
>   Small family concern making rich old-fashioned reds of great character, esp. Bundarra Hermitage and dessert MUSCAT.

Balgownie   Vic. Table ★★★
>   Specialist in fine reds, particularly straight CABERNET.

Berri Coop.   S. Aus. full range   ★→★★
>   Aus's largest winery, selling mostly to other companies. Now developing own name with success; esp. robust oaky reds.

Best's   Central Vic. Full range ★→★★
>   Conservative old family winery at Great Western with good strong old-style claret, hock, etc.

Bilyara   N. Barossa. S. Aus. Table and sp. ★★→★★★
>   Wolf Blass is the ebullient German wine-maker with dazzling products and propaganda. His oaky wines are not for keeping.

Bleasdale   Langhorne Creek, S.A. Full range ★→★★
>   Small family business making above-average reds of CABERNET and SHIRAZ.

Bowen Estate   S.A. Table ★★★
>   Small Coonawarra winery; intense CABERNET SAUVIGNON, and Cabernet blends, particularly 1978.

Brand   Coonawarra, S.A. Table   ★★★
>   Small privately owned winery. Outstandingly fine and stylish CABERNET and SHIRAZ under the Laira label.

Brokenwood   N.S.W. Dry red   ★★★
>   New small winery owned by lawyers blends Hunter wine with Coonawarra from BRAND. Exciting quality of CABERNET SAUVIGNON and SHIRAZ since 1973.

Brown Brothers   Milawa, N.E. Victoria. Full range   ★→★★★
>   Old family firm with new ideas, wide range of rather delicate wines, including several well-made varietals from various districts, a refreshing change from the blood-and-guts style of the area.

Buring, Leo   Barossa, S.A. Full range ★→★★★
>   "Château Leonay", old white-wine specialists, now owned by LINDEMAN. Very good "Reserve Bin" RHINE RIESLING.

Château Tahbilk   Central Vic. Table ★→★★★
>   Family-owned wine-estate making CABERNET, SHIRAZ, RHINE RIESLING and Marsanne. "Special Bins" are outstanding.

Château Yaldara   Barossa, S.A. Full range ★
>   A showpiece of Barossa, popular with tourists. Sparkling wines are a speciality.

Conteville   W. Aus. Table   ★★
>   New winery north of Perth. Richly flavoured reds and light dry muscat table wines, also experimentals from Mt. Barker in the south.

Craigmoor   N.S.W. Table and Port ★→★★
>   The oldest Mudgee winery. Robust reds and whites, and port matured in rum barrels. Also CHARDONNAY.

d'Arenberg   McLaren Vale, S.A. Table and dessert ★→★★
>   Small-scale old-style family outfit s. of Adelaide. Strapping rustic reds; CABERNET, SHIRAZ and Burgundy.

Drayton   Hunter Valley, N.S.W. Table   ★★
>   Traditional Hunter wines, Hermitage red and SEMILLON white, from the old Bellevue estate.

Elliott   Hunter Valley, N.S.W. Table ★★
>   Long-established grower. "Tallawanta" reds and "Belford" whites are in the bosomy, deep-flavoured Hunter style.

Emu   S.A. Table and dessert ★
>   Bulk shippers of high-strength wine to Britain and Canada.

Enterprise Wines   S.A. Table ★★→★★★
>   Tim Knappstein, ex-Stanley, concentrates on RHINE RIESLING and CABERNET SAUVIGNON, made in an old brewery in Clare.

Evans and Tate　W. Aus. Table ⋆⋆→⋆⋆⋆
> A paint manufacturer's hobby of increasing importance. Big, soft, Rhônish reds from both the Swan Valley of W.A. and the south west corner.

Gramp　Barossa, S.A. Full range ⋆→⋆⋆⋆
> Great pioneering family company, now owned by Reckitt & Colman. Range includes sweet fizzy "Barossa Pearl", good standard CABERNET, etc., and some of Australia's best RHINE RIESLING: Steingarten. Typed labels on special wines.

Hamilton's　S. Adelaide and Barossa, S.A. Full range ⋆
> Big family business making popular rather light and "modern" wines, e.g. Ewell Moselle and Springton Riesling.

Hardy's　Southern Vales, S.A., Barossa, etc. Full range ⋆→⋆⋆
> Famous wide-spread family-run company using and blending wines from several areas, incl. a CABERNET, reliable light St. Thomas Burgundy and good Old Castle Riesling.

Henschke　Barossa, S.A. Table ⋆
> Family business known for white wines, esp. RHINE RIESLING.

Houghton　Swan Valley, W.A. Table and dessert ⋆→ ⟦⋆⋆⟧
> The one famous winery of W. Australia. Soft, ripe "White Burgundy" is the top wine. Now also excellent CABERNET.

Hungerford Hill　Hunter Valley, N.S.W. Table ⋆→⋆⋆
> Big new winery with over 1,000 acres and modern ideas.

Huntingdon Estate　N.S.W. Table ⋆→⋆⋆
> New small winery; the best in Mudgee. Fine award-winning reds and clean SEMILLON and CHARDONNAY.

Kaiser Stuhl　Barossa, S.A. Full range ⟦⋆→⋆⋆⋆⟧
> The Barossa growers' co-operative. A fine modern winery with high standards. "Individual v'yd." Rieslings are excellent. So is "Special Reserve" CABERNET.

Krondorf Wines　S.A. Table
> Rejuvenated old winery in Barossa Valley, S.A.; doing well with classic varietals.

Lake's Folly　Hunter Valley, N.S.W. Table ⋆⋆⋆
> The work of an inspired surgeon from Sydney. A new style for the Hunter Valley: CABERNET and new barrels to make rich complex California-style reds. Also excellent CHARDONNAY.

Leasingham　See Stanley

Leconfield　S.A. Table ⋆⋆⋆
> The oldest living wine-maker in Australia, Syd Hamilton, makes Coonawarra CABERNET SAUVIGNON wines of great style.

Lindeman　Orig. Hunter, now everywhere. Full range ⋆→⋆⋆⋆
> One of the oldest firms, now a giant owned by Phillip Morris Corp. Its Ben Ean "Moselle" is Australia's best-selling wine. Owns BURINGS in Barossa and Rouge Homme in Coonawarra. Dessert-wine v'yds. at Corowa, N. Victoria. Many inter-state blends. Pioneers in modernizing wine styles.

McWilliams　Hunter Valley and Riverina, N.S.W. Full range ⟦⋆→⋆⋆⋆⟧
> Famous and first-rate Hunter wine-makers at Mount Pleasant and Lovedale (HERMITAGE and SEMILLON). Pioneers in RIVERINA with lighter wines, incl. sweet white "Lexia" and fine varieties.

Mildara　Murray Valley, S.A. Full range ⋆→⋆⋆⋆
> Sherry and brandy specialists at Mildura on the Murray river also making fine CABERNET and RIESLING at COONAWARRA.

Morris　N.E. Vic. Table and dessert ⋆⋆→⋆⋆⋆⋆
> Old winery at Rutherglen making Australia's best brown "liqueur" muscat. Now owned by Reckitt & Colman.

Moss Wood　W. Aus. Table ⋆⋆⋆
> Tiny 29-acre v'yd. on Margaret River. CABERNET SAUVIGNONS with rich fruit flavours not unlike the best Californians.

Orlando See GRAMPS

Penfold's Orig. Adelaide, now everywhere. Full range ★→★★★★
Ubiquitous and excellent company: in BAROSSA, HUNTER VALLEY, RIVERINA, COONAWARRA, etc. Grange Hermitage is ★★★★, St. Henri Claret not far behind. Bin-numbered wines are usually outstanding. "Grandfather Port" is remarkable.

Petaluma S.A. ★★★
Very promising newcomer, a recent rocket-like success with (N.S.W.-grown) CHARDONNAY and RIESLING, now centred around new winery in ADELAIDE HILLS.

Quelltaler Clare-Watervale, S.A. Full range ★→★★
Old winery n. of Adelaide known for good "Granfiesta" sherry and full dry "hock". Recently good Rhine Riesling.

Redman Coonawarra, S.A. Table ★★★
Small new winery making only COONAWARRA claret of SHIRAZ and CABERNET of top quality.

Reynella Southern Vales, S.A. Full range ★→★★★
Red-wine specialists s. of ADELAIDE. Highly esteemed rich CABERNET and "Vintage Reserve" claret.

The Robson Vineyard N.S.W. Table ★★→★★★
Tiny HUNTER VALLEY winery. Wide range of varietals; CHARDONNAY and HERMITAGE consistently show winners.

Rosemount N.S.W. Table ★→★★
Bustling newcomer in Upper HUNTER. Agreeable RH. RIESLING and Traminer/Riesling blend.

Rothbury Estate Hunter Valley, N.S.W. Table ★★★
Important syndicate-owned wine estate concentrating on traditional HUNTER wines: "Hermitage" and long-lived SEMILLON. New plantings of CABERNET, CHARDONNAY, PINOT NOIR.

Visitors to Australia are invariably surprised by the quality of the wines – particularly the instantly likeable not-quite-dry white Rieslings. The reds need a little more understanding.

The characteristic flavour of good Australian reds is powerful, broad, low in acidity, sometimes even slightly salty. They are ripe and soft enough to drink fairly young, but repay keeping for a good ten years. Above all they are remarkable value for money – the best sell for an absurdly small premium over those which are merely good.

Ryecroft McLaren Vale, S.A. Table ★→★★
Specialists in typical sturdy CABERNET and SHIRAZ.

Saltram Barossa, S.A. Full range ★→★★★
One of the smaller wineries making a notable CABERNET, "Mamre Brook" and good "Selected Vintage" claret and RHINE RIESLING.

Sandalford W. Aus. Table ★→★★
New small winery with contrasting styles of red and white varietals from Swan and Margaret rivers.

Saxonvale N.S.W. Table ★★
Large newcomer at Fordwich, N.W. of Hunter. After early difficulties now making very good SEMILLON and CHARDONNAY. Also CABERNET, SHIRAZ.

Seaview Southern Vales, S.A. Table and dessert ★★
Old-established winery now owned by Toohey's Brewery. Well-known CABERNET, SAUVIGNON and RHINE RIESLING.

Seppelt Barossa, S.A. Central Vic. and elsewhere. Full range ★→★★★
Far-flung producers of Australia's best "champagne" (Gt. Western Brut), good dessert wines (from Rutherglen, the Murray Valley, Barossa), the reliable Moyston claret and some good private bin wines from Gt. Western in Victoria.

Smith's Yalumba   Barossa, S.A. Full range ★→★★★
> Big old family firm. Best wines incl. Rhine Riesling from Pewsey Vale above Barossa, good "Galway Vintage" claret, "Galway Pipe" port and Chiquita sherry.

Southern Vales Wine Co.   S. Aus. Full range ★→★★
> Co-op in McLaren Vale developing fine table wines, esp. dry white varietals.

Stanley   Clare, S. Aus. Full range ★→★★
> Important medium-size quality winery owned by Heinz. Among Aus.'s best RH. RIESLING and CABERNET SAUVIGNON and complex Cabernet-Shiraz-Malbec blends under Leasingham label.

Stonyfell   Adelaide, S.A. Full range ★→★★
> Long-established company best known for "Metala" CABERNET SHIRAZ from Langhorne Creek.

Taltarni   Victoria. Table ★★→★★★
> Dominique Portet, brother of Bernard (Clos du Val, Napa), son of André (Château Lafite), produces huge red wines in Avoca.

Taylors Wines   S.A. Table ★★
> Large new red wine producing unit (CABERNET SAUVIGNON and HERMITAGE) turning to whites (RHINE RIESLING, generics).

Tisdall Wines   Victoria. Table ★★→★★★
> Echuca river area, making local wines plus finer material from central ranges (Mount Helen CABERNET SAUVIGNON, CHARDONNAY, RHINE RIESLING).

Tollana   Barossa, S.A. Full range ★→★★
> Old company famous for brandy, has latterly made some remarkable CABERNET and RHINE RIESLING.

Tulloch   Hunter Valley, N.S.W. Table ★★
> An old name at Pokolbin, with good dry reds and "Riesling".

Tyrrell   Hunter Valley, N.S.W. Table ★★→ ★★★
> Up-to-date old family business at "Ashman's". Some of the best traditional Hunter wines, Hermitage and RIESLING, are distinguished by Vat Numbers. Also big rich CHARDONNAY and delicate PINOT NOIR becoming known in Europe.

Valencia   W. Aus. Full range ★→★★
> W. Aus.'s largest company owned by Thos. Hardy, located in Swan Valley. Interesting white varietals of CHENIN BLANC from Gin Gin w. of Perth.

Vasse Felix   W. Aus. Table ★★
> The pioneer of south western W.A. Elegant CABERNETS that have been compared to St. Julien.

Westfield   W. Aus. Table ★★
> Generally recognized as the most consistent producer of table wine in the Swan Valley. CABERNET and Verdelho show finesse.

Woodleys   Adel, S. Aus. Table ★★
> Melbourne-owned; well-known for Queen Adelaide label claret and Riesling.

Wyndham Estate   Branxton, N.S.W. Full range ★→★★
> Frantic marketers of full range, but some fine Hunter varietals occasionally emerge. Geo. Wyndham's original estate is now a tourist attraction.

Wynns   S. Aus. and N.S.W. Table ★→★★★
> Large inter-state company, originators of flagon wines, with winery in RIVERINA and vineyards at Coonawarra, making good CABERNET. Owned by Toohey's Brewery.

New Zealand

An infant wine industry already making an international impact with fruity and well-balanced table wines from the classic grape varieties. Progress has accelerated since new vineyard areas were planted in the early '70s on both North and South Islands. There are now over 10,000 acres. White grapes predominate. Müller-Thurgau is the most planted variety.

The general style of wine is relatively light with fairly high acidity. The distinctive flavours of grape varieties are well marked and critical opinion sees a very bright future for the industry. The principal producers are:

Cooks
> Progressive new company at Te Kauwhata nr. Auckland, North Island. Fine CABERNET and RIESLING: also CHASSELAS, PINOT GRIS, Pinot Meunier.

Corbans
> Old-established firm at Henderson, nr. Auckland, now owned by Rothman's. Known for flor sherry, also CABERNET, CHENIN BLANC.

Glenvale
> Old-established fruit company with 250 acres of vines at Napier, HAWKES BAY. Formerly mainly sherry; table wines increasing.

Hawkes Bay
> The biggest vineyard area on the east coast of North Island.

Marlborough
> Recently developed vineyard area at north end of South Island, now with 1,300 acres.

Matawhero
> Very small POVERTY BAY producer with high-quality GEWÜRZTRAMINER, CHARDONNAY.

McWilliams
> Winery at HAWKES BAY. Related to the major Australian company. Wines include Baco Noir (see New York), Cresta Doré and, increasingly, CABERNET.

Montana
> The largest winery, originally at POVERTY BAY; pioneer with fine wines and in planting at MARLBOROUGH. "Riesling-Silvaner" (MÜLLER-THURGAU) and CABERNET both very successful.

Nobilo's
> Yugoslav family firm, pioneers with new varieties, incl. good CHARDONNAY, MÜLLER-THURGAU, CABERNET and PINOTAGE; also with carbonic maceration.

Penfolds
> Founded 1963 by the Australian company. V'yds. at Henderson, nr. Auckland, North Island. Experimental CABERNET, PINOTAGE, "Autumn Riesling".

Poverty Bay
> Important wine area near Gisborne, east coast of North Island.

Villa Maria
> Yugoslav family winery nr. Auckland. Riesling-Sylvaner and CABERNET both successful.

Wairau Valley
> Vineyard area in MARLBOROUGH with microclimate giving fine ripe grapes.

South Africa

South Africa has made excellent sherry and port for many years, but has taken table wine seriously only in the last decade. Since 1972 a new system of Wines of Origin and registered "estates" has started a new era of competitive modern wine-making. Cabernet Sauvignon reds of high quality are already well established; the signs are that Chardonnay, Sauvignon Blanc and other superior grapes now being introduced will be similarly successful.

Allesverloren
Estate in MALMESBURY with over 325 acres of v'yds., formerly well known for "port", now specializing in ripe, powerful, deep reds, incl. CABERNET and TINTA BAROCCA. Distributed by BERGKELDER.

Alphen
Estate originally at Constantia, owned by the famous Cloete family (see GROOT CONSTANTIA), now at Somerset West with a new winery. Expert direction should make good wines.

Alto ★★
STELLENBOSCH estate of about 200 acres high on a hill, best known for massive-bodied CABERNET and a good blend: Alto Rouge. Distributed by BERGKELDER.

Autumn Harvest
Popular low-price range from STELLENBOSCH FARMERS' WINERY.

Backsberg ★★
Name formerly associated with commercial blends, now a prize-winning 400-acre estate at PAARL with notably good, relatively light, CABERNET. Also Sauvignon Blanc.

Bellingham
Top brand name of UNION WINES. Reliable reds and whites, esp. SHIRAZ. The GRAND CRU is well known.

Benede-Oranje
Newly demarcated wine region in the Orange River irrigation area. The northernmost region.

Bergkelder
Big wine concern at STELLENBOSCH, member of the OUDE MEESTER group, making and distributing many brands and estate wines, incl. FLEUR DU CAP, ALTO, HAZENDAL, etc. Now combined with STELLENBOSCH FARMERS' WINERY. See Cape Wine and Distillers Ltd.

Bertrams
Major wine company owned by Gilbeys with a wide range of well-made varietals esp. CABERNET.

Blaauwklippen ★★
Estate s. of STELLENBOSCH growing Zinfandel and Pinot Noir as well as the usual varieties.

Boberg
Controlled region of origin for fortified wines consisting of the districts of PAARL and TULBAGH.

Bonfoi ★★
Estate in STELLENBOSCH district. White wines (esp. CHENIN BLANC) marketed through the BERGKELDER.

Boschendal ★★
Estate in PAARL area being developed on old fruit farm. Emphasis on white wines. Also a charming restaurant.

Breede River Valley
Demarcated wine region east of Drakenstein Mtns.; hotter than coastal area. Being upgraded to produce good light wines, esp. at Robertson and Worcester.

Bukettraube

New German white-wine grape with acidity and muscat aroma, popular in S. Africa for blending.

Cabernet

The great Bordeaux grape particularly successful in the COASTAL REGION. Sturdy, long-ageing wines.

Cape Wine and Distillers Ltd.

The holding company for the reconstructed liquor interests of Oudemeester, STELLENBOSCH FARMERS' WINERY, etc.

Carlonet

See Uitkyk

Cavendish Cape ★★

Range of remarkably good sherries from the K.W.V..

Chenin Blanc

Workhorse grape of the Cape; one vine in four. Adaptable and sometimes very good. Alias STEEN.

Cinsaut

Bulk-producing French red grape formerly known as Hermitage in S. Africa. Chiefly blended with CABERNET, but can make reasonable wine on its own.

Coastal Region

Demarcated wine region, includes PAARL, STELLENBOSCH, Durbanville, SWARTLAND.

Colombard

The "FRENCH COLOMBARD" of California. Prized in S. Africa for its high acidity and fruity flavour. An element in many "Steens".

Constantia

Once the world's most famous muscat wine, from the Cape. Now the southernmost district of origin ("Constantia and Durbanville"). See also GROOT CONSTANTIA.

Delheim ★★→★★★

Winery at Driesprong in the best and highest area of STELLENBOSCH, known for delicate STEEN and GEWÜRZ-TRAMINER whites and also light reds: PINOTAGE, SHIRAZ and CABERNET.

Drostdy

Range of sherries from BERGKELDER.

Edelkeur

Excellent intensely sweet white made with nobly rotten (p. 47) STEEN grapes by NEDERBURG.

Estate wine

A strictly controlled term applying only to some 60 registered estates making wines made of grapes grown on the same property.

Fleur du Cap ★★

Popular and well-made range of wines from the BERG-KELDER, Stellenbosch. Particularly good CABERNET; RIESLING less good.

Gewürztraminer

The famous spicy grape of Alsace, successfully grown in the TULBAGH area.

Grand Cru (or Premier Grand Cru)

Term for a totally dry white, with no quality implications. Generally to be avoided.

La Gratitude

Well-known brand of dry white from the STELLENBOSCH FARMERS' WINERY.

Goede Hoop ★

Estate in STELLENBOSCH district. Pleasant blended red bottled and sold by BERGKELDER.

Groot Constantia ★★

Historic estate, now government-owned, near Cape Town. Source of superlative muscat wine in the early 19th century. Now making CABERNET, PINOT NOIR, PINOTAGE and SHIRAZ reds. The CABERNET is best. Also a blend, Heerenrood.

Grünberger ★★

Famous brand of not-quite-dry STEEN white from the BERGKELDER, though flagrantly dressed up as a German Franconian "Steinwein".

Hanepoot

Local name for Muscat of Alexandria, widely grown for sweet dessert wines.

Hazendal ★★

Family estate in w. STELLENBOSCH specializing in semi-sweet STEEN, marketed by the BERGKELDER.

Jacobsdal ★

Estate in STELLENBOSCH district, overlooking False Bay. PINOTAGE bottled and sold by BERGKELDER.

Kanonkop ★★★

Outstanding estate in n. STELLENBOSCH, specializing in high quality and particularly full-bodied CABERNET, PINOTAGE and Pinot Noir. Changed hands in 1981.

Klein Karoo

The easternmost S. African wine district, warm and dry, specializing in dessert and distilling wine.

Kerner

Flowery grape variety recently introduced from Germany.

Koopmanskloof ★

STELLENBOSCH estate making good dry Chenin Blanc "Blanc de Marbonne".

K.W.V.

The Kooperatieve Wijnbouwers Vereniging, S. Africa's national wine co-operative (now independent) originally organized by the State to absorb embarrassing surpluses, now at vast and splendidly equipped premises in PAARL making a range of good wines, particularly sherries.

Laborie N.Y.A.

New K.W.V.-owned estate on Paarl Mtn. Showpiece cellar, restaurant and guesthouse. CABERNET will be the speciality.

Landgoed

South African for Estate; a word which appears on all estate wine labels and official seals.

Landskroon ★

Family estate owned by Paul and Hugo de Villiers. Mainly port-type wines for K.W.V. but recently some good dry reds. Pinot Noir, TINTA BAROCCA and CABERNET.

Late Harvest

Term for a mildly sweet wine. "Special Late Harvest" must be naturally sweet.

Malmesbury

Centre of the SWARTLAND wine district, on the w. coast n. of Cape Town, specializing in dry whites and distilling wine.

Meerendal ★★

Estate near Durbanville producing robust reds (esp. SHIRAZ) marketed by the BERGKELDER.

Meerlust ★★★

Beautiful old family estate s. of STELLENBOSCH making outstanding CABERNET marketed by the BERGKELDER. Now adding Merlot, etc. for balance and complexity.

Monis ★→★★

Well-known wine concern of PAARL, with fine "Vintage Port" now merged with the STELLENBOSCH FARMERS' WINERY.

Montagne ★★

Relatively new but successful estate of 300+ acres near STELLENBOSCH. Wines incl. CABERNET, SHIRAZ and PREMIER GRAND CRU. Owned by Gilbeys.

Montpellier ★→★★

Famous pioneering TULBAGH estate with 350 acres of v'yds. specializing in white wine. Produced the first two whites to be officially designated SUPERIOR (RIESLING and GEWÜRZ-TRAMINER), also CHENIN BLANC and méthode champenoise sparkling wine.

Muratie ★

Ancient estate in STELLENBOSCH, best known for its port and Pinot Noir. 160 acres of v'yds. also grow CABERNET, RIESLING, STEEN and CINSAUT.

Nederburg ★★→★★★★

The most famous wine farm in modern S. Africa, now operated by the STELLENBOSCH FARMERS' WINERY. Its annual auction is a major event. Pioneer in modern cellar practice and with fine CABERNET, "Private Bin" blends and EDELKEUR. Also good sparkling wines and RIESLINGS.

Olifantsrivier

Northerly demarcated wine region with a warm dry climate. Mainly distilling wine.

Oude Libertas

Popular range of mid-quality wines from STELLENBOSCH FARMERS' WINERY. The STEEN and CABERNET are best.

Overberg

Demarcated wine district in the Caledon area, Coastal Region.

Overgaauw ★→★★★

Estate w. of STELLENBOSCH making good STEEN and Sylvaner whites and very good CABERNET.

Paarl

South Africa's wine capital, 50 miles n.e. of Cape Town, and the surrounding demarcated district, among the best in the country, particularly for white wine and sherry. Most of its wine is made by co-operatives. See also Boberg.

Paarlsack ★

Well-known range of sherries made at PAARL by the K.W.V.

Pinotage

South African red grape, a cross between PINOT NOIR and CINSAUT, useful for high yields and hardiness. Its wine is lush and fruity but never first-class.

Piquetberg

Small demarcated district on the w. coast round Porterville. A warm dry climate gives mainly dessert and distilling wine.

Premier Grand Cru

See Grand Cru

Riesling

South African Riesling makes some of the country's better white wines, but is not the same as Rhine Riesling, which has only recently been planted in any quantity in S. Africa.

Rietvallei ★★

New ROBERTSON estate. Fortified Muscadet.

Robertson

Small demarcated district e. of the Cape and inland. Mainly dessert wines (notably MUSCAT), but red and white table wines are on the increase. Includes Bonnievale.

Roodeberg ★★

High-quality brand of blended red wine from the K.W.V. Has good colour, body and flavour and ages well in bottle.

Rustenberg `***`

Effectively, if not officially, an estate red wine from just n of STELLENBOSCH. Rustenberg Dry Red is a go Cabernet/Cinsaut blend. The straight Cabernet is outstan ing. Also Pinot Noir.

Schoongezicht `*`

Partner of RUSTENBERG, one of S. Africa's most beautiful c farms and producer of agreeable white wine from STEE RIESLING and Clairette Blanche. Now registered as an estat

Shiraz

The red Rhône grape, recently gaining in popularity in Africa for rich deep-coloured wine.

Simonsig `**→***`

Estate owned by F.J. Malan, Chairman of the Cape Esta Wine Producers' Association. Produces a wide range, in WEISSER RIESLING and a successful "Méthode Champenoise"

Simonsvlei

One of S. Africa's best-known co-operative cellars, just ou side PAARL. A prize-winner with both whites and reds.

Spier `*`

Estate of five farms w. of STELLENBOSCH producing reds a whites. The SHIRAZ best.

Steen South Africa's commonest white grape, said to be a clone the CHENIN BLANC. It gives strong, tasty and lively wine, swe or dry, normally better than S. African RIESLING.

Stein

Name used for any medium dry white wine.

Stellenbosch

Town and demarcated district 30 miles e. of Cape Tow extending to the ocean at False Bay. Most of the best estate esp. for red wine, are in the mountain foothills of the region

Stellenbosch Farmers' Winery (S.F.W.)

South Africa's biggest winery (after the K.W.V.) with sever ranges of wines, incl. NEDERBURG, ZONNEBLOEM, Lanzera OUDE LIBERTAS and the popular TASSENBERG. Also "Vinot Light". See Cape Wine and Distillers Ltd.

Stellenryck

Good-quality BERGKELDER range, esp. for RIESLING a CHENIN BLANC.

Superior

An official designation of quality for WINES OF ORIGIN. T wine must meet standards set by the Wine & Spirit Board.

Swartland

Demarcated district around MALMESBURY. ALLESVERLOREN the best estate.

Swellendam

Demarcated district of the s.e., with Bonnievale as its cent Dessert, distilling and light table wines.

Sylvaner

Recently introduced variety. OVERGAAUW makes a pleasa version.

Taskelder `*`

Range of good value wines from the STELLENBOSCH FARME WINERY, including CH. LIBERTAS, Lanzerac Rosé, LA GRATITU and Tasheimer.

Tassenberg `*`

Popular and good-value red table wine known to thousands Tassie. "Oom Tas" is a low-price dry amber-white.

Tawny

As in Portugal means port-style wines aged in wood.

Theuniskraal [★★]

Well-known TULBAGH estate specializing in white wines, esp. RIESLING and GEWÜRZTRAMINER. Also STEEN, Semillon. Distributed by the BERGKELDER.

Tulbagh

Demarcated district n. of PAARL best known for the white wines of its three famous estates, MONTPELLIER, THEUNISKRAAL and TWEE JONGEGEZELLEN, and the dessert wines of its co-operative at Drostdy. See also BOBERG.

Twee Jongegezellen ★★→★★★

Estate at TULBAGH. One of the great pioneers which revolutionized S. African wine in the 1950s, still in the family of its 18th-century founder. Mainly white wine, incl. RIESLING, STEEN and Sauvignon Blanc. Best wines: "Schanderl" and "T.J.39". The name means "two young friends". Now also producing a CABERNET grown by a reservoir to get the "Médoc" effect.

Uiterwyk ★★

Old estate w. of STELLENBOSCH making a very good CABERNET SAUVIGNON and pleasant whites.

Uitkyk ★★

Old estate at STELLENBOSCH famous for Carlonet (big gutsy CABERNET) and Carlsheim white. Now over 350 acres. Distribution by BERGKELDER.

Union Wine

Company with HQ in Wellington, Boberg area. Brand names Culemborg, BELLINGHAM and Val du Charron.

Van Riebeck

Co-operative at Riebeck Kasteel, MALMESBURY, known for pioneering work in white wine technology.

Verdun ★

Estate w. of STELLENBOSCH, best known for its Gamay red, but also a good SAUVIGNON BLANC.

Vergenoegd ★★

Old family estate in s. STELLENBOSCH supplying high-quality sherry to the K.W.V. but recently offering deeply flavoured CABERNET and excellent SHIRAZ under an estate label.

Weisser Riesling

A fairly recent introduction from Germany. Considerably finer than the S.A. Riesling, which it is replacing.

Welterrede ★

Progressive ROBERTSON estate. Colombard and blended whites.

De Wetshof ★★★

Pioneering estate in ROBERTSON district. Prize-winning Riesling marketed by BERGKELDER. Also a sweet noblerot white, Edeloes.

Wine of Origin

The S. African equivalent of Appellation Contrôlée. The demarcated regions involved are all described on these pages.

Worcester

Demarcated wine district round the Breede and Hex river valleys, e. of PAARL. Many co-operative cellars make mainly dessert wines, brandy and dry whites.

Zandvliet ★★

Estate in the ROBERTSON area marketing a light SHIRAZ through the BERGKELDER. Later will add a Cabernet-Merlot blend.

Zonnebloem ★★

Good-quality brand of CABERNET, RIESLING, PINOTAGE and PREMIER GRAND CRU from the STELLENBOSCH FARMERS' WINERY. The Cabernet is vintage-dated and ages well in bottle.

QUICK REFERENCE VINTAGE CHARTS FOR FRANCE AND GERMANY

These charts give a picture of the range of qualities made in the principal areas (every year has its relative successes and failures) and a guide to whether the wine is ready to drink or should be kept.

♦ drink now   ━ needs keeping   ∕ can be drunk with pleasure now, but the better wines will continue to improve

0 no good   10 the best

Combinations of these symbols mean that there are wines in more than one of the categories.

FRANCE

| | Red Bordeaux | | White Bordeaux | |
	Médoc/Graves	Pom./St-Em.	Sauternes & sw.	Graves & dr.
80	4–6 ━	3–5 ━	5–8 ━	3–6 ∕
79	5–8 ━	5–9 ━	6–8 ━	6–7 ∕
78	6–9	6–8	4–6 ∕	7–9
77	3–5	2–5	2–4 ♦	6–9
76	6–8	7–8	7–9	4–8
75	9–10	8–10	8–10	8–10
74	4–6	3–5	0	6–7
73	5–6 ♦	5–7	0–4	7–8
72	2–5	2–4 ♦	2–4 ♦	4–7
71	5–8	6–8	8–9	8–10
70	9–10	9–10	9–10	9–10
69	1–4 ♦	0–3 ♦	6–7 ♦	8–9
68	0–2	0	0	0
67	5–7	6–8	7–10	8–10
66	7–9	8–9	4–7 ♦	7–8 ♦
64	2–7 ♦	5–9 ♦		
62	4–8 ♦	3–6 ♦		
61	10	10		

| | Red Burgundy | White Burgundy | | |
	Côte d'Or	Côte d'Or	Chablis	Alsace
80	3–6 ━	4–7	5–8	3–5
79	4–8 ━	6–8 ━	6–8 ∕	7–8 ∕
78	8–10	7–9	7–9	6–8
77	2–4	4–7	5–7	6–7
76	9–10	7–9	8–9	10
75	0–5 ♦	4–8	8–10 ♦	9
74	2–5 ♦	5–8	6–8	6–7
73	4–7 ♦	8	7–8 ♦	7–8 ♦
72	4–9	5–8	1–4 ♦	3
71	8–10	8–10	7–9 ♦	10

Beaujolais: 79 and 80 are the vintages to buy and drink. Mâcon-Villages (white): 79 and 78 are good now.
Loire: Sweet wines of Anjou and Touraine. Best recent vintages: 79, 78, 76, 73, 71, 70, 69, 64.
Upper Loire: Sancerre and Pouilly-Fumé 80, 79, 78 are all good now.
Muscadet: Drink the new vintage.

GERMANY

	Rhône		Rhine	Moselle
80	5–7	80	4–7	3–7
79	6–8	79	6–8 ━	6–8 ━
78	8–10	78	5–7	4–7
77	4–6	77	5–7 ♦	4–6 ♦
76	6–9	76	9–10	9–10
75	0–5	75	7–9	8–10
74	4–7 ♦	74	3–6 ♦	2–4 ♦
73	5–8 ♦	73	6–7 ♦	6–8 ♦
72	6–9	72	2–5 ♦	1–4 ♦
71	7–9	71	9–10	10

N.B. Fully detailed charts will be found on pages 24, 25 (France), 77 (Germany)